WHAT THE ROBIN KNOWS

WHAT THE ROBIN KNOWS

HOW BIRDS REVEAL THE SECRETS OF THE NATURAL WORLD

Jon Young

with science and audio editing by Dan Gardoqui

HOUGHTON MIFFLIN HARCOURT
Boston ⌖ New York   2012

For information about permission to reproduce selections from this book,
write to Permissions, Houghton Mifflin Harcourt Company, 215 Park Avenue South,
New York, New York 10003.

www.hmhbooks.com

Illustrations by Kiliii Fish Photo & Design

Library of Congress Cataloging-in-Publication Data
Young, Jon, date.
What the robin knows : how birds reveal the secrets of the natural world / Jon Young.
p. cm.
Includes bibliographical references and index.
ISBN 978-0-547-45125-1
1. Birdsongs. 2. Songbirds—Behavior. 3. Bird watching. 4. Nature observation.
5. Philosophy of nature. 6. Young, Jon, date.—Travel—New Jersey. 7. Natural
history—New Jersey. I. Title.
QL698.5.Y68 2012
598.8—dc23   2012002403

Printed in the United States of America

DOC 10 9 8 7 6 5 4 3 2 1

DEDICATION

There are teachers, mentors, elders, and wisdom keepers from every part of this world who have kept alive the ways of their traditional ecological knowledge. Through my relationships with these sources of wisdom, and through the lens of natural history science, I have come to offer this book. Through the hope, curiosity, and deep belief of those I have mentored, I have gained immeasurably. This book is sourced from their stories and their sit spot experiences.

Therefore I dedicate this work to both the ancestors of wisdom, indigenous and modern alike. And I dedicate this book to those who sit, watch, and wonder — and ultimately share their stories and questions with others for further learning, reflection, and just plain excitement. These sources continue to build our collective understanding of bird and animal language.

To Tekaronianeken Jake Swamp, once a living friend, elder, and mentor, now an ancestor: you were the first man to tell me that it is good "to give thanks to the birds, for they are the ones who lift us from our troubled minds."

To the children of the wind, who watch, listen, and share their stories and find the power of silence within.

ACKNOWLEDGMENTS

First, let me acknowledge my mentors and ancestors, for without their support this book would not exist.

For the ancestors: Thanks especially to my beloved Aunt Carrie Rozek, the oldest sister of my grandmother Anna Ernish—thanks to you as well. Aunt Carrie helped me to discover the mystery of nature, its silent teachings and the wisdom of the birds' messages to us. Ingwe, my beloved grandfather and teacher, you taught me to believe in the messages of the birds—through you, Ingwe, to your Akamba teachers and mentors, and to the Bushman who showed you so much, so you could inspire me to go on learning and teaching bird language. Thanks to uncles Jake and Gilbert, who shared so generously the wisdom of your culture with me and deepened my understanding and appreciation of the birds and their language at a very deep level.

My living mentors and teachers: To my childhood mentor, Tom Brown Jr., many thanks to you always for what you have offered me and so many others. I could not be writing this book without your vast contribution to my growth as a naturalist, tracker, and bird language teacher. Thanks to the author Jim Corbett, who for many years offered me the only satisfying stories of bird language in print that I could find. Thanks to all the great birders, naturalists, and trackers out there who have provided so many incredible resources and opportunities to learn from.

There are too many people to acknowledge for their contributions to this book and to the source of knowledge, experience, and inspiration that allowed me to be part of the team to create this book. There are many supporters around the world who have contributed time, experience, words, and resources to support this project. To all of you a huge, heartfelt thank-you.

There are a few I have to mention directly. First, Bonnie Solow at Solow Literary, who drew this book from me after hearing me speak about this subject one evening in her town. Thank you, Bonnie. Thank you to Mark and Miki, who helped shape and refine the story from a massive source of words collected over ten years.

Thanks to the group of trackers, researchers, bird language enthusiasts, writers, artists, and other helpers who helped create that massive source of words that we worked from to create this book. That would be the team from OWLink Media and the Shikari Tracking Guild from the mid-1990s right through until 2009, when we began to focus and whittle away at this raw material on bird language and tracking. A special thanks to all of you who provided such important support in terms of facilities to work from, land with suitable habitat—rich with birds and wildlife—and homes for us during this time, resources to support me and my family and members of this team, and belief in us to help us get the work done.

Great thanks to all of you who have worked directly on this book. Thanks to the writer Mike Bryan, who took the job of combing through nearly 200,000 words to find the ones that mattered most. Thanks to Kiliii Yu for your exceptional artistic talent as artist and graphic artist, and your skills and experience in bird language that helped so much in the rendering of the shapes of alarm.

Very special thanks to Dan Gardoqui, someone who I consider a friend, younger brother, and colleague. I began to mentor Dan in bird language and tracking when he was fifteen years old. That was in the mid-1980s. Dan's enthusiasm, focus, passion to learn, and willingness to put in time in the field and in the research have carried him all the way to the top of his field. He is a talented, experienced, and exceptional teacher of tracking and bird language. He is a tireless and skilled researcher—his work included combing through every sentence in this book to find opportunities to link to modern science. He created all of the endnotes and every reference in these pages. Dan, for your work on this project over the last couple of years, and for the last twenty-five or so years of working together closely, thank you. Your hard work has provided an important bridge between worlds of powerful tools.

Dan worked with me and a great team gathered and led by Maureen McConnell, exhibit planner, while she presided over the development of "A Bird's World" exhibit at Boston's Museum of Science natural history section. It was there that Dan worked with Lang Elliott, the exceptional field recordist and owner of NatureSound Studios, to first bring together the five voices of birds we write about in this book. Over the years many people have requested that Dan and I produce a bird vocalization collection organized by these five voices. Working closely again with Lang's help and his recordings, Dan has produced the collection to accompany this book. Thanks to Dan and Lang (and to Maureen for this original opportunity).

Thanks to Josh Lane, experienced naturalist, tracker, bird language teacher, and mentor for the Shikari Tracking Guild for his contributions in shaping the appendix on learning bird language.

Special thanks to the team at Houghton Mifflin Harcourt, especially Lisa White, the editor for this work.

Thanks to my wife for supporting me on this journey and for contributing so much to the work of bird language herself — mentoring and teaching with me all these years. Thanks to those who have helped test, shape, and refine the methodologies in these pages: Dave Hage, Lauren Dalberth Hage, Will Scott, Dan Fontaine, Greg Sommer, Jennifer Bresse, James Stark, Penny Livingston Stark, Rafe Halsey, Ruby Head, Ned Conwell, Nathan Meffert, Calen Kennett, and all the other staff members, apprentices, students, and other folks who have worked year after year, week after week, and hour upon hour, to create the refined experience of learning bird language for many people over the years at the Regenerative Design Institute, the Shikari Tracking Guild, and 8

Shields Institute. Thanks to all the folks at Wilderness Awareness School, who continue to move this work forward as well.

Thanks to all of you who have sat for hours at a time, for days on end, season after season, at all times of day, in all weather, to get to know the birds and animals of your world. To those folks who inspire me for their long-term commitment to one sit spot for ten years or more. There are too many to list. Thanks to two of you, and through you to all others who make that commitment: Rick Bedsworth, who has visited his sit spot to observe for seventeen years, and Alexia Allen, who visited for more than thirteen years (missing only three days) to learn of those places and those birds, and to push the edges of understanding for yourselves and me. Thank you so much for sharing your stories with this team and me so they could end up here. Thanks to all of you who have pushed the science beyond the edge and into the uncharted territory of interspecies communication.

Thanks, most of all, to the birds, the animals, and to all of our sit spots everywhere. Thank you so much for all you give to us.

CONTENTS

INTRODUCTION:
WHAT THE ROBIN KNOWS

ONE EARLY SPRING DAY when I was a teenager and already keenly interested in birds, I was scouting the vast salt marshes of southern New Jersey, and I saw a ruff. A ruff! This wading bird (considered a sandpiper) wasn't supposed to be on the North American continent at all, but there it was, fresh in from Europe or perhaps even Asia. That was an exciting moment, and so was my teenage discovery of the scissor-tailed flycatcher and the snowy owl, both way out of their respective ranges, and the very rare golden-winged warbler. I went to the trouble of identifying those unexpected birds because I identified every bird I saw and heard. If I couldn't do so on the first encounter, I went back the next day, and the next. If I heard a sound from a bird I hadn't heard before, I grabbed my binoculars and went searching until I found the source—or left defeated, but determined to find it at the next opportunity. In May, when the warblers migrated across New Jersey over the course of just three or four peak days, I was out there aggressively trying to sort them out—fifteen or so species at my hangout, as well as a couple dozen others in New Jersey. At Rutgers, where I studied anthropology and natural history, I was probably the first one to sign up for the annual one-day bird count that began in the Brigantine National Wildlife Refuge—a major point along the Atlantic Flyway in southern New Jersey—and concluded at Helyar Woods near the campus. Success for our van full of varied birders began that day before dawn with a singing Chuck-will's-widow and concluded after nightfall with an eastern screech-owl. That very long day's scouring yielded ninety-six species. While that may not be so impressive to some really good birders, it was my best day up to that point. I was eighteen years old.

I've had a lot of great birding moments in North America, the Hawaiian Islands, Europe, and Africa, and I've drawn solid lessons from them, but this fact remains: the American robin in my yard has much more to teach me as I sit quietly beneath a tree first thing each morning (with my binoculars on my lap only rarely these days). For one thing, this bird is so handy. For another, it's one of the most expressive of all birds, vocally and in its body language. Was the robin driven into the tree by something in the thicket, or was it drawn up by curiosity (which is to say, mild alarm)? If I know this bird, I know the answer. I know when there's a cat in the vicinity. I know when there's a dog, not a cat, in the vicinity. Of course, the robin also advises me about what seems to be its greatest fear: the deadly accipiters winging furtively through the neighborhood. Likewise for the song sparrows, even though they're virtually invisible to most folks walking around the neighborhood (*song* sparrows, not *house* sparrows). These elusive little brown shadows that bustle on the brown earth at the sides of the yard — *shreep shreep shreep* — then hop to the top of the bush (almost always the top), flip their wings, flip their tails, peer down intently — *shreep shreep shreep*. They also know all about the cat and the dog and the sharp-shinned hawk. For learning bird language, song sparrows are great allies.

Is a junco hanging around this morning? When feeding, this small gray bird favors the shadowy patches of open ground that match its coloration perfectly. If I haven't really engaged my wide-angle "owl" vision (pretty much the opposite of narrow-angle binocular vision), if I'm not calm and quiet enough to detect subtle movements and hear subtle sounds, this modest creature will always get the best of me and remain undetected. I may unwittingly step on its saucer-size, carefully woven nest of rootlets, moss, pine needles, and grass. So it stands to reason that juncos are masters of subtlety: any songbird that feeds on the ground and often nests on the ground, with danger therefore a constant companion, had better be wary. Sometimes I think the deer have the juncos in their front pockets. When one of these little birds finally bursts off the ground and flies away, flashing its dark gray and white tail pattern, the deer's huge ears — veritable radar dishes — swivel instantly in that direction. For them, the tiny twittering alarm must be like a screaming siren.

Robins? Sparrows? Juncos? *Boring!* I've heard this lament from the occasional first-day student, but I've never heard it from a third-day student. It just doesn't happen, because the complaint is so wrong, and it doesn't take anyone long to understand why. When we really see and hear and begin to understand these and other birds, the revelations are fun, enthralling, even vital.

My name for the study of birds' behavior and accompanying vocalizations is "deep bird language," and I believe — and will attempt to demonstrate in these pages — that it's the key to understanding both the backyard and the forest. Here's a little demonstration of how it works. (I'd put this in the "fun" category.) I was meeting some people at a new mentoring center in California. A board member was showing me around the facility, about which everyone was justifiably proud. In the main part of the building, a converted suburban house, the two of us were in a backroom that had a sliding glass door opening onto a backyard and swimming pool. Through this door, I spied a small brown bird on the ground right outside, helping itself to something trapped in a spider web. As I edged closer, I realized that these were baby spiders in their own web, and the bird was plucking them up, one by one, with its long curved bill, as effective for this job as a pair of tweezers. When I got too close to the glass door, the bird, a wrentit, hopped off and went to ground at the base of an overgrown hedge only a few feet away. If it raised an alarm call at that moment, I could not hear it through the glass door, with some ambient sound coming from another room and my host speaking continuously as he pointed to photographs and told me stories of this place. I enjoyed the stories and was quite engaged, even if my attention seemed elsewhere.

Perched in a nearby tree was a robin, singing away. I couldn't hear the song, but seeing its head flip this way and that—its mouth open, its throat moving, its body relaxed—I knew the bird was singing (*listen to audio file 1, for example*). I turned back to the wrentit, and just as I did, it flew up five feet, something over waist height. Now it was almost in my face, a few feet away. I could barely hear the *chut!* alarm, but I could see the pumping tail. (*The alarm call is in audio file 3.*) This was the same bird that had retreated from me a few moments earlier, so I concluded that something else had startled it even more. Out of the corner of my eye, I saw that the robin had quit singing and was rigid except for its tail, which was now also pumping in alarm. Let's see ... two alarmed birds in a suburban yard, one of them a ground dweller who has jumped up five feet—not ten, not fifty, but five. When I tell this story to a lay audience and ask for guesses about the cause of the alarm, everybody knows the answer.

On the scene, however, when I turned to my new friend and said, "Hey, there's a cat coming," he didn't know what to make of my prediction. He hadn't seen what I'd seen. Frankly, he was in a completely different frame of mind at the moment.

"What?"

"A cat's coming. Look!" I pointed down to the ground outside the glass door, where the cat would surely slink past shortly. When it did a few seconds later, my friend's jaw dropped, but only because he hadn't been following the story outside. Any thoughts about my psychic powers were erased by my real-world explanation of what had happened between the wrentit, the robin, and the cat.

Backyard Learning

There's nothing random about birds' awareness and behavior. They have too much at stake—life and death. Nor does random luck determine who among us has really close encounters with them and the other animals. As cosseted humans who have lost much of our sensory keenness, we are at a great disadvantage, but we can do much better. The birds' language can be loaded with meaning for us as well, if only we pay close enough attention. We have ears; we can tune in, too. If we understand the birds, we can meet just about any animal we want. Without this understanding, many well-meaning seekers find the fox only when she's running away or leaping across the midnight road in the glare of the headlights. I'd much rather find her lying on a mossy bed in dappled sunlight in the early morning, lazily licking her paws, grooming herself, and gazing over the landscape with soft eyes, ears angling this way and that as she picks up and listens to the nuances carried by the wind. This fox is tuned in to the tapestry of bird song on all sides. The animals know the importance of this language, and they listen to it. This is how they learn about us, and the birds' alarms give them so much advance warning of our approach that they can choose the manner and timing of their own retiring departure. Only rarely do they actually have to run away.

We are often (usually, to be honest) a jarring, unaware presence in the world beyond the front door. Even when we're "bird watching," looking for different species—in many cases for particular species—there can be a sense in which we're hunting. If we hear the call of a black-throated green warbler and want to have a look at it, we more or less ignore the other birds, so intent are we on locating that beautiful warbler. The robin may rebuke our sudden incursion, the chipmunk may chip at us, the squirrel may race up the tree and wave its tail, but we're only peripherally aware of these messages, if at all. *(The robin's agitation call is in audio file 2; examples of chipmunk alarm calls are in audio files 66 [terrestrial alarm] and 68 [alarm near hole].)*

If we're in bird language mode, however, we're moving with a whole different frame of mind and venturing into another realm of awareness and intention and curiosity. We're holding multiple questions in mind simultaneously. We're not focused on a single species. We're monitoring several species consciously and perhaps quite a few others unconsciously. We don't have "hunting" intentions. We have diffuse awareness, curiosity, perceptions, and questions. We're always aware of the ripples that we are creating as we go. What is the robin's first alarm call? What is the junco's? Ground predator or aerial predator? Are these alarms for me, for that orange and white cat who's been hanging around the past couple of days, or for something else? Or maybe we have the opposite circumstance. At this time of morning on a calm, sunny spring day, there should be much more vocalizing and activity over in that diverse edge habitat. Two days ago, those trees and hedges were buzzing with multiple species. Why not now? How "big" is the silence in that area? Does it extend from ground to canopy, or are the grosbeaks up in the treetops as vocal as ever? Although we can see in only one direction at a time, when we're in bird language mode, we're hearing information from all directions all the time. The experience is multidimensional and involves many different senses. We're walking carefully, slowly, stopping and looking (but not sneaking, which fools no one out there), adopting a relaxed body posture that reflects a relaxed, receptive brain, not a hunting brain.

One of the first pleasant tasks for anyone interested in the methodology of bird language is to select a private place among the birds to visit as often as possible. It may be in the forest, the suburban or urban park, or the backyard. Regardless, it will be the main venue for figuring out what's going on, for connecting the dots, for gathering the stories of the birds and their context. So I call it simply the "sit spot," but it could be called the "medicine area," in reference to the depth of connection and understanding one can absorb and gain. In this book, it merits a chapter of its own. In your sit spot, it's not as important to know every bird by its scientific name as it is to know that that robin over there is an individual like you and me. Let's call him Bill, the male who owns this territory. Consorting with him this year is Sally. What happened to Betty, who had that very distinctive brown mark on one side? She was with Bill for the past two seasons. She's gone now; that's all we know. How long will this new mate last? What about Bill himself? That remains to be seen. (The names may be silly. The point is not. You, too, can attain such knowledge in your sit spot, should you so desire.)

Thus my two main subjects in this book:

- What's really going on in the world of the birds?
- How can we access that world through our awareness of deep bird language so that we can also see more wildlife?

Am I a "bird whisperer"? No, but I listen to *their* whispers—and their songs and companion calls and alarm calls—very closely. I watch their behavior very closely. If you're a student of bird language, this degree of observation becomes almost automatic. You develop new resources with and for your brain. This approach only makes sense, because, after all, which is older, our language or their language? The sectors of our brain that can understand their language are deeper than the sectors that manage our own. Add up all the accumulated experience and knowledge and input from these ancient yet newly discovered instincts, and you end up with "gut feelings" of uncanny accuracy. That venerable saying "A little bird told me" takes on a whole new meaning. You may just feel in your gut that a certain alarm call is due to a raccoon coming through— nothing else, definitely a raccoon. You don't know why you have this hunch, but you do, so you go out and check, and there goes that masked bandit. Such feats of the "adaptive unconscious" are the subject of Malcolm Gladwell's bestseller *Blink: The Power of*

Thinking Without Thinking. They are manifest in many fields. A basic knowledge of bird language will produce many fascinating examples.

The Science of It All

I've mentioned my teenage days as a birder, but my fascination with birds began even earlier, with my great-aunt Carrie, who was keenly in tune with the natural world. Her mother, my great-grandma Novak, had a special relationship with a robin in her yard. She would recite a poem to this bird while she tapped on the open palm of her upturned hand, and the robin would hop forward and touch its bill to her finger. Aunt Carrie was the first one to take me to Barnegat Bay, to stand in silence for long periods watching and listening to the sounds of water lapping on eelgrass and the cries of gulls and other seabirds. This was my first connection with a natural place, still unsurpassed.

When I was ten years old, I met Tom Brown Jr., now well-known as the author of seventeen books and field guides about the wilderness experience. Aunt Carrie and Great-grandma Novak had primed me to hear Tom's mesmerizing stories; their own stories of bird language had inspired curiosity in me as far back as I could recall. Tom was just twenty-one, but he took me under his wing (a metaphor I don't use lightly), and we spent a great deal of time together in the 1970s. When he opened his school in 1978 (today called the Tracker School), I was one of the first instructors, at age eighteen. Tom Brown writes, "Need is essentially equivalent to results. For anything you undertake, the greater the need, the greater the results." I agree. Creatures in the wild—and the backyard counts as the wild for birds—have the highest possible need for results. We used to have this need, and indigenous people still do. Those of us who study and teach deep bird language follow in the path of those living wild. We aren't doing anything new. Not one thing. That old line about standing on the shoulders of giants is true. I want to make this point as loudly as any in this book. We only borrow the old ideas that have been developed and studied by native hunter-gatherers all over the world, who needed this knowledge and acquired it to the extent that their responses became almost intuitive.

Native people still living in subsistence patterns possess a sophisticated and necessary knowledge of place that is absolutely beyond most of us today. Their brains are trained in the most natural ways possible. Their values and knowledge are bedrock for understanding bird language. By comparison, our modern-day work in this field might seem almost recreational. I'm a little hesitant to write that word, but it's true. I hope and believe that the study of deep bird language is one way to ensure that native knowledge of the natural world receives the respect it deserves. And I mean *scientific* respect.

Native knowledge, scientific knowledge: two ways of paying supremely close attention. Or I could say that native knowledge is science without all the trappings. Throughout this book, I'll refer to published studies that touch on various points about bird language. They fall into three general categories: ornithology, psychology, and neuroscience. Sometimes these studies are reported in the popular press with astonishment. A report of one study showing that red-breasted nuthatches can understand when chickadees are in distress quoted a doctoral candidate who worked on the study as saying, "No one has ever seen this behavior before. There are a fair number of animals that respond to other animals' alarm calls. But this is the first example of subtle information from a call being interpreted by another species."

Actually, native scouts have understood and used their knowledge of such intraspecies and interspecies communication for thousands of years. This principle is introduced on the first day of bird language class, then effectively demonstrated in the first week. Science is in catch-up mode when it comes to bird language, but this is nothing new. For most of Western history, acupuncture was dismissed out of hand by the medical establishment. Not anymore. Many modern medicines, including aspirin (salicylate), cough medicine (hydrocyanic or prussic acid), and the purgative ipecac are the synthesized versions of original herbal forms used for eons by the natives. These are just a few examples of indigenous skills and knowledge that contribute to our lives today. Tracking is another.

Louis Liebenberg is a South African scientist who has worked with San Bushmen to monitor wildlife populations in the far reaches of the Kalahari Desert. His early academic background was physics and math, but he became interested in the origins and philosophy of science, and now his CyberTracker software is used by ornithologists, zoologists, conservationists, and many other professionals around the world. Liebenberg believes that the tracking and other skills practiced by the San, including understanding bird language, are crucial for the evolution of the human brain and are fundamentally true to the scientific method. He says bluntly that the so-called primitive hunter-gatherers are on a par with, and doing the same thing as, the professional scientists who work with him. His book on the subject is titled *The Art of Tracking: The Origin of Science*.

Recently, I spent several weeks with two communities of Bushmen, one living the old way in the Kalahari, and the other more modernized in the Okavango delta, a remote subsistence setting in Botswana. I say that these and other trackers and scouts in the native traditions around the world are professional scientists. They use traditional techniques and knowledge to make their living. They cannot afford to be too far off base in their thinking and conjectures. A wrong assessment, a wrong decision, or a wrong action in the bush can mean curtains. These people are very grounded in the real world. You can watch them at work on the video *The Art of Tracking: The Story of the Skill, Not the Kill* (available at http://find.lib.uts.edu.au). It's a great documentary, though the title is misleading: tracking is hard-earned scientific knowledge, not an art. It is incredible to me that this extremely complex and multidimensional discipline has almost vanished. Thanks to the help of individuals like Louis Liebenberg, at least some of this vast cultural knowledge is being preserved for our benefit.

Remember Lord Baltimore, the native scout hired by the railroads to track Butch Cassidy and the Sundance Kid? Until those lovable, photogenic thieves leaped off the cliff and floated downstream to (momentary) safety, they could not shake their nemesis. That movie character was based on the exploits of a host of native scouts, for whom tracking two men crossing hardpan on horseback was little more than child's play. Any experienced animal tracker can study the ground, the bent twigs, and the flattened grass and show us where a dozen deer got up from their midday lay and slipped off into the trees a couple of minutes before we came along. He or she can identify exactly where a red fox paused in her tracks for a moment to check out the reaction of a Pacific wren a hundred yards away, or exactly where the fox slipped off her favorite trail and waited two minutes under a fallen log for us to get out of the way. I grew up tracking — and in the "old way," using all the senses, the whole body, to imitate and to tell stories, and trying to understand the entire ecology and how each member of the ecosystem fits into the dance of life. I still track this way. It's great stuff, a lot of fun, and tremendously rewarding. And I now believe that deep bird language raises traditional animal tracking to an exponential power. The additional skills and perceptions afforded by bird language keep us from sinking into a state of focused self-absorption. They keep us as alive as we're ever going to be.

I've had some magical experiences in the natural world, and some of them have involved birds. My point here is that I'm certainly no ninja. It's just that the more keenly our antennae are tuned to the sounds, sights, and other sensory input from our world, and the more of our brains we engage, the more we get in touch with our ancient instincts and the instinctive abilities that all animals automatically manifest. Numerous studies have found that people living in many different kinds of landscapes all over the world nevertheless respond viscerally to one scene: a vast plain with a body of water viewed from slightly above. Why the universal appreciation? The consensus hypothesis holds that this is the landscape of the African savanna, where all human life is rooted in evolution. I think this could be right. The experience and the memory of that life are buried deep in our synapses, memory fields, and instincts. So are many other experiences and memories of the natural world, now almost lost to most of us, but not to the scouts.

Many birders know or have heard about exceptional birders who just seem to have "the eye" — that is, a seemingly innate talent for visual discrimination so finely tuned, and a personal database of knowledge so deep, that their instincts for quick identification are amazing. A ghost of a shadow may flit between branches twenty-five yards away, and a birder with "the eye" will murmur, "Dusky flycatcher" (as opposed to the very similar Hammond's flycatcher). Such skill comes only from years and years of the closest possible study of the respective birds' silhouettes, flight patterns, colors, and sizes. To the lay observer, this is borderline mystical, but these amazing blinks have nothing to do with mysticism. They're all about talent, motivation, practice, and connection (and some luck). They're not supernatural. They're only *super-natural*. The hyphen is crucial.

The Best Bottom Line

In bird language, the idea is to look at bird culture as an anthropologist looks at human culture. Each species occupies a different niche in the environment, subtle though the difference may be to us. (It could be glaring to the birds.) Some species catch insects on the wing; others scratch insects from under the leaves. The better we understand the whole ecology of a given place, the better we become at looking at this world from the birds' perspective, and the better we will be at learning the birds' language. Every living being has a purpose, a mission, a life strategy, a set of gifts, and a set of weaknesses. Set aside any assumption that its behavior is random and meaningless. Such a categorization applies to birds and other animals about as much as it applies to people, which is *not at all*.

Reflecting on San culture, a friend told me about something a San Bushman said.

> If one day I see a small bird and recognize it, a thin thread will form between me and that bird. If I just see it but don't really *recognize* it, there is no thin thread. If I go out tomorrow and see and really recognize that same individual small bird again, the thread will thicken and strengthen just a little. Every time I see and recognize that bird, the thread strengthens. Eventually it will grow into a string, then a cord, and finally a rope. This is what it means to be a Bushman. We make ropes with all aspects of the creation in this way.

In my recent visit to a subsistence community in the Kalahari, I was able to experience these relationships between the San and the land directly. The San are some of the most nature-bonded people I have ever spent time with.

The San have developed such keen awareness that it's virtually impossible for them not to acquire an understanding of the birds' perspective, or at least an appreciation of that perspective. One of the most striking things I observed was their ability to imitate everything in nature—for example, the movement of grasses in the wind or the head movements of a walking giraffe—using their hands and arms, as if they were performing a puppet show. And they practice all the time. Through this form of storytelling—which is what imitation really is—a great deal of understanding, awareness, and connection emerges. These elements are essential to understanding bird language. As awareness grows, appreciation grows, too. As appreciation grows, so does empathy.

Empathy: that's a dangerous word in science, of course, because it's taken to entail a loss of rigorous, critical objectivity. An even more dangerous word is *anthropomorphism*, the assumption, acknowledged or implicit, that birds and other creatures live with the same mental and emotional capacities as we do. In science, anthropomorphizing is a grave error, though maybe a little less grave than it used to be, because ornithologists as famous and respected as Konrad Lorenz (*King Solomon's Ring*, featuring a jackdaw) and Alexander Skutch (*The Minds of Birds*) were brazen enough to venture the notion that the attitude of the scientist or any other observer does matter.

I agree. Attitude matters supremely. In all my years of teaching and mentoring bird language to thousands of people all over the world, I've compiled a lot of objective observations, and the evidence is clear: those who succeed are those who adopt an empathetic point of view in their study of the birds. This doesn't mean that I believe birds or other wild creatures or even beloved pets are subjectively "happy" and "sad" in the way that people are. It's impossible to know this. It does mean that while empathy can lead to a loss of objectivity, it can also open doors. There's a Catch-22 lurking here: people with little experience of the natural world and no real experience with birds announce to me that they don't "believe" in bird language. They ignore or even deny the studies about predator-specific vocalizations in black-capped chickadees and red-breasted nuthatches, about mockingbirds who remember people, about the sudden silence that accompanies the flight of the Cooper's hawk through the trees. They miss the logical, evolutionary connection: birds are vocal because birds are listening. (Animals are listening, too, but for different reasons.) With their negative attitude, these folks never open their senses to bird language. They don't learn anything, and then they repeat, smugly, "See, there's nothing going on."

It happens. Rarely, but it happens. Meanwhile, the great majority who are open to new understanding *do* open their senses and *do* reap the reward. And what's unusual about this? Isn't the same true of music? Are the notes on the page "the science of harmonics" or "music"? Both. As a fiddler, I understand that music is rooted in the science of harmonics, and there are many rules for composition and playing. But to get the most out of the experience — composing, playing, or listening — we can't be strictly logical and observe and analyze the sounds in a detached manner. There has to be an investment from the heart, spirit, soul, and body, too. In fact, that investment is the whole point and the whole reward. Any musician knows about the times when, in the middle of a performance, *Try this!* pops to mind, and the new fingering idea works — or doesn't work. Such instantaneous improvisation is the heart and soul of jazz.

This is my third subject in this book. The first two — learning what's really going on out there, and learning how we can access that world through the awareness of deep bird language, so that we can see more wildlife — are, unquestionably, the meat and potatoes of my work. The third is the dessert: my conviction that understanding the birds really does help us to understand ourselves and, if we wish, make some changes. Tom Brown says, "Too often we walk in arrogance." How true, and when we do, the birds pick up our attitude *instantly* and tell us the truth — if only we're prepared to hear it. I've staked my professional life on the conviction that the awareness required to understand and connect with the birds really does change lives.

As it happens, a study published in 2009 in *Personality and Social Psychology Bulletin* confirms my hypothesis. The researchers divided a cohort of 370 women and men into two groups, one viewing photographs of the natural world, the other viewing photos of cityscapes. The former group then scored higher on tests measuring connectedness, empathy, and sharing. There have been other such studies, all with the same results. And remember, these studies involve experimental subjects looking at photographs. Meanwhile, deep bird language is a multidimensional, full-contact nature sport! It influences our psyches much more than any array of pictures or 3-D movies possibly could. And surely this goes double for kids, about whom Richard Louv raised the alarm with his 2005 bestseller, *Last Child in the Woods*. Louv portrays a "denatured" generation untethered from the natural world, immersed instead in an electronic world that functions as a parallel universe. Is this what we want? Is this what's good for our children? As a father of six, I don't think so. The kids are all right, but like all kids in all times, they need help. I know that bird language is a wonderful way for parents and adults to help children connect with their deepest instincts and selves.

I'm a true believer because I have no choice. Too many times, I've seen a radical transformation in children and adults who simply take the time to tune in—not just show up, but really tune in—and learn a thing or two about what the robin already knows.

WHAT THE ROBIN KNOWS

Chapter 1

A CACOPHONY OF HARMONY

I N BIRD GUIDES and CDs, the birds' songs may be the only vocalizations mentioned, which makes sense. For identification purposes, they are by far the most valuable of the many vocalizations. In bird language, however, the songs are not enough. In fact, they're just the beginning. Observers of bird language listen to, identify, and interpret five vocalizations:

- Songs
- Companion calls
- Territorial aggression (often male to male)
- Adolescent begging
- Alarms

I think of these categories as a medium-fine filter for all the sounds the birds produce. The finer filter would include certain migratory flight calls, whisper songs, and copulation calls. In this book, we can dispense with them because we're not analyzing bird songs or the other vocalizations for their own sake. Our emphasis is on situating the birds *in the habitat,* so we can understand what's going on in this habitat as a whole. Our focus on the five vocalizations will get pretty microscopic, but the purpose is macroscopic. We want to think about birds and their habitats as anthropologists consider humans and their cultures.

The first four vocalizations—all but the alarms—are what ornithologists call "maintenance behavior." I prefer the term "baseline." Quite simply, baseline is the backdrop against which everything else plays out. I joke about knowing specific birds by the gas they pass, but this kind of specific knowledge isn't what bird language is really all about. It's fundamentally about recognizing patterns and identifying and understanding the disturbances within these patterns. To identify the disturbances, we first have to understand the patterns. Baseline is the environmental condition collaboratively created by all the animals and birds—all their creeping, crawling, hopping, grazing, prowling, and flying; all their barking, howling, chattering, grunting, whinnying, and singing. It is the intricately woven tapestry of the preferred status quo, and every creature adds its particular contribution to this "baseline symphony," as Tom Brown likes to call it. Again, we learn this from having a seat in the great concert hall where this symphony is best experienced —nature. The seat in the hall is the sit spot. Working with bird language, we learn the parts of each instrument in the great orchestra. When any one of them is out of tune, it's time to investigate. Something outside the baseline is going on.

The songs, companion calls, territorial aggression, and adolescent begging are the norm. It may be noisy in the trees, but these four vocalizations are actually a cacophony of harmony. (Or the baseline may be quiet by the shoreline, because the sandpipers, plovers, and curlews usually go about their business in near silence. Every major type of habitat is different, with a different-sounding baseline. Colonies of shorebirds meeting songbirds at the forest edge is like two orchestras playing quite different tunes at quite different volumes, side by side.) The fifth vocalization—the alarm call—is the most complex phenomenon to analyze, not necessarily phonetically and certainly not aesthetically, but in terms of its practical value for understanding what is happening to disrupt the baseline harmony.

So understanding baseline is fundamental to understanding bird language. What *should* be happening in the trees? The first thing is the dawn chorus, that amazing phenomenon that I discuss in detail in Chapter 4. The chorus is followed immediately by the morning bustle. Assuming no immediate predatory threats and alarms, the specifics of this burst of activity vary with the ecology of a given habitat; the season; the temperature and other weather conditions, such as wind, fog, and humidity; impending weather; the status of the migrant pool; the nonbreeding juveniles from last year; the breeding pairs; the nesting situation—many factors. A very cold morning in the mountains close to our house near the California coastline may yield a throng of varied thrushes feeding in great numbers in the wood-chip mulch, especially if the rain was heavy in the previous few days. The moisture must be perfect for an abundant bloom of some kind of fly larvae, now almost frozen and motionless for easy gleaning. The thrushes will go beyond their normal scratching mode and dig some small excavations. Looking at these small, fresh holes, I might think a herd of digging skunks with sloppy tendencies had moved through. But no, it was this flock of thrushes: baseline for this time of year. Not the kind of baseline we see every day, but still a manifestation of the all-important baseline. Let's follow the baseline as it evolves through an average day in a generic temperate mixed-forest habitat.

As the sun gets a little higher, the thrushes move back into the brush and trees up the hill, where I am more used to seeing them—more "normal" for them on this land. The robins and other songbirds are still singing, but their pace slackens a bit as some individuals drop out of the choir to begin foraging. They've slept all night; it's time for breakfast. (Some birds, such as thrushes in winter, will start feeding at the very beginning of first light, when it's still pretty dark.) Unless there's a particular abundance of fruit or worms, the songbirds will stay in their respective territories. They'll remain there throughout the day (after all, one of the main reasons they moved in was satisfaction with the food supply), but doves, for example, may jump from their roosts and fly several miles to a big meadow or field loaded with seeds. They may be joined in this subtle daily migration by band-tailed pigeons, mixed flocks of blackbirds, or finches, all seeking the best food and water. This activity varies from day to day, and it is why campers and trackers and birders would benefit from getting up early and closely watching these early morning mini-migrations. The birds are practically drawing a map of the immediate landscape for us to use. *Here* is the water, *here* are the berries, *here* are the cold morning–stilled grasshoppers. The local baseline ecology is laid out for all who care to observe. With the very first silvery tint of light in the eastern sky, the crows are out on dawn patrol, indicating with dips, looks, or calls the foxes and owls who are still hunting (and the French fries and rats in the parking lot). Ravens are reliable guides for finding caribou, elk, and moose. (In the old days, native hunters reciprocated by leaving the gut pile for their overhead allies.)

Ravens preferentially associate with gray wolves as a foraging strategy, especially in winter, and more than one experienced wolf specialist has told me that wolves keep an eye on the ravens for the same purpose, at any time of day or year. I learned about this while assisting on several wolf-tracking projects in the West. Using the birds as a first alert greatly improved our odds of finding two wolves (without radio collars) in a million acres of wild country. If the birds were busy eating grasshoppers in the cold morning, we moved on, but if they were gathered low in the trees and acting somewhat skittish, we paused, because ravens gathered in a focused group could be protecting a carcass and keeping their eyes out for other nearby scavengers, including wolves. (This telltale behavior was easy to pick up even for the new volunteers on the project. Ravens also have more subtle maneuvers that clued-in naturalists follow.) Always keep an eye out for what I call "dip looks," with the raven (or crow) flying along in a normal, level flight, then suddenly looking down and dipping in flight ever so slightly. I head straight for the ground directly below any dip look, especially if I'm more involved in straight tracking than in bird language, because you'll often find a carcass, a group of hiding coyotes, a bobcat, or an eagle on the ground with a kill.

As the breeding season progresses, the migrants leave, and the breeding pairs are all that remain behind. They are not idle, and I am often drawn to sit and watch with little Finch, my son, in the growing warmth of the March morning. There are some tussles between rivals and some courtship activities. Even the crows may turn sweet: that male (I presume) is offering his mate a stick, and she takes it gingerly. The birds are preening, showing off, resting and fluffing up in the sunlight, bathing, rolling in the dust (or an anthill, so the annoyed insects will release some formic acid on their feathers and skin to drive off the lice). For a given bird, much depends on how many mouths there are to feed. If you see a song sparrow fly in, hop around, get an insect, fly off, come right back, hop around, get another insect, fly off, come back — I promise you, this bird is not leading a bachelor's life. If he were, he would hang around one good source of food. The more flying around, the more likely it is that this bird has other mouths to feed. The flycatchers nesting under the eaves of my house stand by and watch for their nestlings to defecate, then quickly swoop in to catch the offering and carry it to the forest edge, ten yards away. Then they return to the perch to sing and presumably watch for an insect to catch or for the next sibling's release. If the feeding seems fairly casual, if the bird is just hopping and feeding, hopping and feeding, it's probably responsible only for itself — unless it's collecting a bill full of worms or insects. In the early spring before the chicks arrive, and then in the autumn after they've left the nest, the morning feeding has a more relaxed, empty-nest rhythm.

By late morning, say eleven A.M., the feeding frenzy has tapered off, and the singing has almost ceased. Almost. The Wilson's warbler, house finch, and field sparrow are still spilling over with song, and they will be the entire day. Listen (hard) for the towhees still scratching in the dirt. Otherwise, the baseline now is much quieter. A new student of bird language walking into the woods at this hour might even believe that she is responsible for this relative silence, but that's not really true. She does have the birds' attention, and as we'll see later, their reaction will depend on her attitude and behavior. But all in all, energy and vocalizing are way down now. This late morning semi-hush feeds into the midday all-out hush, when the buzzing of the crickets and the cicadas looms large by contrast. But now hear the beautiful voice of the meadowlark and the prairie warbler. Even in the heat of the day, some species still feel the urge to emote, and they indulge this urge. These isolated tunes are the soundtrack of that delicious midafternoon laziness we humans can't and don't indulge often enough. This could be the best baseline of them all.

During the morning bustle, there had probably been a lot of alarm activity, because feeding time for songbirds is also feeding time for the raptors hunting songbirds, and in the spring the raptors are joined by all the opportunistic nest robbers, both ground based and aerial. During the general midday slowdown, this predatory activity slows down, too, but in a few hours overall activity picks up again in the golden light of late afternoon. The birds are singing again, quite likely with a different song than in the morning. Where available, the insect hatches that are more common in the late afternoon are on the menu. The birds that specialize in taking these bugs on the wing—flycatchers, warblers, swallows, cedar waxwings—are guaranteed to be busy right now. In the forest, the deer are moving again; the foxes are on the prowl; the bears are resuming their silent, invisible forage wander. Right at sunset, the singing comes to a peak. Though not as remarkable and glamorous as the dawn chorus, it's certainly noticeable to the most casual listener, sort of a last gasp before roosting. As the sunset progresses, the singing drops off quickly, leaving the lonely songs of the robin and the thrush to dominate the cooling, contemplative twilight. Some of them may sing into the dark of later twilight—for me, bittersweet melodies, the last musical embers of a dying day. With the western sky still glowing pink, the nighthawks make their move. The birds that roost together during the night are flocking up and flying overhead: ducks, geese, doves, blackbirds, and, in the winter, robins, siskins, goldfinches, and other songsters. The horned owls may already be calling.

And then, finally, the robins and thrushes join the mocking-birds, thrashers, flocking sparrows, California towhees, and various others in a roosting-time shout-out. To our ears, this sounds like birds going bonkers, with many loud arguments and screaming matches. A first hypothesis might be that a cat or some other nocturnal predator is sitting right below a crowded roost, teasing the tired birds. Or maybe somebody has been murdered, with a lot of recriminations in the flock. But every time I've investigated (quite a few times), I've found nothing of the sort going on. Apparently, the birds are just tired and cranky. *(For American robin agitation and alarm calls, listen to audio files 2 and 3.)* I call this the "robin roosting ruckus," because they seem to be the ringleaders. Other species also get weird just before bedtime, but in my experience the robins are the weirdest. There might be enough light left for you to catch a glimpse of one of them speeding away from the scene in an evasive, darting flight. In Europe I've watched the very same behavior with the robin's close cousin the blackbird (like a black robin; same genus, too). Are these birds trying to fool the early owls by making a lot of noise in faux roosts, then sneaking out the back door to their real ones? I don't know, and I don't believe anyone else does either. Trying to figure out who's sleeping where can be confusing —teachers of tracking and bird language courses often pose such a challenge as a game—but know this: many of the birds are not actually roosting where they issued their last calls.

The mockingbird, which quite likely was the herald of the dawn chorus, is also quite likely the last bird standing fourteen, fifteen, sixteen hours later. In my experience in New Jersey, it was the only bird that bookended the day in this way, and with the same song out of a repertoire that may include more than a hundred. (On the West Coast, so far, I have neither encountered nor heard about any bird that behaves this way.) The mockingbird may even continue singing throughout the night, off and on . . . and on . . . and on. The whip-poor-will is out and about, along with other local goatsuckers (yes, that's what they're called), such as the Chuck-will's-widow, the common poorwill, and the common nighthawk. Of course, the owls will be active, generally throughout the night — the barn owls with their ghostly hisses and shrieks, the barred owls with their *who cooks for you? who cooks for you all?* call. Highlighted against the overpowering surround-sound chorus of katydids on summer nights in New Jersey, the screech-owl always got my concerned attention. If you haven't heard one before, it will get yours, too. Although it has a quieter kind of call, this owl can be pretty frightening. On group expeditions, campers sometimes report hearing a woman screaming during the night. I take these concerns in stride, as it is almost certainly just a screech-owl. (Along these same lines, the sound of a pair of raccoons in territorial conflict can be misinterpreted as the Jersey Devil himself: intense, frightening, bloodcurdling — even more surprising and chilling than a midnight catfight.)

I understand that the nocturnal frog chorus keeps some people from sleeping. This is good! It provides an opportunity to lie there and speculate about why the frogs have suddenly stopped croaking. Like the birds, they have their reasons. Maybe a raccoon has passed by, or did the distant rumbling of a train give the frogs pause? Or was it the much more distant, barely discernible hum of an airplane high overhead?

And so the cacophony of harmony cycles around, and soon enough the birds will be at it again, the thrushes singing the opening notes of the dawn chorus.

It's All About Energy

In its simplest terms, baseline is the daily routine sans known danger. It can be quiet and peaceful and lazy, or active, at times even raucous, as with the songbirds' shout-out prefatory to roosting. It is always dynamic. Every species has a distinctive mode for every time of day, every ecological niche, and every season. Generalizations about baseline vocalizations may be necessary, but they are always subject to modification. If we have a good sense of them, we can handle the permutations. Without this sense, misinterpreting the roosting shout-out as a general alarm call will be only the last of many mistakes in interpretation we've made that day.

At all times, baseline conserves energy, because conservation of energy is a major priority for all animals, but especially for birds, almost all of whom run on a very lean energy budget. (A chickadee startled from its roost on a very cold night in the dead of winter loses the vital heat trapped in its feathers. This bird may well die by dawn.) I could not spend too much of my own energy explaining the importance of this principle for understanding baseline and, therefore, deep bird language. This is why researchers have written hundreds of dissertations and books on various aspects of energy conservation and baseline, or "maintenance behavior," as they are manifested by many different species. I imagine that plants, too, are operating under the same imperatives, in their slow-going, plantlike way.

First imagine trying to feed your own hungry self off a landscape. Have you ever tried this? Now imagine feeding five starving teenagers off the landscape, and you'll know why birds conserve energy, particularly when they're also singing to mark their territories. Conservation of energy is why the ground bird who knows that a particular cat can jump only four feet off the ground will ascend to a branch five feet up, but not fifty feet or even fifteen feet, which would be a waste of energy. If a song sparrow and a weasel share a yard, the bird knows this animal. He sees it every day. If the weasel is feeding its young, the song sparrow watches it pass by maybe a dozen times in a single morning. (I once watched a weasel go back and forth many times within a ten-minute period, delivering shrews to its nest under the foundation of an old shed.) The sparrow knows *this* specific weasel, knows how quick it is, how far it can jump, its favorite routes. For this time and place, the weasel is not so much a cause for alarm as part of the baseline situation, relatively speaking. Why should the sparrow waste energy worrying about it? Instead, the sparrow simply watches to make sure the weasel is just passing through, then gets back to other maintenance chores.

But what about those midday songs of the hot-day singers — the prairie warblers and field sparrows and meadowlarks mentioned above, also the spotted towhees, canyon wrens, wrentits — and the all-night singing of the mockingbird? And what about the dawn chorus? Isn't all this a waste of energy? I seriously doubt it. It all surely serves some purpose and is somehow advantageous for these species in the long run. It's all part of baseline, and our idea should be to identify these apparent anomalies with the intention of perhaps eventually figuring out why such "wastes of energy" are no such thing for the birds. Bird language is a tool for helping us first to become aware of the principles at play as we spend more and more time in the sit spot, and then to think about them.

It's Not Random

There's nothing random about birds' awareness and behavior, because they have too much at stake — life and death. Random behavior is a waste of energy, and any species that consistently squanders energy is ruthlessly eliminated from the game of life. (I can think of only one exception, and maybe this biped species will eventually pay the price.) In a very basic sense, all living creatures seem to be geared to one issue: eating and avoiding being eaten long enough to produce as many offspring as possible. That's what it's all about. Very few venues in nature ensure an overabundance of food, and even if one did, the animals wouldn't know this. And if they did know it, the overabundance would not be guaranteed in the future. Animals have evolved under dog-eat-dog conditions, and that's where their instincts are. Thus, pampered poodles wolf down their kibble. They know there's plenty more where that came from, they even know from which jar on which shelf, but they wolf it down anyway. This is a result of instinct, and there's nothing they can do about it. It's the same for bears, cougars, otters, tiny hummingbirds, large geese, and our title bird, the robin: they just don't waste much energy. Kittens and cubs and colts horse around and play games and waste energy because they have that luxury—until they don't, because they've grown up. If you do see the adults running in circles and chasing their tails, you can bet that life is good, food is plentiful, and danger is not a factor. In fact, odds are you've stumbled upon some domesticated animals—or a really productive salmon run. Herding dogs who can and will run all day—and if they're pets, possibly drive unsuspecting new owners crazy—and water dogs who will swim all day didn't evolve under, and they don't live under, conditions of scarcity. They were artificially bred under, and they live under, conditions of plenty supplied by their human benefactors. Their behavior is, in evolutionary terms, artificial.

In a very real way, baseline grants animals permission to be lazy. Birds and other animals have exactly as much of a work ethic as they need and not an ounce more. If a deer isn't grazing, what is it doing? Resting. (And even when deer feed, they're resting, their legs dangling from their bodies like wet noodles as they swing to the next position of "standing rest." They are not even trying. They are so relaxed—and so alert at the same time: baseline.) If a wolf isn't hunting, what is it doing? Hanging out. And when wolves are hunting, they still conserve energy, working together for maximum efficiency—one on the thicket trail, driving the rabbit into the open field, the other in that field a couple of paces behind, ready to pounce. Or they may work it the other way around, one chasing the rabbit into the thicket, where the other is working the trail. Or a pack may work together to drive an elk into shallow water or mud, where the killing is a lot easier (conserving energy) and less dangerous. Wolves, coyotes, and foxes conserve energy with their basic locomotion, loping along in a beautifully relaxed manner—harmonically rhythmic, I judge, when I'm in my musician's frame of mind.

Wake Hunting: The Ultimate Energy Conservation

A number of years ago, a group of behavioral scientists in San Francisco figured out that the local population of sharp-shinned hawks had learned to follow the joggers in the Presidio, an open-space preserve within the city. This is a popular place to jog, walk, sit, and enjoy a beautiful day. Since it's busy with people, it's also busy for the wildlife who are disturbed by the people. (The numerous coyotes in the Presidio hang back in the thickets during the day and head out at dusk, to forage at night. You might also glimpse one coming home at dawn.) Common sense would suggest that there's not a lot of good, standard baseline for the birds of the Presidio on a sunny Saturday, at least not along the trails that people follow, but people's habitual use of the trails with their habitual day-in-the-sun body language must create another kind of baseline for the birds. They're used to all this. Nevertheless, when someone is out of sync —a jogger wearing headphones, say—agitated birds may squirt out recklessly, possibly right into the talons of the sharpies who have learned to lurk close behind these joggers, waiting for just such an opportunity. Energy conservation for the sharpie.

In the bird language and tracking communities, the hawks' strategy is called "wake hunting," a well-established energy-saving strategy used by many species all over the world. (The dolphins cavorting in the boat's bow wave may well be having fun—I think they must be—but they're also getting an almost free meal from the abundance of small fish that are disoriented and involuntarily trapped by the pressure and chaos within the wave.) In Monmouth County, New Jersey, where I grew up, the farmers' tractors were followed by a dynamic cloud of robins, crows, gulls, and other birds, gleaning the worms, grubs, voles, and other delicious, maybe injured morsels unearthed from the dirt. On Kauai, the moment my friend starts up the lawn mower, the cattle egrets quickly fly in and alight in the trees, on the fence, everywhere. *Come on, Scott, get to it!* When he finally does, the egrets follow in the machine's wake and pick off the fleeing insects and any maimed mice. In the Lakota hunting tradition, my late friend Gilbert Walking Bull told me, the location of deer is reliably revealed by the magpies who follow them around, presumably because the grazers kick up from the dirt and shake loose from the branches a lot of worms, caterpillars, and insects.

Check out the wake behind the rumbling diesel utility trucks: a Cooper's hawk may be following behind (especially if there's good cover by the road), ready to seize choice morsels that are flying away from the din. Cooper's hawks aim to pick off songbirds that burst from the right-of-way in front of speeding cars. They are not the only hawks to utilize roads and cars. Red-tailed hawks and other hawks routinely take up positions along roads and highways, and not only to monitor the adjacent fields for small mammals. (As we'll see, the birds' tightly woven network of awareness and alarms makes it difficult for the hawks to pick them off as they feed on the ground.) This is shrewd conservation of energy by the hawks. Some of my colleagues, and I myself, have even changed the way we drive, slowing down, eyes trained on the landscape and the rearview mirror, looking for raptor shadows, monitoring their overall impact.

A family group of Harris's hawks may understand that the songbirds' alarm behavior in the presence of one of them presents a good opportunity for the others following close behind, sort of a cooperative "net on wings." This could be very efficient wake hunting. (The birds' alarms for hawks are considered in detail in Chapter 3.) It is well-known that Harris's hawks cooperate in group hunting of small mammals, especially desert cottontails. I can't prove it, and I don't believe anyone else has either, but I'm fairly certain that Cooper's hawks also hunt cooperatively in pairs, one following opportunistically in the wake of another. I say this because from September to May every year, I work with a skilled group of trainers and trainees on solving the mysteries of bird language, and many of us have observed two Cooper's hawks converge on one target at the same moment, usually resulting in success for one of them. Maybe these were just coincidental attacks, but I doubt it. We have seen too many such incidents. Moreover, very often when we lead group bird sits, two Cooper's hawks are evident, not just one. We've also seen these accipiters take advantage of the wakes caused among songbirds by loud jets, airplanes, helicopters, and passing trucks, or by golden eagles or gusts of wind, just as a bobcat or well-trained native hunter or nature photographer uses a gust of wind while stalking prey to cover the sound and motion of his own approach. My colleagues and I have seen that such disturbances fairly typically cause the songbirds themselves to pause for assessment. Have they learned that these disturbances may "mask" the approach of an accipiter, so they should take no chances and go on high alert?

In California and Washington, I've seen perching jays in the backyard imitate the call of a hawk, then zoom right at the birdfeeder with the intense cry of alarm they issue when a hawk really is on the wing. *(For an example of a red-tailed hawk mimic call by Steller's jay, listen to audio file 64.)* (I know of one study of this behavior, which concludes that what seems to be going on—clever deception—may be what actually *is* going on, or it may be something else altogether.) This is a different kind of wake hunting, and I have sometimes seen the other birds and squirrels in the area fall for the trick and scatter, allowing the jay to take over the feeder without any hassles. But I don't think this ruse would ever work twice in quick succession. I've seen it tried, but without success.

Of course, some predators are also scavengers, which is just about the easiest wake hunting. Coyotes are known to wait patiently while a badger feverishly digs out a ground squirrel colony. I've seen the same behavior among jackals and honey badgers in Africa. Predatory and especially scavenger birds always seem ready to jump in on the action. Broadly defined, wake hunting is ubiquitous throughout the natural world, but my all-time favorite observation of it in any species was from my office in Redmond, Washington: a Cooper's hawk that cruised right above the cars on the city streets of the old downtown, matching the vehicles speed for speed, just above their antennas and just below the canopy of overhanging trees, poised to pick off starlings by sharply swooping up and into the branches in a sudden arc of death. The cars provided the hawk perfect cover, and the starlings were too busy chattering and maybe ignoring the cars to notice the very sudden winged danger. I think this is *advanced* wake hunting. It could even be viewed as another sophisticated form of tool use, which is the subject of intense research by animal behaviorists. Comparing the hawk's shrewd use of the cars for cover and the famous chimps' use of sticks to retrieve ants from an anthill, I might propose that by our standards, the bird's behavior is more sophisticated.

Why Bird Language Works

Of course, that hawk's energy-conserving, wake-hunting baseline may become the starling's energy-*expending* nightmare, if not death. Clearly, baseline must always be thought of as species specific. Within a given species, baseline must be a very comfortable mode of being. The animals are confident in their sensory awareness and their ability to respond to all provocations accordingly. This awareness allows them to avoid danger, and avoiding danger conserves energy. It is in their best interests to have as early a warning of trouble as possible, not only, obviously, to escape death and live to breed another day, but also to avoid the trauma of the fight-or-flight response, which triggers several biological reactions, all of them energy-intensive. Heart rate increases, adrenaline surges, stored energy is consumed, the body's overall resistance suffers, and susceptibility to starvation and disease increases. And then either the fight or the flight is hard work. (I've chopped a lot of wood in my day. It's hard work, but nothing compared with the drain of taking a final exam or meeting a production deadline. The mental energy these tasks require, and the anxiety they produce—the adrenaline and other hormonal surges—are even more debilitating for the body than sheer physical exercise.) Consider the master elk herd bull who has earned the right to mate with all the cows in the herd. Granted, mating is energy expensive, but just as expensive is all the stress and anxiety used in warding off the competition. This elk bull is virtually trapped in a constant state of fight-or-flight, and the choice is mandated by instinct: fight if necessary. He cannot eat enough, he cannot rest enough, and he's using up his fat and bone marrow reserves at an alarming rate. That is why, when winter sets in, this huge, majestic, vital, and powerful animal is the elk most likely to die in late winter or early spring. The expenditure of all that energy can kill it. In effect, the alpha male's "sacrifice" helps conserve the energy of all the other bulls, and may the best one win during the next rutting season. The system works.

The energy equation is also why territorial systems have evolved in so many species. The energy required to establish and maintain a territory, with its assured though restricted resources, is less than the energy required to fight over unrestricted resources all the time. The energy equation is also why there's a lot of displaying and bluffing in the natural world: it's cheaper than fighting. (Most of the other elk bulls choose not to fight. They'll wait until next year.) It's why the big cats quit the chase the instant they start losing ground to the prey (which happens frequently with individual hunters; groups fare better, statistically). You will never see a lion chasing and chasing while she loses more and more ground. Only well-fed house dogs will do that!

Energy conservation explains why animals have evolved to place such a high priority on the voices and body language of the birds and other animals in the vicinity. *This principle lies at the heart of bird language.* It is the subject of a great deal of research and a great deal of further discussion in this book. The birds, the deer, and the squirrels will always heed warnings long before the danger gets there, if at all possible (and it usually is). This whole dynamic is exactly why studying bird language works so well. It's just much easier and energy-efficient for every creature if there's time to casually hide or fade into the shadows. Among deer, which buck is going to survive—the one who maintains what I call the baseline or information-gathering gait, or the one bounding through the forest in a blind panic on the first day of hunting season? The latter is the easier target for all the predators, especially the hunters. Meanwhile, the bucks who don't panic, who learn to walk slowly and take everything in stride, to heed the warnings of the birds—they're the ones who remain untagged year after year. *Oh, here come some more of those bipeds, but no big deal. I've seen them plow through here a dozen times. They rarely leave the trail, and when they do, they make so much noise I have plenty of warning and plenty of time to hide. And if they're a little more subtle than that, I can rely on the birds. And if absolutely necessary, I can even hide in plain sight within ten feet of them, because they're looking, but they're not really seeing.* That's what some bucks figure out through time, not in so many words, of course, but in general intuitive wisdom. Keen awareness, relaxing, not panicking—it all saves energy and prolongs life for more breeding. The oldest bucks are often revered by traditional hunting peoples the world over. They've earned that respect. They radiate the wisdom of the hardest lessons learned in nature.

In many cases, baseline is straightforward analysis: the singing bird, for example, is a bird in baseline. In other times and places, and with other species, baseline can get tricky. For example, in the otherwise quiet trees, crows love to yell back and forth, and they're not waiting politely for the others to speak their piece. It's a real din. By contrast, in urban areas with a lot of street noise, the crows may hang out on rooftops and flip their wings and wag their tails a lot, much more than they would in the trees, and with much less yelling back and forth. Do they do this in the city because they can't hear each other above the city traffic? It seems to me that all this expressive body language is baseline behavior. If we're tuned in, we can know this. If we were to observe this body language in the trees, we would know that something else must be going on, because in the trees this is not baseline behavior.

In flight, killdeer are highly skilled and noisy acrobats, showing off their bold maneuvers. *(Listen to audio file 52 for an example of a killdeer flight display call.)* Nighthawks have a special thing they do with their wings, diving and whirring air through them with a dramatic vibration (hard to describe in words; you need to see it and hear it). Hawks have their own maneuvers. Corvids on the wing do all kinds of weird things. With any of these species you don't know well, you might think, *Oh, that was really unusual. Something must have alarmed that bird.* Maybe, or maybe what you observed was just the strange baseline behavior of that species. While feeding, the inimitable mockingbird will suddenly jump a foot in the air and flutter its wings rapidly in display. The bird might do this three or four times, quickly, then settle back down. Was it alarmed at something? No. This strange dance is normal for mockingbirds. Many birds ruffle their neck feathers and make them stick out at odd angles. They may ruffle all their feathers, or as many as they're able to, in effect inflating themselves, presumably in an effort to look bigger and more imposing. This is standard behavior during the courtship displays of several species. The wing and tail feathers of the spotted towhee have little black and white patterns that the birds expose periodically in a steady rhythm while feeding, like little black and white flashers. Ruffed grouse thump their wings against their sides to make their territorial call: it sounds like an alarm, but it's just their kind of song.

It's easy to misinterpret many of the birds' actions. For that reason, it's important to know the baseline for a particular species in a particular habitat. The best way to do that is to become familiar with the species' baseline vocalizations, starting with song.

Chapter 2

IN THE BEGINNING IS THE SONG

First Baseline Vocalization: Songs

Songs are universally emblematic of birds, difficult to miss (with a few exceptions, such as the tiny tune of the junco), and simply beautiful. Logically enough, our bird language focus is on those species known as the songbirds, which are also the perching birds: thrushes (including the robin), sparrows, chickadees, nuthatches, wrens, warblers, tanagers, and the rest. Passeriformes is the taxonomic order, and it takes up the second half of most guidebooks, because these species are more than half of all bird species. All have relatively pointy bills of average length with which they eat mostly seeds, worms, insects, nuts, or fruit. As we'll see, other birds are important for various reasons in understanding bird language, but the passerines have the greater evolutionary investment in vocalization, and they are our main allies as we go forward.

Our ideal bird language allies are songbirds who

- are pretty common year-round in our region,
- feed or nest on or near the ground (where we are),
- establish relatively small territories (that we can keep track of).

I've introduced the robin and junco as ideal teachers. So are the song sparrow, catbird, cardinal, red-winged blackbird, common yellowthroat, towhees, thrushes, and wrens. The aesthetic quality of a species' song is not a factor in understanding bird language. The hermit thrush is a good teacher because it fulfills the three key requirements, not because its song happens to be so beautiful.

Some areas of North America—such as the Jersey shore around its tip at Cape May, where many types of habitat overlap or touch, and where the peninsula attracts most species—boast of well over two hundred species, resident or passing through. Of these, a solid fifty are good teachers of bird language. (In my limited experience throughout North America, I've found that the Pacific Northwest rainforest has the lowest number of total species, a few dozen on a good day, with fewer than twenty of these dependably serving as bird language teachers.) How do you determine which species to focus on in the beginning? Experience will be your guide. You can hear the bird, but can you see it reliably? Is it around most of the time? Is it singing? If the answers are yes, this bird will be a good partner in the journey. Through the years, I've come to love and listen to all the songbirds, while focusing on a few key species. You'll probably develop the same attitude. You'll even come to appreciate the crows and ravens and other corvids. Those birds can really get to me when I'm enjoying a quiet respite in the yard —and that's their intention, I believe: disruption and mayhem for the sheer fun of it. Technically, the corvids are passerines—songbirds—but their behaviors and vocalizations are so out of kilter in so many respects that I've promulgated the Bird Language Corvid Disclaimer Clause, explained in Chapter 7.

A study reported in the journal *Nature* in 2006 showed that a small group of European starlings (considered an invasive species locally, and not a popular one with many birders) learned to make grammatical differentiations between their songs' "sentences." This was some heavy science: the birds were subjected to more than fifteen thousand trials. The results surprised the researchers, who concluded that European starlings have a more complex language capability than previously thought. I am sure there will be more such discoveries in the years to come. We are just beginning to tap into this vast world of communication and bird song.

Almost all of the songbird species have a distinctive generic song, but within some species, such as the Bewick's wren, the generic song can be modified in distinguishable ways by individual birds. *(Listen to audio files 13 and 14 for examples of Bewick's wren song.)* Donald Kroodsma, whose book *The Singing Life of Birds* had a tremendous impact on ornithologists and birders when it was published in 2005, discovered that these wrens sing between ten and sixteen songs. The Bewick's wrens in different regions of North America have different variations. Those in different neighborhoods within the same forest also have different variations, even though the neighborhoods can be remarkably small. For instance, a male offspring may sing different songs than his father just a few territories (that is, a few hundred yards) away. Birds born early in the season develop more songs, and various times of day are marked by different song frequencies.

All this variation can be confusing for veteran birders, ornithologists, trackers, and bird language folks like me. Even aces can have trouble identifying a new species on the basis of song alone. The phonetic transcription on the page is one thing, but the voice in the field is another entirely. *Could that have been a western tanager?* Maybe. Most field guides say that this tanager's song is similar to a robin's song but raspier. Even if you know the robin's song (*plurrri, kliwi, plurrri, kliwi*), what does "raspier" sound like? Was that bird you just heard a western tanager or a robin—or a scarlet tanager or a rose-breasted grosbeak—all of whose songs are suggestive of a robin's? Moreover, many birds are vocally quick on the draw, and their songs from the trees can sound a lot faster to the ear than the transcription on the page may indicate. Most experienced birders know this, and newcomers learn it soon enough. They also know that you have to work with what you have. Today, that's a lot more than was available when I started birding. Digital audio sources, for example, are helpful (see Appendix B: Audio). But the resources themselves can get confusing. An Internet search for a species' song may yield dozens of different examples.

In theory, you don't even need to identify a bird in order to get some bird language value from it. But I've never met a soul who could abide not knowing the species. It's just the way we humans are. On a recent trip to Africa, a new venue for me, I listened to all the bird language and began to piece it together, which was exciting. But I didn't know the species, which was frustrating. Guess what? I figured out those species as fast as I could.

Baseline and Territory

In bird language, songs are all-important for (1) confirming baseline conditions and (2) establishing the birds' individual territories. On the first point, the principle is simple: the singing bird is not worried for its life. The singing bird establishes the absence of immediate danger, helping to confirm baseline. The corollary is also important: the mildest provocation or disturbance will cause almost any bird to stop singing instantly and either maintain silence or broadcast an alarm until its sense of safety—relative peace and harmony—is restored. The restoration of baseline can be shockingly sudden. As we'll see in Chapter 3, the deathly quiet that accompanies the visitation of a hunting Cooper's hawk may yield to vigorous singing just one second after the predator's departure.

So we listen to the songs for pleasure, but we think about them as proof that baseline reigns in this little patch of the world. This is why I say that for bird language purposes, it hardly matters whether the song is simple, such as the olive-sided flycatcher's *quick! three beers*, or wonderfully complex, such as the songs of the hermit thrush and the Pacific wren. What's important is the information it conveys about baseline (or its absence) and about territory.

Understanding the concept of territory and using the birds'

songs to map out their territories is absolutely critical for understanding baseline and whatever else is happening. It necessarily follows that a very interesting, if perhaps overstimulating, time to begin a course in bird language is the spring, the season with the most action and variety. Birds' innate sense of territoriality follows them year-round and can be discerned in different manifestations in different seasons, but birds are most territorial and most committed to singing during the early stages of courtship, breeding, and nesting. As the young become fledglings and are able to follow their parents, everyone becomes less territorial by necessity. It takes a lot of energy to feed teenagers all day long, with nothing left for song. In the cold of winter, or in other seasons or regions with serious food or water shortages, singing also falls off or stops altogether. I don't recommend starting your bird language studies in the middle of January in the state of Maine. There may be plenty going on with alarms and other communication, but the singing component of bird language is at its lowest ebb in the deepest snow. Wait three months.

Primarily, we are talking about the males' songs. It's no coincidence that testosterone production in many male passerines is triggered diurnally, just as the songs are. Females do sing, and some fascinating studies have found that female red-winged blackbirds, who are among the most diligent female songsters, have elevated testosterone during the breeding season. *(Female red-winged blackbird song and calls are in audio file 29.)* This is well-known and documented in the ornithology and birding communities. But the redwings are the exception. Unlike their mates, most female birds I have observed seem to be more action oriented than song oriented, as we'll see.

The experts agree that the most elaborate songs have the best chances of attracting a good mate. We know that male canaries actually grow new brain cells in the spring while they are developing and singing their new songs. After mating season, their brains return to the original size. The female's logic (or, more accurately and less anthropomorphically, her instinct that has evolved under selective pressure) might go something like this: *Well, you've got that great song, so you've got the energy required for breeding and parenting. And maybe you're a pretty good listener, too, so you'll probably pay attention to predators. So, okay, let's go.*

This hypothesis makes sense to me, but who knows if it's right? Understanding bird language doesn't mean we can read their "minds" and instincts. All we know for certain is that there must be some kind of meaningful relationship between the males' songs and the females' breeding decisions. For the purposes of evolution (and these purposes do count in the long run), the females seem to be in charge. They make the decisions that count.

Once a female has chosen her mate, the male's song is all about securing territory for breeding, nesting, and feeding. The song is a straightforward declaration of ownership: *Posted! This is my land. This is my reproductive partner! I'm guarding her closely. Keep out!* Birds can fly, but many of them, certainly the songbirds, are anchored in surprisingly small territories much of the time. I've often wondered what would happen if several birds were airlifted from their respective territories in the middle of the season and dropped down a mile away. I don't know of any such study, but I'll hypothesize that the birds would first try to find their original homes, for one simple reason: territory is security. Within territory, the birds know all the hiding places, the safe roosts, the food resources, the local predators' patterns, the local nest robbers, and the best escape and avoidance strategies and routes. They have more or less memorized the territory, which requires time and energy.

Within the borders of his territory of a few thousand square feet, a male robin, for example, is very visible, demonstrative, and vocal. But should he venture forth to pluck that juicy worm that he's spied just beyond the border, he will adopt a different strategy. For starters, no singing, because *outside* his territory may be *inside* his close neighbor's territory. This bird will probably stick to forest edges and shadowy places, move a bit more slowly, and dispense with tail-

or wing-flipping displays. The border is all-important: a couple of yards either way is the difference between cocky and furtive.

With their territory established, many male songbirds assume a visible post from which they can observe their domain and sing all day without moving much at all. Technically, they have multiple perches for singing, but in my own observations over the years, I have tended to find only two or three per bird. These "post-up birds" include robins, cardinals, mockingbirds, juncos, catbirds, grosbeaks, doves, thrushes, finches, thrashers, sparrows, towhees, and blackbirds.

By contrast, some male songbirds seem to be on the move almost all the time, either circling the perimeter of their territory, around and around, or crisscrossing the entire territory, singing all the way, maybe all day long. The yellowthroat, yellow warbler, Wilson's warbler, and other warblers are in this category, as are many of the vireos, cuckoos, titmice, chickadees, and wrens.

On a warm spring day in a rural area of New Jersey, I measured one yellowthroat's territory at about fifty yards across, which seems typical for this species, depending on habitat. (Dense, swampy thickets adjacent to mixed edges of forest and scrub are very productive foodwise, and thus result in smaller territories for yellowthroats.) It took that beautiful bird, with its brilliant yellow throat and amazing mask of shimmering black, about fifteen minutes to make the circuit. His song lasted four or five seconds: *witchity-witchity-witchity-witchity . . . witchity-witchity-witchity-witchity . . . witchity-witchity-witchity-witchity. (Listen to an example of common yellowthroat song in audio file 25.)* The average pause while he flew to his next location on the perimeter was eight seconds. Around and around he went. It was mesmerizing.

Over a period of days, careful observation of the neighborhood yellowthroat in all-out territorial mode will probably yield several instances of him cutting across his territory or doing something else out of the ordinary. Why? These aberrations aren't random; something no doubt prompted them. To solve this puzzle, we need to tune in to the other birds' actions and vocalizations, especially any alarm calls. With experience in bird language, we should be able to figure it out.

Observing the pattern of singing of any territorial songbird should yield a good map of its territory. When in doubt, we can also determine those invisible lines by "pushing" the bird. For instance, while a robin is on the ground feeding, we can walk toward it and see how far in one direction it will move before it hits the invisible fence and doubles back or makes a ninety-degree turn. Then we can push it in another direction. This technique sounds invasive and disrespectful, and it can be if carried too far. I'll never actively disturb a bird's feeding, but if I'm walking around my yard doing chores, cutting the grass, or landscaping, I have no qualms about keeping an eye out for a particular bird's movements. One way or another, watching a bird over the course of several days shortly after he has set up shop will yield quite an accurate map of his territory.

A territory fifty yards in diameter may seem small to us, but for a territorial songbird, that's quite an estate. By contrast, the Pacific wren in western Washington's temperate rainforest with whom I shared a few weeks during the spring, his busy singing season, defended a plot only about fifteen yards in diameter. That's not much space, but it was near a beaver lodge and very rich in insects and other invertebrates at that time. He was thriving, and the tight confines belied the high energy of this explosive little ball of feathers. Like all the wrens (nine species in seven genera in North America, and eighty species of true wrens in twenty genera worldwide), the Pacific wren feeds on insects and spiders, which are especially good sources of energy. To sing, it takes a deep breath—where does it put all that air? —and then lets loose for up to ten seconds without pausing: *ka-wa-miti-go-shi-que-na-go-mooch . . . ka-wa-miti-go-shi-que-na-go-mooch . . .*

And this song is loud. The wrens put out the most volume per ounce of any bird that I know, with the Carolina wren the loudest of them all. *(Audio files 17 and 18 have examples of Carolina wren songs.)* New birders or bird language students, or just passersby who hear a wren for the first time, will invariably look around for a very large bird, for surely such mass would be required to produce such volume. Matching this little brown ball with this astounding aria takes an act of will, at least it did for me on my first encounter with it in a red-cedar forest in western Washington. Wrens also bob around and often skip up to higher branches. Finally out of air, they stop, maybe drop to a lower branch, recuperate, take a deep breath, and half a minute later start all over again. All for the sake of a few hundred square feet.

The bird's airspace extends maybe twenty feet up. That's all. You will rarely if ever hear the wren singing from a higher altitude. The junco goes a little higher, maybe twenty-five feet. This is also the maximum for the yellowthroat, who will more likely be making its circuit at chest height. The song sparrow is singing from a spot just above my head. The robin may be about head-high, too, or it may nest considerably higher (here in the Santa Cruz Mountains of northern California, occasionally as high as forty feet). I have seen — or, rather, heard — robins ascend to the heights of the redwoods for some high-altitude singing, but this is unusual (except for wintering flocks). For these and many other birds, all that open space higher in the trees, all that open sky above the treetops, is of no interest. It doesn't seem to exist for them.

Meanwhile, in a fully mature forest with a high canopy, the black-headed grosbeak, the black-throated green warbler, the western tanager, and the red-eyed vireo are singing and nesting high in the trees and rarely if ever dropping down to the sub-canopy, let alone the head-high brush zone. This is why they are *not* good allies for our investigations in bird language. We can't find them! Although there are bound to be some outliers in these two groups of birds, my experience in numerous sit spots tells me that they have different worldviews.

Chapter 3

MORE CACOPHONY OF HARMONY

ONE AFTERNOON YEARS AGO in New Jersey, I stepped out of the forest with a stringer of bluegills (a favorite pan fish) and happened to hear a little noise and some barely discernible scurrying sounds under a bush. It was a strange little noise, as if it were coming from a tiny tambourine. I had heard it before, but it was so quiet and apparently insignificant, I had never paid any attention to it. The sun was nearing the horizon, but on that afternoon I decided to find out who was responsible. I crept closer . . . closer . . . closer, and finally I was looking at a small brownish bird with black and white head markings and a little spot of yellow. *(Listen to an example of the white-throated sparrow's contact call—"seep" call—in audio file 44.)* I didn't see a second bird, though I could hear a rustling of wings, which indicated there must be at least one more back in there somewhere.

Having seen the bird, I continued on the trail home, where I worked over my mess of bluegills, presented the soon-to-be-delicious little fillets to my mother, and then headed for the bird guides to identify the new bird. At first I thought it might be a white-throated sparrow, but the throat didn't quite match up. I found no other candidate. The next day, at the exact same bush, I found the same bird again, this time with his companion, and got a better look at the white throat patch and the beautiful little yellow spot right by the eye on one of them. The birds were nothing spectacular, but I was impressed by them. Something stirred inside me. I think this was the first time I really recognized a songbird — not just looked at and saw it, but *recognized* it. I was eleven years old. And yes, it was a white-throated sparrow, a cool little creature, and what an intriguing sound it made.

Talking this through with Tom Brown, I changed my mind about the sound I'd heard. Maybe it was more like a quiet sleigh bell than a tiny tambourine, or maybe I should think of it as a "rattling" kind of whistle. At about the same time, now that I was listening to everything more closely, I heard another little sound from the bushes. It was similar to the white-throated sparrow's call, but softer and thinner. This one really did sound like a tiny tambourine! And the birds responsible for it also seemed to be making another sound, something like the one I can produce by clicking my tongue off the roof of my mouth: *ttsch ttsch ttsch ttsch*, in a staccato rhythm of about one call per second. Along with those calls, I sometimes glimpsed black and white tail flashes as the birds moved off when I got too curious, then made still another little sound when they finally fluttered off. Tom and I looked through the books, and I finally found my bird: the junco. I realized I'd seen a couple of juncos at a neighbor's birdfeeder, but it wasn't until I saw these primo little birds in the wild that I got hooked on them. *(Dark-eyed junco contact calls: listen to audio files 6 [first is song, then contact calls] and 8 [similar alarm calls] for examples.)*

The little tambourine sound is the junco's companion call, given out (in that instance in New Jersey) among a small flock of individuals, perhaps even an immediate family, who had arrived in late autumn and, as it turned out, stayed through the winter. Maybe the circumstances — autumn; still warm and often breezy; bluegills still biting; calm, peaceful baseline — combined with the plaintive quality of the junco's call (and the white-throated sparrow's similarly plaintive single-whistle call) to seal the deal for me.

In any event, songbirds' companion calls are the sweetest and most calming aspect of my personal bird language experience. Although I've spent a lot of time alone in the woods, I am, at heart, a

social person who enjoys and probably needs the sustained relationships of tightly knit communities, with a lot of mentoring up and
down the line. Thus, I'm naturally biased in favor of companion
calls.

Second Baseline Vocalization: Companion Calls

To recapitulate, in bird language we concentrate on five vocalizations: songs, companion calls, territorial aggression (usually male-
to-male squawks and the like), adolescent begging, and alarms. The
first four of these are part of the baseline—our best resources for
understanding the baseline patterns for a given species, so we can
then recognize and understand the alarm calls that break those patterns.

Some guidebooks discuss some of the companion calls, usually
under the rubric "contact calls," but for many folks these calls play
a distant second fiddle to the songs. *(For examples of various contact
calls, listen to audio files 16 [Bewick's wren], 20 [Carolina wren], and
30 [red-winged blackbird].)* There's also a natural tendency among
beginners in bird language to concentrate on the loudest (and often
closest) birds. This would be okay if it didn't usually inhibit hearing the quieter birds and the quieter vocalizations—the companion calls. So I urge beginners also to find the recessive birds, such as
the juncos, and their easily missed companion calls. As discussed in
some detail in Chapter 4, if you learn to listen to the silence, you'll
hear more of everything else. And the best understanding of baseline comes from understanding the quietest sounds, which are the
companion calls. They are not spectacular, like many of the songs;
they don't teach us as much as songs do about territories; they don't
teach us as much as alarms do about predators. But more than any
of the other vocalizations, they *do* teach us about the relationships
between the birds, especially paired couples and gathered flocks
of families and mixed winter groups. Companion calls are like the
gently humming, rhythmic, mesmerizing throbbing of the crickets,

locusts, katydids, and other buzzing insects. They sound very different, of course, and they are not nearly as loud. But for those paying full attention, the twittering among the birds as they are feeding, moving comfortably through the underbrush, and "talking" to one another evokes the same feeling of harmony and well-being.

Another advantage of companion calls for bird language students is that they are reliable year-round vocalizations. In the dead of winter in colder climes, when only a hardy band of chickadees may be vocalizing and no one is begging, singing, or fighting, the bird language student can rely on the companion calls. If you have songbirds, you'll always have these calls. And not only songbirds use them. Ducks and geese keep up a quiet conversation, and along the wave line, small, fast-running sandpipers make the tiniest sounds, which you might be able to catch against the hissing of the water in the sand. As quail walk along, they whisper their little *pwrt pwrt pwrt* sounds in time with their footfalls. And, of course, ravens and crows seem to talk incessantly, if not quietly.

I was introduced to companion calls by the white-throated sparrow and junco, but the best of all bird language teachers in this regard is, I believe, a pair of mated cardinals. Their basic exchange is a simple little *chip . . . chip* back and forth, back and forth. *(The first part of audio file 33 has an example of northern cardinal contact calls.)* Each couple has a distinctive rhythm. Maybe five seconds is the standard interval between calls. They're scratching and feeding and busy, but they're also intimately aware of each other, even though they might be fifty feet or more apart. If the male, say, is making too much noise foraging and doesn't hear the female, she'll say, *CHIP! Chip! Chip!* If he fails to reply because he has just snared a juicy grub, she will quickly and more insistently say, *CHIP! CHIP! CHIP! CHIP!* And so it continues, back and forth:

Are you there?
Yes, are YOU there?
Yeah, I'm here!
Don't do that to me!

Sorry.

Okay.

Everything all right?

Fine.

Okay.

Dear?

Yes, honey?

You still there?

Yes, dear.

Chip.

Chip . . . Chip . . . Chip.

Is that imagined exchange the most egregious kind of anthropomorphizing on my part? Only the translation into words. The intent of those little *chip*s must be just about as I've translated them. Spend a few hours on a few different days with a pair of cardinals feeding in the grass in peaceful baseline and tell me otherwise. The rhythms particular to a specific pair will become very apparent. Always, the point is a return to harmony and security. Those cardinals, they're so codependent.

Not by coincidence, perhaps, my most dramatic companion call story concerns a pair of cardinals. It took place close to my home in New Jersey many years ago, near a mixed second-growth deciduous forest — very mixed, lots of species of trees and shrubs — a great place for learning bird language and a great place for a pair of cardinals to live. On that fall day, the two cardinals were feeding beneath the trees, the male about twenty yards to my right, the female ten yards to my left. This is about as far apart as I would expect any pair of cardinals to get. I was strolling and pausing in a very relaxed fashion toward the small creek not far away. The two birds were exchanging a *chip* call every five seconds or so. Now I have to bend the rules of time, because it would take a speed-reader longer to finish this paragraph than it took for the ensuing drama to unfold, which was about ten seconds, I estimated in immediate hindsight. The male to my right uttered a *chip,* and the female to my left did not reply in the accustomed time. This created tension in me immediately—and in the male, who issued a more insistent *chip-chip*, a companion call asking, *What's up?* Then I heard his wings beating furiously as he headed toward me on his way to where the female had been feeding. At the same time, I caught a flash of brown to my left and just ahead. This was the female in sudden flight, and behind her was a sharp-shinned hawk closing fast. The female cardinal was heading for a wall of brush and vines, perhaps hoping to lose the hawk in this tangle. Just as the hawk was about to reach the female, the male burst onto the stage at a dead, bright red sprint and flung himself right between his lady love and the hawk. It was a Superman-like maneuver—just amazing. Distracted, the sharpie faltered and swerved to pursue the male, but the male had too much velocity and a trajectory almost perpendicular to that of the other two birds. Even the sharpie, with his incredible turn-on-a-dime agility, couldn't pull it off. The male escaped and continued in evasive flight to my left, along the wall of vegetation. He was gone in a split second. The female was back in the brush somewhere, not visible. The hawk banked, landed on a branch, peered left and right, gave up on the cardinals, and glided off in pursuit of other prey.

I was stunned. This was one of the most powerful scenes involving birds I had ever witnessed. Was it an incredible act of courage, as we would define it? That's one interpretation, which could be challenged. What can't be challenged is the lesson I learned about the bond between those two cardinals and the importance of baseline companion calls for maintaining that bond. When the male's *chip* went unanswered, his *chip-chip* asked a question. When the answer was not instantly forthcoming, he took action, and just in the nick of time. The sharpie nearly had the female in its talons before the bright red guy intervened. Almost without a doubt, the "missing" companion call had saved the female cardinal's life.

The first question any student of bird language should ask is, Where were the alarm cries for the sharpie? I'm not sure. Strolling toward the creek, I had been alert, but I hadn't heard them or the deafening silence that often follows the initial alarm. One factor may have been the season, late autumn, when there is not a lot of bird coverage in that forest. But there *were* songbirds around, and it wouldn't take many to virtually guarantee that at least one would have seen the hawk. From that moment, word would have spread instantly. Maybe I missed the scattered alarms and didn't pick up on the silence. If so, that's a demerit. In any event, all kudos to that brave cardinal!

One Native American story holds that if one cardinal dies, its mate isn't long for the world either, for their spirits are joined forever. They are two bodies but one spirit. I came across that story in my research at Rutgers about ten years before this cardinal incident. Just weeks later, I found the molten red feathers of a cardinal that, by the look of things, had been dispatched by a sharp-shinned hawk. The feathers were in a circle under an umbrella of vines. Apparently, the hawk had perched in those vines under cover while taking its meal. As it happened, this male and his mate were the only cardinals in the neighborhood, which I knew pretty well. Within a few days of my discovery, I realized that the female had disappeared. She never returned. Had she left to find another mate, or had she, as the Native American story suggests, also given up the ghost? All I know is that I never saw or heard from that bird again.

The following year, a new pair of cardinals moved in, and the female was definitely not the same one. Something about her was different. I can't tell you how I knew this; I don't have any objective, scientific evidence of it. Maybe it was a super-natural *Blink!* moment. Something was also different about how this new couple used their territory, but why shouldn't it have been? They were different birds. I missed the other two. *Grief* might seem too powerful a word to apply to anyone's sense of loss about two birds in the wild, but I was very much haunted by the Native American story and by "my" two cardinals.

One day along the Skykomish River in Washington, a male song sparrow, perched in a curtain of knotweed and cottonwood

branches, caught my attention with its song: *seet-seet-seet-to—
zeeeeee-tipo-zeet-zeet. (Audio file 9 has an example of song sparrow
song.)* He then dropped to the ground. After spending a couple of
minutes watching his incessant, nervous flitting of wings and tail
while scuffling and "hunting," and his continuous contact calling
—louder than usual, insistent and more frequent—I finally realized
that this bird was the only song sparrow around. *(Audio file 11 has
an example of a song sparrow's contact call.)* Where was his mate?
He had one, because I knew this pair well. This was wintertime,
when the song sparrows and most other songbirds have a feeding
area rather than a defended nesting territory, so the missing mate,
not territorial anxiety, was the reason for this display behavior. The
male was nervous, and he was acting his anxiety out.

The female finally returned, and when she did, the male immediately settled down. (I was working with some other trackers. In
their hasty scramble over the bank of the slough on their way from
the cars to the tracking location, some of them must have separated
the paired birds.) Obviously, these sparrows depended on each
other, because he had put a lot of energy into locating his mate as
quickly as possible, broadcasting his position with his insistent, nervous behavior and querulous calls of concern.

The junco's seductive companion call is just about my favorite, but you have to listen closely to catch it. These birds feed head
to ground, and they don't really lift their heads to call. The result
is a muffled *stip*. The same holds true for the white-crowned and
white-throated sparrows and the other scratch feeders, who move
in flocks, scratching with their feet, thereby producing a rhythmic,
rustling *shhrrt . . . shhrrt . . . shhrrtt*. Since these little birds feed under
bushes and brush, they often lose sight of one another, and they're
diligent with their scratch-and-call, pause, scratch-and-call, pause,
scratch-and-call. The intrepid birds breaking new ground on the
leading edge of the flock are the most diligent. I've always found
these rhythmic pulses, this peaceful feeding of a flock, mesmerizing: the sweetest, most peaceful baseline in the forest. The compan-

ion calls of these ground feeders is also invaluable in the study of bird language, because they teach us *attention*. Only with close attention and wide-angle deer hearing (the equivalent of wide-angle owl vision) can we find and learn from these quieter companion calls.

Finding large flocks feeding together is more likely in the winter, of course, when the territorial imperative is diminished or absent. Mixed flocks are common: sparrows, titmice, chickadees, kinglets, nuthatches, brown creepers, yellow-rumped warblers, waxwings, siskins, and bushtits all bustle around together, truly a (quiet) cacophony of harmony, each species with its slightly different little *chip* or *stip*, or a wispy *seeeet* with rising inflection. *(Listen to audio file 49 for an example of black-capped chickadee song, which they often begin singing in midwinter.)* When this contact chorus stops in its tracks, something is up. Nervousness among robins flocking in the winter is a great barometer of neighborhood tension.

The companion calls of the ground-scratching spotted towhees are a special case. Like the juncos, they may vocalize and scratch in rhythm, but just as often they do not vocalize at all. Instead, their rhythmic scratching alone serves as the "all's well" signal. *Scratch, scratch, scratch, scratch.* Then they pause and listen. *Scratch, scratch, scratch, scratch.* This companion call is aural but not oral. (I sometimes believe that towhees can hear in the subsonic range, because they seem to respond to cues before all the other birds and are often the first to leave the scene when danger or a disturbance approaches.) On top of all the aural cues, the spotted towhees also use visual cues, as do the juncos and other ground feeders who make a lot of noise while feeding and may not be heard no matter how much noise they make. These towhees flip their wings and flash their black and white tail feathers, rhythmically and methodically, once every few seconds: *flip . . . flip . . . flip . . . flip.* You could calibrate a metronome by this action. (I exaggerate only slightly.) Most birds catch our attention by a sudden movement that interrupts the stillness—such flitting and flashing is some kind of alarm signal —but with these towhees, it's exactly the opposite. Their unusual stillness indicates that something is afoot. Without knowledge of their baseline behavior—their peculiar scratching habit—we could easily misinterpret the importance of their stillness. (What about the mockingbirds? Is their strange dance while feeding in the grass —leaping straight up a foot or so, fluttering the wings, exposing the white patch—a token of their companionship, or is it just an idiosyncrasy, like the other aerial stunting of these terrific birds? I still don't know.)

One of my favorite birds to work with in the call category is the bobwhite, a type of quail. This is not a songbird and not one of our usual bird language allies, but in their specialized habitat, you can learn a lot from quail. *(Listen to audio file 58 for an example of a bobwhite vocalization, made mostly by unmated males in the spring.)* They have a basic companion call while feeding (a soft *took* or *pitoo*) and a different "covey call," or "flock call," to bring everyone back together following a disturbance that has scattered the flock (*hoy-hoypoo* and *koile*). *(Listen to audio files 59 [northern bobwhite] and 56 [California quail] for examples of quail flock calls.)* The designated flock caller (the alpha male?) hops onto a high point and calls and calls and calls—*come-right-here . . . come-right-here . . . come-right-here* (the accepted English-language translation of *hoy-hoy-poo*)—until all the birds have returned to the fold. If a good human mimic of this call happens to be in the field and beats the real caller to the punch following a disturbance, the birds will scurry to the phony call until they get to within six feet or so, which is just out of clear eyesight, given the ground cover that prevails. (Quail rely on ground cover, of course.) There they will stop, perhaps sensing that something is wrong, and make a weird little sound, something like *pitoo* issued over and over in a quail whisper. This is their secret handshake/companion call, and if the phony caller can't return it convincingly, the birds will circle all around, but they won't get any closer. If the caller does produce the secret handshake, the quail will break cover and walk right over. I've had quail almost in my lap. That's a lot of fun.

Emphasis, Context, Response: Nuance Matters

Listening to a Spanish, Italian, or German opera, you, like me, may have no idea what the words of a particular aria mean, but you don't need this knowledge to understand the feeling they convey. You can tell if it's a song of pleasure, jubilation, triumph, or tragedy. The singers' talent and the music itself make the emotional component and the overall story quite clear. In the same way, you don't need to know exactly what the birds are saying to one another with their companion calls in order to pick up and understand the flow. *Understanding* bird language does not equate to *translating* bird language.

Think about the English word *really*. Depending on subtle differences in enunciation that don't show up in phonetic transcriptions, that word can express astonishment, sarcasm, dismay, irony, reassurance, and a good deal more. By the same token, if you know a pair of birds or a flock well enough, if you understand in your bones the baseline norm for a certain patch of the world twenty-five yards across—your favorite sit spot—you'll begin to detect the same kinds of distinctions between *chip* and *CHIP, shhrrt* and *SHHRRT, tsip* and *TSIP,* and *pseet* and *PSEET.*

Your awareness is that keen, your knowledge of place that encompassing, your empathy that powerful. You'll definitely understand that the two robins flitting around, making all kinds of racket (*cheenk! cheenk! cheenk!*), and whapping their wings in the brush are not issuing dire alarm calls because they see a boa constrictor. You'll know this because the song sparrows are still feeding peacefully, confirmed by their exchange of companion calls barely discernible "below" the noise generated by the robins. The towhee hasn't raised an eyebrow either. The wood thrush farther away is still singing. The other birds are saying, in effect, *Nothing dangerous here. Just a couple of proud robins beating themselves up because their hormones are raging. Let's pretend we don't hear them.* Simply put, no one is paying any attention except for the two male birds. Even their partners are standing by quietly. *Men!*

Third Baseline Vocalization: Territorial Aggression

And so we turn to the third baseline vocalization of songbirds (and many other birds): your generic, ho-hum, male-to-male aggression. Two male robins are scuffling? Note their location as a likely point on the border between their territories. In the spring and summer especially, during mating and nesting, territorial behavior reflects the high investment the birds have in finding a mate and setting up a territory. Within this territory, each male knows all the hiding spots and feeding areas. He knows the regular predators and the safe perching areas. This is important information for him. He doesn't want to have to move and learn these details about a new neighborhood. So he defends this territory, often several times a day. When another robin trespasses, his actions will almost certainly be followed by a sudden outburst from the rightful owner. The ensuing squabble and maybe chase will be energetic and brief, the better for saving everyone's energy. The phonetic transcription of the aggression call hardly matters. *(American robin's agitation calls are in audio file 3.)* The robin's *cheenk!* will always be accompanied by intense body language. This holds true for the other songbirds, too. In short, there's no mistaking this territorial aggression action for anything else in the bird language repertoire. Scolded, and perhaps wing-slapped (for lack of a better term), for a few moments by the owner, the trespasser will probably retreat. The owner will immediately relax, secure in his alpha status. (I've seen robins also chase away flickers and other woodpeckers if the intruder's chosen tree happens to harbor the robin's nest. The defender's loud, aggressive behavior is the same as that employed against another robin, and the scuffle is also short.) In most cases, the trespasser likely wasn't attempting to actually take over this territory; he has his own territory. It was all an unfortunate mistake. At least that's how it seems to me.

As with our own real estate, so it is with the birds'. Some of it may be more desirable, high-rent terrain, with good access to food, water, and cover, and with relatively less danger from nest robbers and other predators (mainly because the property owner knows all the escape routes and strategies). Birds who have successfully established such territories may pay a price, however. Because resources are plentiful and predator stress is low, *competitor* stress may be high. The turf battles between long-distance migrating birds may be the most intense of all. These birds have come a long way to breed, often thousands of miles. Their investment is high. Interlopers should be ready for a battle. Some male red knots leave their wintering home in Tierra del Fuego a week earlier than their peers, thus getting a jump on the ten-thousand-mile race to Nunavut. This one week slightly increases their risk of encountering bad weather, but it's a risk the early migrant is willing to take. He arrives first on the breeding territory and finds a location that meets all of his courtship, mating, and rearing needs. Six days later, the leading edge of the main flock of red knots arrives and pushes the edges of the early bird's territory. As a first warning, the owner scolds them. Then he tries serious posturing. If necessary, he may try to physically drive them off. As always, it's a matter of energy. After such a long migration, all sides in the territorial struggles in Nunavut have energy issues.

Sometimes a collection of robins who are spread over a meadow or a suburban neighborhood and who have been fiercely defending their patches of turf (and airspace) suddenly drop all hostilities. Or so it seems when you find them gathered on a nearby lawn, or even on a small patch of that lawn, for some peaceful side-by-side dining. What's with this contradictory "flock" behavior? The only answer is a great abundance of food—so much food that there's no reason to be possessive about it. In fact, with food everywhere, there's almost no way to be possessive about it. Likewise with the grizzlies, who fish shoulder to shoulder in the salmon-bearing rivers of Alaska and Canada. Tussles there are rare. In other times and other places, however, they do tussle. With birds and bears, if scarcity is a factor, you won't find communal dining in any season.

Given a consistent food supply in winter, say, communal feeding among groups of birds may vary wildly, being within the realm of the normal—baseline—one day and verboten the next. I'm pretty sure that the change is tied to the transition into the nesting season. Early in the season, in the transition from winter to spring, the "one flock, one mind" mode hasn't yet been superseded by the mating mode. *If you step one foot closer, I'll drill the feathers off your nape!*

Where I live in California, tall Douglas fir and redwood trees are massed on the northern and eastern edges of my yard, and in the winter as many as two hundred robins may be perched in those branches, a big communal roost. Toward the end of January this past season, however, I noticed that one robin was becoming less and less tolerant of the other dozen feeding on the worms below. From his perch, he began to sing more and more, and soon he was chasing the others away—all of them! He could do this without much trouble because they were nonbreeding migrants with little investment in this turf. They yielded without a fight and moved off to the south, where the living also was easy, with dense clusters of berries on the neighborhood madrones and fire thorns. I concluded (correctly, it turned out) that the boss bird was a breeding male, a real local who wanted to keep these tourists at bay. Even in the spring, with breeding under way, you may see or hear a large group of robins gathered together in the same tree for the dawn chorus. Twenty years ago, I heard at least twenty-five males caroling one morning (that was my estimate; it was still pitch-dark) near the end of April—the twenty-seventh, to be exact. I know the date because that wonderful harmonizing drifted in the window just as one of my daughters was born. It was such an overwhelming moment that we decided to name her Robin.

These days, I'm often in the field around San Francisco Bay, working each week with the same group learning bird language together. In the winter months—that's what we call them, though the blooming flowers and the visitors from colder climes don't corroborate the label—the song sparrows especially sing a lot and, to all appearances, seem to be engaged in territorial defense. The pair bonds seem to be present, and powerfully, even though breeding and nesting may still be two months in the future. The same holds for the varied thrushes, the Bewick's wrens, and the robins. These birds are flocking, but there are also some scuffles between birds of the same species. My guess is that in many of the dustups, maybe most, it's local adults, committed and territorial, versus juveniles and/or migrants. Or maybe some of the local birds just don't have it in them to be territorial right now, so they get pushed around. Again, to fully understand what's happening, we have to know the birds of this area and their territorial behavior. We have to know the baseline in place. Knowing the "technical" natural history facts behind baseline behavior is great but not really necessary. Remembering the *patterns* of the birds' behavior gives us the context for interpreting the stories embodied by the new sounds and activities that don't fit in.

One final significant note about this aggression: I use the term "male-to-male" because the male version predominates, but have you ever seen a mother robin in her territorial mode? I watched one brutalize another female robin, then a minute later strike a hard blow to the back of the neck of a considerably larger Steller's jay. This was in the magnolia tree outside my kitchen window. Generally speaking, and again from my observations, most males of most species are actually fairly low-key and oriented toward the *idea* of defense through song and display and, if necessary, scuffling. Protecting chicks in the nest, a female will be quick to drive away anyone deemed an intruder, and without much fanfare. They're more direct and seem tougher to me. They go for the jugular, almost literally. As another bird, I'd much rather deal with a male.

Aggression Is Not Alarm

There's nothing subtle or profound about the birds' aggressive behavior and vocalizations. They're not going to entice anyone into a lifetime's study, and I don't think it's worth one (unlike songs, which have been so studied by many people, and also unlike companion calls and alarms, which are still waiting for such lifelong devotion). The most important point for bird language students to understand is that this aggressive behavior and these calls are part of the baseline. I say this for two reasons. First, as noted, the other birds don't pay much attention to intraspecies disputes. They understand that the racket is not an alarm call, so they go about their business. Second, if a real alarm concerning a real predator is issued during an episode of territorial struggle, the two fighting birds will instantly forget their dispute and become the best of friends as they hide together, side by side in the same thicket, while their worst nightmare—say, a Cooper's hawk—glides silently past.

Fourth Baseline Vocalization: Adolescent Begging

In the spring and early summer, however, that Cooper's hawk is not thinking about the adult robins as direct targets. Relatively speaking, at this time of year, those adults are too much work. The predator is looking instead for the adolescents, who are easier pickings. Nature abhors a vacuum, and it also seems to abhor adolescent behavior. In virtually every ecological niche other than human society, hungry and demanding self-absorption often comes at a fatal cost. Chicks, virtually all of them, beg: *I WANT MY FOOD, AND I WANT IT NOW!* Phonetically, there's not a lot of difference in the begging voice from species to species, just variations on the *sssssss!*, the *squawk*, and the guttural *aahhh!* Since nestlings are everywhere and easy to hear, these differences can be learned pretty quickly. Young birds simply cannot keep their mouths shut, and they therefore announce their presence and their vulnerability unmistakably. The mother grabs a berry and stuffs it into the nearest gaping mouth. The other two, three, or four gaping mouths are still squawking—even more intensely when Mom or Dad feeds another sibling. The one with the berry is satisfied for about as long as it takes to swallow, blink an eye, and shake the head in a distinctive manner customary in many species. Then the chick joins the others in their demands as if it had never been fed.

This fourth vocalization in bird language is restricted to the nestling and fledgling season, when the young birds are stuck in or near the nest, utterly dependent on their parents for food. Fortunately for them (and their parents), this dependence lasts for only several days to a few weeks, depending on the species. Then they take flight and are somewhat on their own. The overall nesting season lasts three to five months, from sometime in March or April into June, even July, depending on the location. For some species, and in some specific locations, nesting can start even earlier.

Like the territorial aggression calls, the begging calls aren't subtle or worthy of a lifelong study, but they're important enough to warrant designation as a separate baseline vocalization within bird language. *(Audio files 12 [song sparrow fledglings] and 48 [American goldfinch fledglings] have examples of begging calls.)* For these few months of the year, they contribute significantly to the fund of bird vocalizations filling the air. Also filling the air are the hawks, especially the accipiters, and among them *especially* the Cooper's and sharp-shinned hawks, who are intent on combing the begging kids out of the trees. How easy it is! Children seem particularly good at catching birds of this age with their bare hands, and I remember doing the same. A small child's skill is nothing compared with an agile bird-hunting specialist's skill. All these predators have to do is listen for those rhythmic, incessant begging calls. The rest is like taking not the candy, but the baby itself. And the accipiters are joined by the corvids, the peregrines, the cats, the raccoons, the foxes—

just about all of the predators and opportunistic feeders. Who would want to miss this feast?

Of course, the wiser parents know when a predator is in flight, because the birds' alarm calls—perhaps a wave of alarms followed by a tunnel of silence—are leading and trailing the hawk all the way. The parent robins pause, stiffen, crane their necks upward, flick their tails nervously, and emit an insistent and questioning *cheenk! cheenk!* One or both then call out in alarm, and both dive headlong into the thicket behind the berry bushes. Some of the juveniles may be able to set aside their single-minded obsession with food, notice that their parents have ditched it, and follow them into stillness and silence (though not into the thicket). But there's usually at least one who is more self-absorbed than the others, more concerned about its own needs at the moment, still begging at the top of its tiny lungs: *Hey! Where you going? What about me?* Listening carefully from the ground, we can hear this chick, and then—a sudden silence, a muffled thud, maybe a little shriek, or perhaps the flash of a swooping gray figure and a puff of feathers. Instantly, the Cooper's hawk is flying off with a meal for its own nest. Some of the remaining chicks, not necessarily all of them, are finally stunned into silence. The trauma of such a brush with death—inches away, with the wind from the hawk's descent lifting their breast feathers, the hawk's wings perhaps hitting one or more of them directly— leaves a definite imprint, which will likely never go away. Awareness grows, but how quickly? The fate of those who don't learn from this experience is almost guaranteed.

After the attack, the parents call to each other from their cover nearby. It's not a companion call exactly, but something else, sort of a post-alarm call, similar to the other calls, but less intense and in a different pattern. Reassured, the mother comes out of hiding. In the distance, she hears other alarms for the hawk going off, including the sudden surge in excitement among a group of jays as the hawk passes by with its limp catch in its grasp. The father also emerges.

The chicks pick up the cues of relative safety and resume begging, and both parents study them. Are they searching for the missing sibling? The father issues a quiet, questioning call, something like a companion call, and assumes a more relaxed posture. I have seen both parents preen and shake, as if releasing a terrible energetic burden from their bodies, if not from their brains, because they do remember. We know this because, only a couple of minutes after the hawk's attack, when alarm calls from other birds are heard approaching from the same direction in which the hawk flew off, the parents hit the deck again. Quite likely, the same predator is returning for a second helping, knowing that acting swiftly gives him an edge over the other predators. The chicks, who have resumed begging, fall silent this time—some of them. But the odds are pretty good that at least one will not yet have learned the lesson and will be unable to restrain its primal instinct (even more primal than the fear of hawks), and now we hear this chick begging in the sudden silence, and then . . .

Establish a post near a hawk's nest during nesting season, and you will be astonished by how often the parents fly in with a songbird to feed their young. I've watched a Cooper's hawk deliver a bird to one of its own two or three chicks three times within half an hour. The parent had found the ultimate larder. Seeing this, I wondered how many songbirds a single hawk nestling requires to get through its six weeks in the nest. On average, according to careful observation, it needs sixty-six. That's a lot of songbirds who don't make it (many of them are likely fledglings). This is why it's not unusual for a nesting pair of songbirds to lose an entire clutch and have to start all over, and this is why we find robin eggs in July. I've seen a pair of mated robins try to raise three clutches in one summer. The third clutch made it at least until the fledgling stage; who knows what happened after that. At that point, the fledglings and parents moved out of my yard.

The world of wildlife, though lovely during baseline, can

quickly turn brutal: one life prolonged, one life lost, the way of the world.

We've now covered the four baseline vocalizations, leaving the fifth vocalization, alarms, for last. Before we get into that complex category (see Chapter 5), let's get immersed in the habitat where the best learning takes place—your sit spot.

Chapter 4

THE SIT SPOT

P EOPLE OCCASIONALLY SAY, "Jon, I can't even identify the different birds that come to my feeder. The robin, the cardinal, sure, at least the males, but not most of the others. How in the world can I use their songs to figure out their territories? How can I ever identify and understand the companion calls? How can I distinguish scuffling males from alarmed males? How am I ever going to understand the baseline vocalizations?"

My answer is, practice. The only "talent" required for understanding the birds is awareness, and we all have that. What really counts is practice — *motivated* practice. Even in fields such as chess and music, which we tend to think of as dominated by talent and "genius," it turns out that sheer talent is easier to come by than the motivation to practice and learn for eight hours a day. For the deepest learning and achievement to happen, the deepest visceral connection with the subject is necessary. In education, sparking this connection is the primary goal; the learning follows. A lot of careful research in recent years has confirmed this, some of it neatly summarized in a 2009 *New Yorker* piece by Malcolm Gladwell, author of the book *Outliers*. Anyone with even a modest amount of motivation can become adept at bird language, and it doesn't require practicing eight hours a day.

But practice where? In your sit spot, which we sometimes call the "secret spot" or, more charmingly and more respectfully of the native tradition, the "medicine area." Earlier in the book, I used a food metaphor: my first two subjects—what's really going on out there, and how we can access that world through the awareness of deep bird language (and see more wildlife)—are the meat and potatoes; my third subject—understanding how that recognition and connection can change our lives—is the dessert. The sit spot is where the entire meal is laid out for us in perfect detail.

Even for a veteran, making quick sense of any new habitat with multiple species and birds and disturbances is a challenge; for a neophyte, it's impossible. But "quick sense" isn't the idea anyway. *Slow* sense is the idea, and returning to the same habitat day after day builds slow sense. Previously random observations begin to fall into place and come together as a coherent picture. The birds step forward. The intimidating surface of their world begins to yield to our awareness, revealing the hidden recesses and truths.

I helped to develop an alternative program for older teenagers in the rural foothills of the Cascade Range in King County, Washington. On the first day of classes, each teen was sent into the nearby woods to select his or her personal home base for the class in bird language. At the end of every subsequent forty-minute "class" in the sit spot, the teens and the facilitators returned to the gathering shelter and reported their observations. I loved those sessions (so much so that I now use them as a model for a yearlong training in California). We learned so much about the birds, the animals, and the participants themselves. I remember well the saga of one young man who had grown up in nearby Seattle. I'll call him Jack. His experience with the natural world had been limited to city parks. His experience with birds had been limited to pigeons and crows. No surprise, and not his fault. It's where a lot of people are today—both children and adults. In the beginning, Jack's time alone in his sit spot was a real challenge. He could not for the life of him figure out why people would want to do this—go into the woods, sit there, pay attention, otherwise do nothing—much less be required to do so as part of a high school experience.

At first the birds all around Jack didn't even exist for him. He refused to give them any importance at all. He rebelled against the whole idea. The first day he said, "There weren't any birds around. I didn't see any." True and not true. Those woods were well occupied by a variety of common birds, but most of them probably did flee on the arrival of this intruder (known as the "bird plow," alarm shape number one, as we'll see in Chapter 7). Jack's mind was so busy rebelling that his senses shut down and he didn't see or hear any of the birds who took a chance and stayed put. In a way, he was *refusing* to see them, but maybe the experience was so new to him, and the senses required for this kind of quiet attention were so undeveloped, that he literally *couldn't* see them. Regardless, my job is to help people recover their latent instincts and develop them into new patterns and habits of perception and awareness. I also try to build good thinking skills, research abilities, and background knowledge, but it's hard to get going in those departments without triggering the keener awareness, deeper connection, and motivation to use them. That's what I set out to do with Jack.

The teaching tool of choice is what Tom Brown Jr. calls the "sacred question," which is actually three questions: "What did you observe? What is this telling you? What is this *teaching* you?" I use it in all of my programs, because it drives people deeper into any question.

With rebellious Jack specifically, over the following months, with the help of those three questions, "no birds" became "a few birds," which morphed into "some little brown noisy birds," then into "flocks of little black and white ones that stayed in the trees" and "other birds I couldn't really see." One day Jack announced that he had seen some "Pacific wrens" (those "little brown noisy birds") and some "chickadees in the trees" (those "little black and white ones"). *(Listen to audio file 50 for an example of the multipurpose call of black-capped chickadees.)* Then the "chickadees were feeding and calling in the trees." Then "the Pacific wren seemed upset because another Pacific wren came close to this one's favorite stump." (An understanding of territory is often a revelation: *This bird* lives *here! This is her address. No wonder she lets me know that she's not happy when I barge in.*)

Bird language is about acquiring some "jungle etiquette," and the sit spot is where this starts to happen. Little by little over the course of that school year, Jack identified by species the birds he couldn't even see a few months earlier, differentiated one from the other ("the male Pacific wren that hangs out by the east bank beaver lodge"), built some connection with them, and then finally *recognized* them, San Bushman–style. The key was his basic but growing awareness and practice. Instead of flushing out the wrens and chickadees and robins and sparrows with a major bird plow, Jack learned to sit quietly and watch, listen, learn, and connect. As a result, he changed.

Where, Exactly?

Jack's personal growth wouldn't have happened if he'd just charged into those woods every day in a different direction. It happened because he had one place where his own rebellion and the intimidating natural world yielded to his newfound awareness, connections, and understanding. He also had the advantage of the program itself, which provided easy access to a sit spot and the discipline to visit it every day. A daily dose of bird language medicine is recommended, which is why I say that the single most important factor for anyone interested in the subject is choosing a first sit spot that is *convenient*. Any place more than a two-minute walk from the door may be too far. The sit spot must be accessible on a moment's notice, so when you have some time, you don't have an excuse. In the beginning, this is vital.

In the city, a tree on the edge of the park up the street is just as effective as a tree in the country. In fact, it can be more effective, because the birds are more concentrated. There are plenty of birds in the city (I've heard city dwellers complain about the dawn chorus outside their apartment windows), and those birds seen and heard every day are the ones to learn from, because they have the most to say to us. There are Cooper's hawks and sharp-shinned hawks and owls living in most cities. Often there are peregrine falcons and red-tailed hawks as well. There are certainly nest robbers (crows and probably some jays, possibly magpies, certainly rats and squirrels and cats). One year, on the eve of St. Patrick's Day in London, right by a busy street along the Thames, I watched a red fox sniffing and investigating unseen trails and stories in the grass along the walking path under a streetlight. In Seattle, a coyote got stuck in an elevator, and a cougar sauntered right by a homeless camp beneath an overpass. But it doesn't take cougars to learn bird language, or even coyotes. A housecat will do just fine.

Know all your neighbors. This is what it comes down to.

In the backyard, a spot near a hedge or underneath a tree is theoretically better than one in the middle of the lawn. But the middle works, too. You can create an awesome backyard sit spot with different kinds of feeders. Birdbaths can also be great teachers. Many resources can help you set up your yard as a more diverse habitat for birds and find the best sit spot. My family composts outdoors, and our compost pile is a fine mini–sit spot. Even for bird language learners whose primary sit spot is in the middle of a great bird habitat such as a northeastern deciduous forest, a secondary pad in the backyard is highly recommended. When you have fifteen minutes and are too tired even to flip through the channels mindlessly, flop down on the grass instead, relax, and open new horizons. I do this all the time. And I have to admit that a lot of my bird language awareness also has come from my dynamic sit spot by the local fishing hole (with rod in hand, I have watched many a story unfold), as well as from my lazy summer wanders in the Pine Barrens of New Jersey.

Today I live at the edge of the woods on top of one of the Santa Cruz Mountains, near the sea. When I'm home, I try to go outside for a bit at first light—just walk out the front door and sit on my wooden bench in the quiet before the dawn. This is kind of a *tempo-*

ral sit spot, also highly recommended. The neighbors' lights are all out, and my family is still asleep. It's my time to take in the morning and feel the day coming. I love these moments. I watch the stars slowly blink out as the eastern sky blushes pink against the azure and silver band of fading night. I take in the morning news. Who's around? The night birds move off to their rest as the day birds start waking up—the towhees first, then the jays. The wings of ravens are squeaking in the darkness; sometimes a horned owl is still calling. A bit later, the robins get going (in winter, hundreds roost on the edge of the property). The dawn chorus is on the way. It takes only five minutes, maybe ten, for me to feel connected. Later in the day, I step out again for a few minutes. I sit on the bench by the front door, or just outside the back door in the sun, in another chair I set there for this purpose. When I have calls to make or conference calls to monitor, I sit there and multitask. My actual sit spot is the bench by my front door, facing the yard, but these secondary sites are perfectly satisfactory—and they're really all part of one larger sit spot area.

Wherever you live, pick a sit spot where you can actually see, not one in the middle of a blackberry thicket—and not one in the top of a tree. You should be down low with the ground birds. I recommend the edge of a pond or a creek, if possible, because almost all creatures will pass by the water, especially in a dry habitat. That's the ideal, but I didn't have water near my first sit spot in New Jersey. I still figured out that the ovenbird lived over in *that* area; the juncos liked to feed around *those* evergreen trees in the winter; the barred owl roosted in *that* holly tree; the chickadees moved through in bands, mixed with titmice, creepers, and nuthatches in winter; and the white-throated sparrows slept in the hemlock hedges in good numbers all winter. To learn this, I had to learn about the bushes, trees, nuts, berries, and insects—all necessary baseline information, since those food sources dictate so much of the birds' behavior. When you pay attention and begin to connect the dots, any place with some birds is a good sit spot to start out. In a big city, there may be fewer dots to connect than in a suburban or rural area, but that's fine. Bird language is universal, and the journey of understanding it is the same no matter where you are.

I read recently that Max Allen, a naturalist, tracker, and nature photographer I have known for many years, had just marked the seven-year anniversary of his sit spot routine. For more than 2,555 consecutive days—and counting—Max made time to find a little ad hoc sit spot, even when on the road. He is to be congratulated and celebrated—especially since his initial reason for establishing a sit spot was to help a young man he was mentoring, who visited his own sit spot every day for a year.

As a kid, I had the same sit spot every day from the early summer of 1971 through the fall of 1978, rarely missing a day. I must have unwittingly sparked a competition by sharing this information with other bird language folks, because several have told me that they've passed my mark. In fact, I've passed it myself. The longest I've had a steady, if not *everyday,* sit spot is eight years. That was thirty miles north of my current home in northern California. As an adult, I can't match Max Allen's streak, but for the past forty years, I have rarely missed a day at a sit spot of some kind somewhere, impromptu though it may be. When too many days go by without that kind of connection, my mood slips. As Max told me, it's difficult to put into words the life lessons and wisdom we learn from this kind of practice, and it's best *felt* in the bones rather than *thought* in the head. So it's not essential that you make it to your sit spot every single day, but it is important to go there as regularly as possible.

When traveling, it's usually pretty easy to find a sit spot that mimics the one back home. If your main sit spot is in a lawn with a thicket edge along one side, a grassy expanse with a thicket edge almost anywhere in North America will almost certainly yield many of the same bird species (or at least species similar in niche and behavior). Alternatively, you can anchor not with a habitat, but with a species. If robins are your best allies at home, sit with some robins wherever you go. Their general behavior may vary from coast to coast, but the five basic robin vocalizations won't. In Africa, Australia, Europe, and Asia, I understand the language of the native birds almost as well as I do that of the redwood forest at home. In the end, it's not about specific species. It's about principles.

Here's an example. The very first day in a new sit spot at a plain backyard feeder in Washington, I got off to a great start when I realized that someone out there had taken my East Coast blue jay, enlarged it slightly, turned it upside down and dipped it in black ink from the top of its crest halfway down its body, and renamed it "Steller's jay." Moreover, all that ink had clogged the bird's pipes. This jay didn't make the *jaaay jaaay jaaay* declarations I was used to, but seemed stuck with some raspy clicking noises like none I'd ever heard. It also made some unbirdlike "gassy" sounds and every variation on *shhh-shhh-shhh-shhh-shhh*, although that monosyllable doesn't begin to do the sounds justice. But then I heard something familiar in the jay's insistent vocalization (if not the tone) of the *chhht! chhht! chhht!* alarm, one of three alarms shared with the eastern blue jay. The body language was also the same: the bird bent way over, bill pointed down, head nodding up and down, up and down. (The intruder provoking the alarm was a species well-known to me in New Jersey: a housecat.) That sit spot is also where I learned that jays will imitate the call of a red-tailed hawk and then issue an alarm about that hawk. *(Listen to a Steller's jay mimicking a red-tailed hawk call in audio file 64.)* If the ruse works, the birds at the feeder will scatter, and the Steller's will take over. On the other side of the world, the Siberian jay has apparently perfected the same scheme. So has the blue jay back east; I remember the first time I heard one almost perfectly imitate the call of a broad-winged hawk.

Binoculars, Journals, and Other Sit Spot Gear

"Should I bring binoculars to my sit spot?" This is one of the questions I'm asked most frequently, and I always say that if you want to bring binoculars, you should bring them and use them as you wish. I've learned a lot with binoculars. In my teenage years, when I was out at my sit spot alone and heard a bird making a sound that I couldn't quite figure out, I used every resource possible. Tom Brown always asked me about the birds I had heard or seen and encouraged me to stay the course until I could identify them with certainty. Later, he encouraged me to get methodical, so I started using a file box of index cards, noting species, date, time, and location for every bird I observed. My first index card is dated 1973, and by the time I was at Rutgers half a dozen years later, I had hundreds of entries and could identify every species in the forests, fields, rivers, estuaries, and shorelines within thirty miles of my home, and in the Pine Barrens as well. I distinguished the year-round residents from the summer residents from the winter residents from the just-passing-through migrants.

What about those binoculars? I believe the day will come, as it did for me, when you feel that most of the time, they belong on your lap. Also on your lap should be your journal, in which I recommend making short notes every ten minutes. (That's at the beginning of your bird language experience. At some point, you will find that you can leave the journal home for nightly "story of the day" back-trail analysis.) The idea of setting such a strict time schedule for note taking usually surprises people. Intuitively, it might seem kind of hypocritical, even counterproductive, given the timeless quality inherent in sitting in nature. I don't want to make anyone obsessive about time, but the ten-minute discipline speeds up the learning curve in bird language study. Experience has sold me on this point. In some schools and bird language programs, a raven call — *kraaah-kraah-kraah* — is broadcast to mark the ten-minute intervals for participants in their sit spots. Using quick shorthand references, they note everything that happened in the preceding ten minutes, including the barking dog, the passing train, and the jet flying overhead. Who would have guessed the correlation between the mild vibration of that jet or a gust of wind and the sudden cessation of the spring peepers' chorus; between the rumble of that train and the Pacific chorus frogs' immediate silence; between the sudden appearance of the sun on a cloudy day and a burst of bird song. These little discoveries are delightful and surprisingly valuable. Discount none of them. The baseline is deeper and more subtle than we can imagine.

Train Your Senses

With bird language, you're at the mercy of your senses. Don't leave home without them. Our tutelage begins with our eyes, since sight is the sense we humans rely on first. "Owl vision" is the ultimate achievement. "Wide-angle vision" might be technically more accurate, but I believe that imitating a creature universally identified with keen eyesight helps us utilize more of our brains. Many indigenous trackers with extraordinary tracking and bird language skills are also prone to imitation. This isn't hard science. This is my sense of things after thirty years of experience with both bird language and cultural approaches to mentoring. Others have seconded that hypothesis. Owls have evolved eyes so large that they have actually outgrown their sockets and are "frozen" in place. They can locate prey even on the darkest nights. Thus "owl vision" it is in this book.

Here's an exercise: Look straight ahead and imagine that your eyeballs are so large that they're stuck and cannot move. To look at, or focus your eyes on, any object, you will have to move your entire head. Now look straight ahead and pick a point or object on which you can train your eyes without moving. Hold that spot as your focal point. If your eyes wander off, bring them back. Always return to that spot. While staring at that point and without moving your eyeballs, notice how you can also see some of the context around that spot—part of the ground or floor, maybe some of the ceiling, maybe stuff on the surrounding wall. This is your peripheral vision coming into play. Build on it by adding to your peripheral awareness the farthest thing you can see to the extreme left . . . to the extreme right . . . as far above the focal point as possible . . . as far below the focal point as possible . . . all without moving your eyeballs from your focal point. By focusing hard on one point, you can actually see much more throughout your field of vision. Now turn your head, change your focal point, and reengage your peripheral vision. This is actually a meditation, in a way, and you can practice it anywhere, anytime. In your sit spot, engage owl vision in moments of deep baseline, when nothing seems to require close attention. Absorb the scene as a whole. This connection is invaluable.

When you have the hang of owl vision, add in the equivalent kind of hearing, which I call "deer hearing," in honor of that animal's incredible auditory receptors, which swivel and turn to catch the slightest sound before any possible danger approaches. Among beginners, there's a natural tendency to concentrate on the loudest (and therefore often the closest) birds. This tendency would be okay if it didn't usually preclude hearing the quieter birds and vocalizations. In the beginning, most people can hear the wind or flowing water, but probably only as a solid wall of sound. They can pick up loud, obtrusive sounds and a collective category they might label "bird sounds," punctuated now and then by a discreet "song." That's about it. Now in your mind, "prick up" your ears. "Twitch" them. Imagine how they feel. In your sit spot, listen to the silence between the sounds, so that you can hear the more easily missed companion calls and the quieter birds such as the juncos. I always try to listen "farther" than I can see. This mental image helps some people extend the range of their hearing.

By listening to the silence, you'll hear more of everything. An enhancement of this exercise is to concentrate on the farthest and quietest sound in front of you, then to the left . . . the right . . . behind . . . above . . . *below* (where even worms and insects moving in the litter at your feet make a little noise, and in time you will hear it).

With keen peripheral hearing, no matter how far away and subtle the bird calls may be, they will jump to your ears. Am I contradicting my usual advice to first learn one bird well? Not really. Learning the robin first doesn't mean learning the robin to the exclusion of the other birds. *(Oh, wow, I'm really into bird language now because I can hear that robin so well.)* Even on the first day, go deeper. Listen to the silence and hear all the sounds around you. There will be many in your sit spot.

I always find it instructive to ask new people how many airplanes they heard while sitting in their sit spots.

"Three?" one might say hesitantly, after a pause.

I may have asked a more experienced individual with a nearby sit spot to be sure to pick up the planes. I turn to her and say, "How many?"

"Seven," she replies.

"No way! I can hear a *plane*. There were three," the new student argues.

"No, there were seven."

The next day, I put that same student in charge of counting planes in his sit spot, and his count goes up.

This exercise may seem silly, even counterproductive, when the main idea is to hear birds. But the main idea is not to hear *birds*. The main idea is to hear *everything*. If you don't notice the planes, what else are you missing? So I like the plane exercise. I like differentiating between the sounds made by the wind as it flows through the branches, the shrubs, the grass — all of them different. Use your ears like radar, sweeping all around you, through 360 degrees, and also up and down. Even in the bedroom in the dead of night, there's plenty to hear. Silence itself has a sound, and listening to it is good practice for picking up the junco's tiny tunes and alarms.

While you are seeing and hearing at your sit spot, you are also sitting on the ground or in a chair, maybe leaning against a tree, and your hands are touching something. What? Feel it! Our skin is the largest organ of the body for a reason. Use it. Is the ground cold? Is a rock or a piece of bark poking you? Is any part of your body crying for attention? What's the feeling inside your shoes, or the feeling of the ground beneath your feet? Can you feel moisture? Is the sun shining on your face? Can you feel its heat? If you can hear the wind, you can also feel it. I call this "raccoon touch," because the raccoon earns a living with its sense of touch. Have you ever watched one investigate the rocks at the edge of a pond? Its little hands touch and turn, reach under and around each rock, hoping for a tasty morsel. All the while, its eyes are directed elsewhere, often into distant space, not really looking at what its hands are exploring.

Learning bird language is all about training, and the right balance in training. If you awaken *all* of your senses, the connections happen faster, understanding is richer, and your bird language experience becomes more and more compelling. Mentoring hundreds of people over the past thirty years has made me absolutely certain of this correlation.

Walk the Walk

Actually, the best time to don your keen awareness is *before* you enter the sit spot. The owl doesn't leave its roost and just blunder blindly into the trees, and the cat doesn't leave the porch for the bushes in a hurry. From its silent and invisible perch, the owl surveys the landscape with those incredible eyes and listens with ears that are as remarkable as the deer's. It sees and hears the squirrels, the mice, the deer crunching the leaf litter, the muskrat digging and feeding, the rustle of the wind blowing in the sedges and the cattails. You could do worse than emulate the owl. At the very least, pause to collect yourself as you approach the sit spot. Take a deep breath, hold it for a second or two, then exhale and relax. Engage your owl eyes, your deer ears, your raccoon skin. Smell and taste the air like a dog. Think of yourself as a lazy surveyor. Definitely do not think, *Hey, look at me! I'm successfully sneaking around in the woods like a cat!* Sneaking provokes alarms. Besides, *you're* going to sneak up on a junco or a fox? Somehow I doubt it. Let's release that kind of naiveté from our mindset. Instead, you're the lazy surveyor getting paid by the hour, with all the time in the world on this beautiful afternoon. Empty your mind of everything except awareness. Channel your ability to multitask in new ways. Walk in the "weight last" style taught to me by Tom Brown, which shortens your stride, slows you down, engages your awareness, and changes the way you conduct yourself. Tom dubbed this style of locomotion "fox walking," and light on their feet as foxes are, the label is fitting. (In Africa, I was not surprised to find the great San trackers employing their own distinctive version of fox walking.)

I remember well the day I learned the value of fox walking for the first time. Tom and I were on our way to one of our favorite fishing holes through a forest we knew well. Tom had talked with me many times about the right way to walk, but of course I knew better than he did, and after walking his way for an hour or so, I always lapsed back into my accustomed swing-and-stomp style, which is pretty much everyone's style: pushing forward with the full weight committed before the other foot hits the ground. On one of these slam-dunk steps, I came down full force on a rusty nail sticking out of a fence board. That nail went through the thin soles of my sneakers and then out the top as well. In between was my foot. Ouch!

In the natural world, fox walking pays immediate dividends. It changes your body language and your impact on the local birds and animals. So instead of swinging and stomping, raise one foot off the ground and let it hang there comfortably. Then slowly lower the foot to the ground, wherever it naturally falls. Don't lean forward. When the foot touches down, the other leg is still bearing all your weight. After the first foot is on the ground, shift your weight, still without leaning forward. Keep your head up. Like the journey of a thousand miles, the road to natural walking begins with this single step. Repeat the process. With very little practice, you will find yourself treading softly, taking shorter steps. If you do encounter a nail, you can react, but that's an incidental benefit. You're changing—softening—your presence in the world. Yes, I've seen the dubious looks that sometimes greet this suggestion. I'm not worried. I know what's going to happen. The people who try it are going to feel the difference very quickly.

An alternative to softer walking is jogging or mountain biking, and I say this only half-facetiously, because I'm convinced that the *untutored* visitor to the woods will see more wildlife if jogging or biking. I've startled deer from close range while jogging. I've almost stepped on a fox, which is very hard to do while walking. Counterintuitively, the jogger's impact seems to be less intrusive than the walker's, even though she's moving faster, not slower, which seems to contradict my lesson about walking. One reason might be that in a way, the jogger is staying ahead of the birds' alarms, but I think the main factor is that the jogger is a little closer to her instinctual, animal self—probably more akin to a coyote in a genial trot, with no hunting intent. In effect, the jogger is distracted from her unaware mind. This phenomenon is a bit of a mystery, but it's also a fact. By the way, the best way to "cheat," so to speak, is by riding horseback. This may be because the birds perceive the horse as the primary animal, not the person on the horse's back, and they're instinctively more comfortable with the horse.

In the native cultures on all the continents I have visited, there are many variations on the "weight last" style of walking. These peoples also use different images for what I call owl vision and deer hearing and raccoon touch, but they do share these concepts, because in many parts of the world, in the city or in the wild, it's dangerous to move without awareness. It's necessary to train the young people to be subtle, quiet, gentle, and both self-aware and other-aware.

Sometimes I present the concept of fox walking this way: Pretend you're a waiter carrying a tray of drinks in fragile crystal. Without thinking about it, you bend your knees a little and tighten your stomach so that your back flattens out, a stance similar to the opening position in tai chi. Then you walk slowly and deliberately, gliding rather than bouncing. The body acts as a shock absorber. If we were able to see a procession of such "waiters" only from the waist up, they would appear to be rolling along on a cart. This mode of ambulation is much more effective in the natural world than the usual swing-and-stomp gait, which is better suited to busy sidewalks.

Or picture a cat, moving as if it has honey in its veins. The slow, deliberate, and powerful movements rely on strong muscles, sure-footed accuracy, much practice, and careful planning. The cat moves forward a few steps, pauses, holds very still, scans the environment. Then it moves forward again, always staying in the shadows, always moving along the edges, in the thicket, or under the cover of darkness. Of all the forest animals, the various cats are most like us in their dominant sense patterns, using their eyes to the greatest effect, their ears less so, and their noses even less. But how do humans tend to move? Like rambunctious house dogs — abruptly, continuously, often looking at the ground as if we, too, could smell its secrets. We can't. Unlike most dogs, but like all cats, we're sight-oriented creatures, for whom slow and steady wins the race. Indeed, when we don't have the usual pressures to push us along in our daily lives, we naturally tend to fall back into a slower, more relaxed, more deliberate gait. As tourists out to see the sights, with no place to be by a certain time, we amble along and look around at everything. It's a more natural way for sight-oriented creatures to move. This is what you want on the way to your sit spot.

The Routine of Invisibility

I call the overall preparatory engagement of the senses the "routine of invisibility." An easy test of its value is simply to employ this routine one day, then blunder out to your sit spot the next day (at the same time), use the routine the following day (also at the same time), and then blunder out again on the fourth day. If you compare your subsequent experiences, assuming roughly the same weather, you'll notice how different they are. One is clearly better. It's common sense, really.

To give you a different perspective on this idea (one that has helped a lot of people learning bird language), imagine two spheres, one representing an individual's *awareness* of the natural world, the other representing the *disturbance* this individual causes. These images are both metaphorical and real. For some people, the sphere of awareness (five feet?) is much smaller than the sphere of disturbance (fifty to one hundred yards or more). In short, they're aware of very little while kicking up a big bird plow, and they have almost no chance of seeing much wildlife. The idea behind understanding bird language is to slowly but surely expand the sphere of awareness and shrink the sphere of disturbance by learning and practicing good jungle etiquette. As the beneficial sphere becomes increasingly larger than the detrimental one, you will start seeing and hearing many more birds and other animals, become more "invisible," and be more welcome in the animals' home. You will see the mink and the fox in repose.

How Bird Language Works in Practice

The most basic way to study bird language is to sit relatively still, quiet, and alert in your sit spot for at least thirty minutes. In the beginning, you may kick up a disturbance — a bird plow — as you enter the spot. If it's in your backyard, probably not, because the birds know you, but if it's in the woods, probably so, and twenty minutes is about the shortest amount of time required for the baseline to recover from your intrusion. (You don't have twenty minutes today? By all means, give it a shot anyway, remembering that if the benefit is marginal, it's not the birds' fault!) While the baseline is recovering, you'll notice that little if anything is going on around you, although you'll probably hear some birds in the distance. After ten minutes, you might notice some chickadees (who don't seem

The Cause of a Big Disturbance: When our disturbance exceeds our awareness in size and scope, we cause a large alarm and a "wake" of disturbance around us. We see very little wildlife, and we often see birds flying away. Part of this wake's signature is a "bird plow," illustrated on page 120. We must adapt our walking and awareness practices to change this.

Awareness Greater Than Disturbance: When we practice the techniques that constitute the routine of invisibility — including fox walking and sensory expansion — our awareness will quickly grow larger than our disturbance, thus bringing us into closer contact with wildlife.

to care what we do), and you might get the feeling that some birds are moving around in the treetops above you (if there are any in your chosen spot). In suburban areas, gray squirrels and rabbits will probably brave your presence, because in these habitats they aren't hunted. In rural and wild areas, where they are hunted, you'll be fortunate to see, much less get close to, either one. The culture of animal behavior, just like the culture of bird behavior, varies. That is, the baseline varies.

After fifteen minutes, you might notice that some singing birds have ventured closer, but it will probably take about twenty minutes of sitting still before the birds in your immediate sit spot start singing and feeding again. If you're fidgeting, this will take longer. That must have been true in my first sit spot. I have a pretty clear memory of myself sitting there early on, not really knowing what to do, just poking at the ground with a stick, looking around, moving around, sweeping off my butt, sitting back down again, and so on. The first bird I remember seeing was a chickadee, but that doesn't mean it was the first bird with the nerve to hang around. I don't believe I was as willfully unaware as sullen Jack, the adolescent who couldn't (or perhaps wouldn't) even see the birds, but I might have been as functionally unaware. I wonder what that chickadee thought of me. One day Tom Brown said to me, "Do you think anything's going to stick around, the way you fidget? They see you from so far away, they hear you from even farther. And then when you finally sit down, you're just as bad." This surprised me, because I hadn't told Tom about my fidgeting, nor had he joined me in the woods. He just knew, because fidgeting is the natural side effect of finding yourself in a new situation. Speaking metaphorically (or maybe not), chaining yourself to a folding chair is a necessary indoctrination to becoming invisible, but you won't need to do this for long. When I was growing up under Tom's watchful gaze, I often wondered why he seemed so distant and quiet so much of the time. This was why. He was stilling the chatter, quieting his mind, connecting and listening: practicing the routine of invisibility.

The Bravest Birds

Which are the bravest birds? After about twenty minutes, you'll find out as some of them follow the chickadees back into the area. The order of birds arriving back at the scene will vary from place to place. Some might be more predictable than others, and it's interesting to note that different people experience different birds, even in the same place. Once the chickadees and sparrows have settled in, the juncos, thrushes, warblers, and eventually towhees also will return. In my experience, the towhees often bring up the rear. It could take them forty minutes to return. The ovenbirds might not come back at all until you're gone. You may hear them, but you will almost never see them. If you do, I'd be willing to wager that this happens later in your bird language journey and that you are taking seriously your preparatory routine of invisibility. This is all sheer speculation, based on my experience and many reports, because I hardly need to repeat that no two habitats, no two sit spots, no two baselines are exactly the same. And this one is *yours*. If you stay half an hour—better yet, forty minutes—on your first day out, you'll already have some interesting information to jot in your journal.

After a handful of visits, the bird plow will diminish. You'll have a surprisingly clear sense of the bravest and the most cautious birds in your area. Some previously unseen birds won't hesitate to feed a foot or two away, completely confident in your benign presence. They'll come to know you as an individual, as surely as your pets do. *(Oh, here's Susan again, a little late.)* Inevitably, one species—say, the robin—will become your favorite ally, and then general knowledge of robins will become specific knowledge of *this* robin, and *this* one. Absorbing the five vocalizations and the behaviors of these specific birds will prepare you to do the same with virtually all the birds. Over time, it will just happen.

If you want to shorten the learning curve and get around those early bird plows, go out in the darkness, before the birds wake up, and get into position before first light. This strategy could prevent the bird plow caused by your arrival, plus you'll hear the dawn chorus.

If possible, use various routes to approach your sit spot. New angles reveal new discoveries. Over time, work out a comprehensive understanding of this quarter acre of medicine. Where are the squirrels today? The towhees? The song sparrows? The tanagers? You know quite a bit even before you sit down. In the beginning, between sunrise and midmorning is the perfect time in the sit spot, with the busiest baseline. Midafternoon is not as good, but take what you can get, and experience as many different times of day as you can. On the laziest summer afternoon with the quietest baseline, there's still plenty to learn. Go in the rain, in the snow, and in the wind, and notice that the animals behave differently under each circumstance. For instance, they behave differently in a drizzle than in a downpour. (I'm not sure mosquitoes make this distinction, but I know they definitely bite more just before rain.) Before a storm or a cold front, bird activity increases. There are harbingers all over the place, waiting to be discovered by you.

You begin to think, *I can do this!* Of course you can, because the human brain is set up for it. Some of this capacity may have shut down, but it's still there, latent. What you're doing is turning on the regions of your brain that have been waiting your whole life for you to do this—a cartoonish simplification, but relevant. Those regions have been working at other tasks all along, but they'll adapt to the bird language challenges without any problem. Unless you're a born mathematician, you'll become adept at bird language a lot faster than you would with calculus. Mutual respect will build between you and the birds and other animals. By recognizing and respecting them in the way of the San Bushmen, you honor them. After a month, say, the juncos, initially very wary of you, are no longer suspicious. They almost ignore you. Now even the more skittish birds, such as the wood thrushes and Pacific wrens, are flitting or hopping respectfully just to the side or flying softly overhead and giving you your well-earned space. ("Soft" flying? This is the style birds use when they are comfortably within the baseline, taking it easy. The flight of tense birds perceiving danger creates a "tighter" tone, a louder wingbeat. I don't know of any studies on this subject, but the difference is obvious to anyone who spends much time with birds. Of course, the best place to learn the difference is the sit spot.) Even the towhees may recognize you, and one day, while you're cleaning the barbecue grill, a female towhee feeds just five feet away. Now that's a rite of passage. You're accepted as a neighbor—not a predator, not an intruder, not a stranger. It's a sweet feeling. And because the birds are not firing off alarms, the mammals are no longer beneficiaries of that early warning system. They don't know you're there. A positive feedback loop is setting up. If you're in the woods, you're well on your way to seeing wildlife you couldn't have dreamed of seeing before. You may find the deer in their day beds, doe and fawn feeding peacefully. You may also see certain bears, but not all bears.

You begin to distinguish between the various alarm "shapes" that I will discuss at length in the following chapters. You recognize that the alarm activity twenty yards away is probably not for you after all. Bird plow aside, a bird that far away isn't worried about you; some other danger has precipitated this event. You conclude that you must have kicked up a small predator that waited for you to pass before "quartering" back and away from your route, a classic escape maneuver for wildlife. The evidence is that alarm you hear following the intruder into the distance. Or you *don't* hear the alarm. The singing has stopped; the birds are quiet. *Huh, I wonder if that's someone approaching.* Half a minute goes by. *Nah, I guess not.* Then you hear the swishing of Gore-Tex and some voices. *I guess so!* Eventually, after months in your sit spot, you figure out who's moving, at what time of day, and how the birds are responding. That's how you learn bird language. You will surprise yourself. (Some tracking skills will also help in this regard, because they will allow you to identify specific animals. With tracking skills, you'll realize that the woods are full of little eyes and ears, and a lot of the brains behind those eyes and ears are really good at hide-and-seek. Without the tracks and signs, you would never know that you lost the game again!)

The Junco: A Detective Story

With awareness, connection, and respect, you'll see that old saying "A little bird told me" in a whole new light. When you take your seat in a sit spot—your favorite one or someplace new on the other side of the world—soon enough the wind is not just a solid wall of sound. It has shape and texture and depth. It brings with it bird language and other tidbits from all directions. These new dimensions and qualities are very complex and almost impossible to describe in words, but there's no need to. Your eyesight, hearing, sense of touch, and sense of smell are focusing in a new way. Old instincts kick into gear. The routine of invisibility hasn't actually made you invisible, but your overall energy and behavior profile has changed. I believe that if researchers could hook up some electrodes without breaking the spell, they'd record different brain waves at this stage than they would have during your early days in the sit spot. Now you are good at being relaxed, and this has changed *your* baseline. You're solving conundrums in three-dimensional spaces, finding the baseline patterns—both around you and in you—and the telltale disruptions.

You're no junco—none of us is—but you're a long way from the hiker who believes that his camouflage clothing is actually camouflage. One day you sense the junco's tiny alarm before you even hear it. The concentric rings emanating from this bird and the approaching disturbance have penetrated your instincts before they've registered in your consciousness. *Blink!* Even the squirrels have begun to accept you and not chatter in alarm as much. You understand that even though they seem to scamper through the trees randomly, they have preferred routes—tree trails—that they follow over and over again, obsessively (as they seem to do everything).

You may see the mink and her young, and you'll be tempted to say, "I guess they just moved to the neighborhood." Much more likely, they've been living within fifty yards of you all this time, and only now does the mother trust you enough to pass by openly. If your sit spot is in the woods where there are foxes around, don't be surprised if a fox passes by, stops and looks at you, or maybe ignores you altogether. If he ignores you, you might think that you were so invisible he didn't even see you. I wouldn't be that smug. If you've been there fifteen days, he's probably watched you for fourteen of them; a hundred days, ninety-nine of them. Remember, this is not a part-time recreational pursuit for the fox. He has invested exponentially more than you in bird language, and he knows exponentially more. Revealing his presence now is totally up to him. You are beginning to understand the wisdom of the native elders when they say that the animals are our best teachers. This is not a metaphor; it's the simple truth.

Of all my great times growing up in the semi-wilds of New Jersey, the juncos around my first sit spot beneath the ash tree were responsible for triggering what was probably the key experience that drove my zeal to understand bird language. *(Listen to audio files 5, 6, 7, and 8 for a variety of junco vocalizations.)* I certainly had every opportunity. I was situated a little less than a hundred yards inside the local forest, with a good view of the high canopy in one direction, a mixture of second-growth and old-growth, twisted, gnarled oaks and ashes and beeches several hundred years old. There were some old black cherries that twisted and reached toward the sky, and a lot of young red maples racing for the sun, quite close together. Many of them died on their way up, leaving long, straight poles standing dead, some tantalizingly close to the canopy. There were plenty of edge species—honeysuckle, sassafras, cherry, locust—the seeds of which were dropped there mostly in the scats of birds perched along old locust fences that were no longer present in complete form. And I loved the aromatic smells of the spicebush and sassafras. This was all private property, linked together with some old abandoned farms and next to a bygone thoroughbred training center that had fallen into decay. But bridle paths still led to hidden ponds and mysterious sandy outliers of pine and sweet fern and beautiful red British soldier lichen encrusting the ground in sunny spots (probably overgrazed horse pastures, but also unique little ecosystems). There were wetlands, with a few great fishing ponds and a couple of streams. The birds didn't complain about any of this. Come spring, the dawn chorus was absolutely mind-boggling—diverse and beautiful. (Just one suburban cul-de-sac poked into one corner of this habitat, but talk about a harbinger. My sit spot is now someone's side yard, with a child's play set right at my old anchor point. The ash tree still stands, though.)

In the beginning, however, none of these details was important to me. Tom Brown had seen that I liked to play with sticks in fires, and he somehow convinced me that I needed a campfire circle on this little hill, where I could look down over the forest and meadow edges and make observations. That's how my sit spot began, with a circle of native limonite concretion rocks set around a fire pit centered on a flat bench of about an eighth of an acre. This sit spot was a very short walk from my house. The bench of unconsolidated loamy forest humus gave me a good view in three directions. The fourth and easterly direction—behind me—was a thicket, at Tom's suggestion. He said, "Make sure you have your back to a thicket so nothing can come up behind you without making a lot of noise. This way you won't be surprised. You never know who's out there."

That comment was a little disarming, but I found out he was right. I did like having my back covered. Initially, I walked the same way from my house to my sit spot, until one day Tom came for a visit and saw the new trail forming from my habitual footfalls. Not a good idea, he said. "This might lead someone to your sit spot, and you never know who's out here." Again, this gave me something a little spooky to think about, but he was right. I began taking different routes, including some deer and raccoon runs. At and around my sit spot, I was beginning to understand the companion calls, the feeding sounds, and the occasional territorial quarrels of the juncos, song sparrows, robins, white-throated sparrows, catbirds, cardinals, towhees, blue jays, crows, bobwhites, Carolina and house wrens, mockingbirds, brown thrashers, wood thrushes, ovenbirds, common yellowthroats, and more. I also caught a lot of fish in the ponds nearby. Without realizing it, I was primed for a major rite of passage, and immersion in my sit spot was a necessary precondition.

This was the year I turned thirteen; I'd been going to that place for about two and a half years. The juncos had been around the whole time, of course, but I didn't know that for at least the first year or more. Finally, I had become aware at times of a very soft *t-th! t-th! t-th!* coming from the thicket behind and to the east of where I sat. Then I figured out that the juncos were making this sound, a tiny interruption in their baseline. It was so subtle, almost inaudible. (Sometimes even serious bird language students have to really penetrate the silence in order to discern the juncos.) Late one afternoon, as I was sitting by my fire beneath the ash tree, I emerged from a dreamy fog, and the truth hit me: that *t-th! t-th! t-th!* was an alarm, quiet though it was, and the cause was something moving behind me unseen. The sensation that something unknown is right behind us gets our attention, especially in the forest, especially if we're alone, and no matter how comfortable we are in the solitude. I had that distinct feeling. I could almost hear some footfalls in the dry leaves. I thought perhaps it was my imagination, but I soon found out otherwise.

Then the other alarms began, including the catbird's little twitter sounds (the *mew* call) and chipmunks warning of a ground approach (*chip chip chip chip chip*). *(Listen to audio file 66 for an example of eastern chipmunk terrestrial alarm call.)* As you will soon see, an alarm joined by two or three species is an almost certain sign that this isn't just an intramural scuffle of some sort. Something else is going on. That was the circumstance that evening. The sun was getting low, the birds had been busy and vocal again as they prepared for roosting, and now these alarms disturbed the baseline in a very local kind of way. I became convinced that something larger was moving in the thicket behind me. I'm not certain, but that may have been the first time I drew such a conclusion, the first time I understood that a consensus alarm has a specific "shape" relating to the location of the intrusion.

How many times had I sat in that same spot and missed the juncos' warning? I think it must have been many times—an embarrassing number, perhaps. Actually, I had been missing an entire dimension of reality—the sights and sounds of the baseline and alarms. Specifically, what animal had I missed back there? The alarm had now faded to the north more than a hundred yards, so I could go in and try to find out. I crawled into the thicket, ducking under some viburnums and honeysuckles hanging over the understory shrubs, elderberries and spicebush. Of course, this invasion set off a series of alarms, too, but what choice did I have? I had to find out what was happening. Not fifteen yards from my sit spot, I found it: an animal run, literally a tunnel through the thicker growth, about as high as my knees. What a surprise. The only way to see it was to get down to that height and look. This was a thoroughfare for some animal, probably more than one, and I had been clueless for a couple of years. I had even crossed the tunnel without seeing it when I entered my sit spot from the east. I studied the options—left or right into the tunnel—and turned left, as the alarms had gone in that direction earlier. In the distance, I heard a chipmunk challenging something, maybe the animal I was now following, if I'd taken the correct turn.

About twenty yards north of my sit spot, the tunnel emerged onto an old wagon road, now the bridle path that led toward my favorite fishing hole. Another surprise. I'd walked along there many times and never realized that the little open area in the undergrowth was an animal run. This was a crossroads, and I had completely missed it. At this juncture was the "hinge tree," as I had labeled it in my journal, a very old (perhaps two hundred years old) black locust tree snag with only a small bit of bark left alive, and as hard and white as bone. Embedded in the dead wood was a rusty, hand-forged gate hinge. I had often found the scat of a red fox at the base of this tree, but I had never seen the animal. Now, emerging from the tunnel, I finally put two and two together: all this time, a red fox had been playing a game of hide-and-seek with me, and winning every time. The juncos' subtle *t-th! t-th! t-th!* had been telling me—trying to tell me—that this fox was passing right behind me, as I sat there so proudly alert. Without a doubt, this fox had paused to take my measure. How many times without my knowing? No telling. But let me put it this way: I smelled fresh fox urine by that hinge tree every time I passed it to fish or wander to a friend's house—several times each week. Now I was smelling it again, and this time it was very fresh.

Before that moment, I'd thought I had it all down pat. I could catch just about anything in water, including fish and water snakes (try that!). I could grab corn snakes warming in the sun. I could pick up a snapping turtle by its tail without losing a fingertip. (Their necks are much longer than they look, and folks make a big mistake picking them up in the wrong way.) I could catch young rabbits and fast lizards. I could even corner quail. What can I say? I was young, naive, learning, full of vinegar, and fired up with the need to find and catch things and generally conquer the world. But now, suddenly, I was utterly humbled. I was Jon, the earnest young student of bird language, the "naturalist," but in this instance I had been as uninformed as the hiker who causes such a ruckus with his bird plow. I was humbled but also tremendously exhilarated by the revelation that this fox had outfoxed me so many times. This was such a profound lesson in the subtlety of what goes on in the wild. I finally understood that there were whole new dimensions, a new universe of possibilities, that I hadn't even imagined. I still feel that way. We'll never catch up with the birds and other animals. That is the beauty of studying bird language and everything that follows.

And I learned this when I was just thirteen years old. What a lucky kid.

Of course, I told Tom about this episode. He was taking apart the engine of his truck. (In my memory, he was often taking it apart. Either the truck was a lemon or he was hard on vehicles, or both. Or, just as likely, my memory has exaggerated Tom's mechanical endeavors.) Tom could have answered my questions immediately, but he never did that. He asked questions in the style of the great mentor he was. He lectured me very little. He never once gave away answers or solved mysteries for me. Instead, he'd emerge from his truck, wipe his hands on a rag, and pick up his field guide, then we'd study it together. Maybe the current mystery was the identification of a new woodpecker I'd seen. How big was it? Was the bill longer than the head or really small-looking? Was I sure it had the telltale white line down its back? In short, was it a downy or a hairy?

Regarding the red fox, Tom rubbed it in a bit. *Yeah, that fox pays better attention than you do, it seems. How many times do you think he looked right at you?* Tom was throwing down the gauntlet. He knew I'd relish the challenge of an awareness adversary. I had to lay eyes on this fox. Sure, the fox was shrewd, but he couldn't always win. In my sit spot, revealing himself would remain his prerogative. Out in the field, though, I could turn the tables. That was my youthful competitive streak. I now understand that this is not really a productive thought if it takes over your whole attitude, but it's a great starting motivation. I learned great lessons from answering Tom's challenges, and if necessary (often) Tom would bring me down to earth during the debriefing.

So I embarked on a quest to see that fox, and I figured it wouldn't be too hard to find him. Foxes refresh their marks on a regular basis. The spot becomes a latrine, in effect. This is standard territorial behavior. The fox's marking also has a very particular musky, oily odor, suggestive of a skunk. In fact, for a long time I thought this smell was a skunk's sign. Then I began to note the correlation between the odor and fox runs and fox scats, and I finally found my first fox den. Case closed: this pungent odor was fox, not skunk. (Now I love to catch this scent on the wind, and I often do. There are a lot of foxes in the world, even in the suburbs, almost all of them padding along, as they prefer it, unseen, unheard, unsmelled — generally *unrecognized* through any sense.)

The game of hide-and-seek with the fox lasted many more months as I followed the clues he *had* to leave, because this was, after all, his home. The contest drove my tracking skills to new heights. I was always stopping, testing the wind for fresh scent, looking around for new tracks, or scouring the ground for feathers or tufts of rabbit fur indicating a kill. And I was listening in the four directions like I'd never listened before. (I didn't exactly know *what* I was listening for, but no matter.) With Tom's questions driving my research, I sketched small maps in my journal, detailing the fox's regular routes and latrines, noting the telltale feathers and fur I thought he was responsible for. I was trying to connect the dots, seeking those behavioral eddies in the landscape that, eventually, helped me determine his most popular visitation zones, the ones he used each and every day, his main lairs and possible den site. And one morning, before first light, hiding on a cliff overlooking what I now believed was the fox's favorite hangout, I saw him. On my own terms, *I* saw *him*. I had turned the tables. What a connection for me.

Getting There

I ended up spending seven years in that sit spot in New Jersey. It wasn't until the fourth year that I realized with a start that a few of the birds had been with me the whole time. It was very likely that the catbird I saw over and over, breeding season after breeding season, who acted like the same one from the previous year, with all the same haunts and habits, was indeed the same individual. This insight very likely applied to any number of species around me. Maybe I assumed (as many people do) that all the birds are about the same age—a year or two, then they die. This isn't right. The average bird has more of a chance of being eaten in its first year, but those who live past the adolescent rites of passage probably live several years, breeding and raising young. As a corollary of the first incorrect impression, I probably also assumed that since birds fly, they're always flying, and long distances at that. It's my sense that most people have this general impression, but it, too, is wrong. Taking migration out of the equation, most birds do not move around much, even after the main territorial season—nesting—has concluded. They're homebodies. I finally understood this. After seven years, I understood so much more about that habitat. I had acquired some pretty serviceable jungle etiquette, too. The chickadees were often very close, even occasionally landing on me.

As it turned out, I was—totally unwittingly—a professional in training. But enjoying deep bird language doesn't require making a career of it. Not at all. Three days a week, half an hour every day, opens the same door, just more slowly. Moreover, students today have one tremendous advantage over those of my generation, even those who enjoyed the mentoring of the likes of Tom Brown: our knowledge of bird language is now codified, more so every day. Even this book, an informal introduction to the subject, presents more information in usable form than I ever had as a beginner. Breaking down the most pertinent vocalizations into the five categories laid out here is a big advantage in and of itself. In that respect, the door does open more quickly for today's students.

Codification means providing the tools for asking the right questions, not providing answers. It means guidelines, not algorithms. In an appendix, I could list one hundred of the most common birds in North America and phonetically describe their songs, companion calls, and alarms. (The phonetic descriptions of the other two vocalizations, aggression and begging, are pretty generic.) I won't do that. With bird language, the learning is in the questioning and the doing. Students accumulate the information, awareness skills, connection, recognition, and wisdom to discover the answers the birds have been providing all along. The student today will understand the junco's modest *t-th! t-th! t-th!* alarm in a lot less time than the two years it took me, that's for sure. I've seen students in structured courses draw amazingly keen inferences after just a few months of facilitated sits, debriefings, motivated awareness, and thoughtful mentoring.

I also see stumped students and frustrated students. This is good. We share these frustrations openly, and they drive all of us to ask more questions, write about a particular situation in our journals, and research it until all the resources have been utterly exhausted. At that point, I may say, "Okay, why don't you just ask the robin what's going on." Which is to say, "Okay, now let your instincts do the talking." They will, eventually, and when they do, the odds are excellent that they'll be sitting in their sit spot. It is the heart and soul of bird language, practice room and concert hall, raw canvas and glorious museum.

[For a recorded session of this process, including a full bird language group debrief, see *Bird Language with Jon Young: How to Interpret the Behavior and Patterns of Nature* (an instructional DVD).]

Chapter 5

AN ALARM FOR EVERY OCCASION

W HEN I MOVED MY FAMILY from New Jersey to Washington State in 1995, our cottage was in Duvall, several hundred feet in elevation above the Snoqualmie Valley in rural King County, in the foothills of the Cascade Range on the edge of a vast wild place. There were no traffic lights in Duvall at that time. The porch of our cottage overlooked a number of excellent avian habitats, including a low salmonberry thicket on the edge of a wetland stream and beaver pond complex. The season was high summer, nearing July, and I couldn't believe how long the days were, even though this latitude in Washington was only about three hundred miles north of New Jersey's. Those long days out west were a lifesaver for me. If there were any vast wild places remaining in New Jersey, even in the Pine Barrens, I couldn't find them—but it was also *home*. I knew those sit spots and those baselines so well, and I wasn't all that happy about leaving them.

One morning as I was sitting on the porch of our new home, something caught my attention. I couldn't see through the berry bushes or the sword ferns, or past a bunch of logs covered with moss, but the persistent *chh-ch-chh-chh-chh-ch-ch-ch-ch* must have been alarm calls from the Pacific wrens who frequented this thicket. *(Listen to audio files 15 [Bewick's wren], 22 [Carolina wren], and 24 [house wren] for examples of wren alarm calls.)* So I decided. I couldn't be sure, because I didn't know the baseline in those foothills, but knowing bird language anywhere gives you a leg up everywhere. You recognize patterns quickly, and with these patterns as a foundation and a reference point, you're able to figure out what the birds are communicating in the new places. Outside our cottage, the males were sometimes into their dueling songs and squawks, but I had quickly figured out their territorial boundaries, and those had not been violated. The birds mostly stayed put. Moreover, the song sparrows, spotted towhees, and some chipmunks confirmed that a good deal of the Pacific wrens' vocalizations were alarms, not male-to-male aggression. I concluded that the wrens were very concerned about something moving around underneath them.

Long experience had taught me that the Pacific wren is a reliable alarm source in the forest. Very few predators can catch and dispatch a wren. I don't think there's a hawk around who can succeed with an experienced adult bird. The weasel or skilled housecat, maybe, on its best day, and only if it gets lucky — that is, if the wren makes a mistake. Supremely alert, Pacific wrens are also supremely elusive. With the light gray or buff stripe above their eyes, little black and white checkerboard highlights, and neat racing stripes on their sides, they are exquisite little jewel boxes that we usually don't see unless they're singing. Hard-wired for producing a big sound (as I've noted, the most volume per ounce of any bird I know), they are otherwise among the greatest of avian illusionists.

Sitting on my porch overlooking the salmonberry thicket, I would say to one and all, "*There*, hear that? That Pacific wren is alarmed . . . Now his mate . . . Now the song sparrow. Hear how the towhee just stopped singing a moment ago? Now he's alarming, too. *See?*" My family and our friends weren't quite as interested in this puzzle as I was. Yet these episodes happened several times an hour. On a summer day, that's a lot. Sometimes the wrens were scolding so fast and loudly that I couldn't concentrate on anything else. *Chh-ch-chh-chh-chh-ch-ch-ch-ch*, said the male; *chh-ch-chh-chh-chh-ch-ch-ch-ch*, said the female. Then they were instantly quiet, and when I could see them at all, they were looking around — to the left, then the right, then directly below. This behavior clearly said they were having trouble finding and following the cause of their concern. Based on my experience in New Jersey, I was formulating a theory, and a few days after I first woke up to the situation in the salmonberry thicket, I asked one of the caretakers on the property, "Are there a lot of weasels around here?"

He was always out and about, and he lived opposite my cottage in a small dwelling on the edge of the same salmonberry thicket, close to all the action. "Nope," he replied. "Never seen any." He added that he'd lived there for more than ten years and was sure there weren't any weasels around. An innocent sort, I believed him. The plot thickened. If it wasn't a weasel, what could it be? A mink? Possibly, because there was a lot of water around. But when I asked about mink, the caretaker replied, "Not while I've lived here." A housecat? I didn't ask him about this possibility, because I knew it was not a cat. I would have seen it or its tracks elsewhere on the property. Snakes? Back east in the Pine Barrens, the pine snakes and rat snakes will grab small birds, but there are no such snakes in Washington. Garter snakes are plentiful in the state, but these are not usually a threat to birds. A species of rattlesnake in the arid eastern part of the state is not that interested in birds, preferring to hunt at night for mammals. Coyote? Much too big and visible to elude inquiring eyes. Fox? Are there any here? Otter? Too noisy and visible. Bobcat? In a place like this, with people living on all sides, never. Cougar? Likewise. Opossum? Big enough to see, nocturnal, moves much more slowly than a weasel, so the alarm for it would have been very static, isolated for long periods in one spot. Raccoon? Big enough to see easily, nocturnal.

I went down the list of feasible alternatives to the weasel and discarded all of them. The alarm pattern among the wrens just didn't fit them. It fit only the weasel. That sporadic blast of alarm, then again, then again, and deep concern and puzzlement between the alarms—looking left, right, down, back and forth—all this was precisely as expected if the danger was visible, then not, then visible, then not; first here, then over there, then elsewhere. Which is exactly how weasels work, using cover such as mouse tunnels and logs to move around unseen, popping into view sporadically. This behavior justifiably causes birds great concern, and this worry was what I saw over a period of a few days in the salmonberry thicket. The predator had to be a weasel, but could the caretaker possibly be unaware of weasels on the property after all those years? Well, they are very elusive. In New Jersey, I'd had to wait patiently for hours to get a glimpse of one that I knew had been within ten feet of me. The field guide confirmed that the whole state of Washington is within the weasel's habitual range, but that proved nothing about my salmonberry thicket. I just didn't know enough about this place yet. Maybe these Pacific wrens were a random varietal and got all agitated and excited and wasted a lot of energy broadcasting alarms for no reason at all. Or maybe there were so many high-octane, nutrient-rich spiders in these thickets that the wrens had nothing better to do than burn all their extra energy by pretending to be alarmed all the time. Conceivable, though barely.

About a week after arriving in Duvall, I drove the nine miles to Redmond to check out my new office — this was my first trip there in the daytime since moving. I counted seven dead weasels along the road. In New Jersey, it would have taken me probably ten thousand cumulative miles to see that many weasel roadkill. Not only were there weasels in Washington, but they were much more common than in New Jersey. My confidence in the caretaker's repeated assurances about the absence of weasels on his property took a big hit that day. My confidence in what I thought the Pacific wrens had been telling me rose accordingly.

Several days later, two other tracking instructors and I were cleaning up a section of the property for our teaching programs. We decided to move an old moss-encrusted Volkswagen square-back sedan that was parked on a minimal road in the forest on the other side of the wetland from my cottage. Maybe someone would want it, for whatever reason. The key was still in the ignition! Someone made a joke about Woody Allen's classic film *Sleeper*, in which the old VW Bug cranks up after many years, but this sedan failed to ignite. We opened the trunk in the front of the car, looking for jumper cables. Inside was a cardboard box, partially closed. Also in the trunk was an odor that momentarily drove us back. It had been a while, but I believed I could identify that distinctive, rank, powerful scent of acrid urine and musk. I was pretty sure what we'd find in that box, and so it was: a big fluffy nest (the VW's insulation serving as a warm blanket) with four squirming baby weasels, soft and grayish brown and in excellent condition, wonderful little creatures. Also inside that box was a pile of a couple dozen shrew moles, the ones on top fresh and floppy (we tested), none stiff with rigor mortis, several bitten in half (with the other half missing; maybe Mom had taken a few bites on the way home).

I say Mom, not Dad, because while my friends and I were standing there, staring into the box, the female showed up with yet another shrew mole. Not happy to see us or the disturbance to her nursery, she made a kind of *chrrrr*ing sound, which echoed in a funny way as she darted through some unseen passageways between the undercarriage and this chamber and popped up on the right side of the box, shrew mole in mouth. She paused for a second to stare, then backed up, disappeared, made that *chrrrr*ing sound again, and popped up in another part of the trunk. We learned that there are at least four ways for a weasel to enter the trunk of a VW square-back sedan from beneath the car. Maybe not a typical weasel habitat, but typically cryptic weasel behavior! We lowered the lids to the cardboard box, then carefully lowered the hood and quietly pressed it into place. We didn't move the car for another few weeks, until the nursery was abandoned.

The car was maybe a hundred yards from the salmonberry thicket near where I was living. As it turned out, nesting season for both weasels and birds had concluded by the time I was able to spend much time observing events there, so I never confirmed that the Pacific wrens' alarms had been targeted at weasels, but the circumstantial evidence was overwhelming—though not ironclad. Being *almost* certain is sometimes the "burden" of the bird language student. I think it's a good burden to have. I never said a word about any of this to the caretaker. Fifteen years later, he may still believe there aren't any weasels around that property. Probably so, if he hasn't learned to tune in to the birds' alarms.

Fifth Vocalization: Alarms

Perhaps a couple of weeks after that business with the weasels, the same two guys and I were tracking along the Skykomish River on a newly exposed sandbar, just over ten miles from my cottage in the Snoqualmie Valley, as the raven flies. A group of foothills separates these two major rivers, which meet a little north of Duvall to form the Snohomish. Upstream from that confluence, the "Sky" drops out of the Cascades to the east and creates some fast-flowing rapids, a real delight to my ears, nose, and soul. The air was fresh and charged with the ions of falling, dancing, frigid snowmelt and salmon-bearing waters and ancient rock riverbeds; the trees were tall and sentrylike, majestic in their draped mosses. I fell in love with this region, a great place to dig into all these habitats — their fishes, mammals, and birds, and their symphony of baselines. I soon had several fine sit spots scattered about before I finally settled on one.

One morning on the sandbar, we were reading the story left in the sand the night before by what seemed to be a breeding pair of gray wolves with half-grown pups. The front tracks of the big male were very nearly five inches from heel to nail mark. His tracks and stride put him in the "pretty darn big" class for this species, probably weighing more than one hundred pounds. We were looking for the perfect set to cast in plaster and bring home for our little nature museum when, as usual, I became distracted by some bird language that demanded my attention. Ravens were calling from a heavily forested area. I knew there was a kill nearby, because earlier I had smelled the decaying flesh of what I suspected was a deer in the cottonwoods somewhere near the river. From the opposite direction of the ravens, a bird let out an alarm call very close: *chh-ch-ch-ch*. Pacific wren? Probably, but it was not too agitated, and not for very long.

One of the guys said, "Ground bird, listen . . ."

Then a series of like alarms tumbled like dominoes through the brush, receding into the forest. Wren, song sparrow, robin, another song sparrow—and kinglet? Maybe. *(Listen to audio files 39 [this alarm is also used as a contact call at times] and 38 [song] for examples of ruby-crowned kinglet vocalizations.)* Investigating in that direction, we found fresh wolf tracks leading away on the same trajectory as the alarming birds. Perhaps this wolf had been studying us as we studied the tracks he'd left in the sand the night before. I liked that idea a lot, but all I knew for sure was that *some* wolf had been watching us and then moved softly away, and when it did, the birds announced the fact to the waiting world—that is, to *all* the other animals, who that morning happened to include three biped trackers in the sand.

As I hope I've made manifestly clear, these birds know more about the mysteries of the backyard and the forest than we can imagine, because they have no choice. It is a jungle out there—even in the backyard—and I don't think we can possibly comprehend the level of awareness that a bird must have in order to survive. When we consider that Cooper's and sharp-shinned hawks are feeding their own young almost nothing but songbirds, well, that's a lot of baby songbirds culled from the nursery.

The birds' wisdom *is* their awareness, and their awareness is their wisdom. We can't comprehend how it feels to be so alert, but we can know the results, because their main tool for surviving is knowing in advance where and what the danger is, then putting into action a strategy for quiet, energy-saving preventive avoidance. The last resort, though not uncommon, is the cry of alarm, followed by the dive for safety.

As the previous chapters have established, four of the five vocalizations we study in bird language—songs, companion calls, male-to-male aggression, and adolescent begging—are integral to baseline. The better we understand baseline for any given species and niche, the better we understand the disruption signaled by the fifth vocalization, the outlier, which is the alarm. Oftentimes that disruption is subtle, but on a somewhat limited basis, it can be a cry of surprised panic. Sometimes it's a silent alarm, with the silence so deep we can actually *feel* it—at once intangible and unmistakable. Usually easy to hear (relatively speaking, even from the juncos, whose alarms, though quiet, are louder than their companion calls), alarms are by far the most complicated vocalizations to analyze. With those Pacific wrens in Washington, I didn't have too many doubts about the weasels, despite the caretaker's denials, if only because I'd been listening to the birds for more than twenty years. Likewise with the watchful wolf by the sandbar. We students of bird language slowly build up our understanding and will never exhaust the subject. This and the next two chapters on alarms (and then the final chapter on the birds' interactions with, and alarms about, humans) are full of observations from my own fieldwork and that of other trackers and bird language types, ornithologists, and researchers in other fields. This is where the rubber meets the road. Still, we're dealing with guidelines and principles, not airtight algorithms, to help us organize our thinking around the sounds and the behaviors we're hearing and observing: Not *if* this, *then* that. Rather, *if* this, then *possibly* that; ask another question. Now *probably* that; ask another question. Finally, *almost definitely* that.

A Phonetics Lesson

With many songbird species, the alarm call is phonetically the same as the companion call, just exaggerated, and unmistakably so. In the case of the cardinal, for instance, whose song is a simple *cheer cheer cheer* and its companion call a simple *chip*, uttered softly and rhythmically, a modest alarm might just be a louder, faster version of the companion call: *chip! chip!* A higher stage of alarm is *CHIP! CHIP! CHIP!* Even though the difference is not strictly phonetic, it will quickly become evident, even for the beginning student of bird language. *(Examples of songbird* chip! *alarms are in audio files 10 [song sparrow], 34 [northern cardinal], and 21 [Carolina wren].)*

The differences in intensity, volume, and speed of delivery will always be accompanied by agitated body language that's also hard to miss—if you can see the bird at all. If it has been feeding, focused on the ground or the bush, it stands up tall and cranes its neck, listening. If the source of the alarm is below, it crouches on the limb and peers intently downward, searching and no doubt listening. Many birds pump their tails nervously; the bird that pumps its tail as a baseline *visual* companion call, such as the American kestrel or eastern phoebe, pumps it faster still for purposes of alarm— or maybe not at all, with the *frozen* tail the telltale signal to others concerned with its message. Previously, I asked whether the mockingbird's bizarre jumping dance, with its sudden movement and flashing feathers, could be a companion call. That remains an open question. How about the dance as an alarm? It definitely has all the behavioral earmarks of an alarm, but missing are the accompanying alarm call and, even more significantly, any response from other mockingbirds or other species. This is the tip-off: if the other birds don't pick up on this behavior as an alarm and react accordingly, the mockingbird's dance cannot be an alarm. Simple as that. It's standard, if puzzling, baseline behavior. (The mockingbird's actual alarm is usually described as a loud, harsh, wheezy *skeeeeh* vocalized while the bird is leaning boldly forward, tail pumping, all this from a prominent perch so that others can see and then join in the action. The mockingbird often swoops—frequently upside down —from perch to perch, while calling *skeeeeh . . . skeeeeh . . . skeeeeh.*) *(Listen to audio file 74 for an example of the mockingbird's alarm call.)*

Unlike the mockingbird but like the cardinal, finches, house sparrows, house wrens, black-capped chickadees, tufted titmice, and chipping sparrows (to name a few) also have alarms that phonetically match their companion calls. Most of the passerines have alarms that *may* phonetically match the companion call or may be distinctly different. The different one is reserved for that very last moment of surprise and evasion from extreme danger. For example, the companion call of the Swainson's thrush is a clear, slightly inflected, whistled note: *feee-ee*. Its big alarm is a short, whistled *WHIT!* issued one time. All alarms are accompanied by context cues of various sorts. As I said, these are not algorithms, these are principles, and the deeper our knowledge of the local baseline, the more reliable our interpretation of the alarms. The lifelong learning curve is the ultimate appeal of what we do.

The robin's companion call seems more visual than audible, as the male appears to be watching everything all the time and seems always to know where his mate is. The calls robins make in feeding flocks are little squeaks that are too hard to render phonetically. The alarm is a collection of startled *chirp*s, *cheenk*s, *chuck*s, *tut*s, *ʒeee-bit*s, and what folks call "whinnies," all accompanied by vigorous, repeated tail flips, none of which can be confused with companionship. Those *chirp*s and *cheenk*s are more or less generic sounds, but the whinny is different. If I had to take a stab at it phonetically, it would be something like this: *seech-each-each-each-each-each-each-each-each!* As always, speed of delivery, intensity, volume, position on landscape, and body language will confirm the alarm. *(Audio file 2 has an example of the American robin's whinny call.)* Without any knowledge of bird language or field experience, observers usually will not detect an alarm. With some knowledge and experience, you can't miss it. You'll definitely know something above and beyond baseline is going on.

We humans may be curious, puzzled, annoyed, startled, frightened, or terrified half to death. Sometimes it's one reaction or another instantly; other times the emotion evolves as new information comes in. Likewise with birds. The difference between a mild and a major alarm is fairly analogous to the difference between our parental *Please stop that* to discourage some minor childish annoyance and the shouted *STOP!* along with an instantaneous grab to prevent a child from bolting out in front of a car. We can hear the intensity of the *chip*s and count the number and frequency of them. The absolute highest stage of alarm is total silence in a good, tight thicket for protection. I've seen plenty of birds also frozen and silent in the open when aerial predators were perched nearby. Perhaps they were caught in the predators' headlights. Just short of this radical response is a string of the basic alarm call — *CHIP! CHIP! CHIP! CHIP! CHIP! CHIP! CHIP! CHIP!* — directed at a ground predator or nest robber from a safe, just-out-of-reach distance.

One morning I was lying in bed listening to events outside when two birds exploded in what I assumed was an alarm. Even a neophyte in the natural world would have picked up on the intensity. Cardinals. (The neophyte would not have picked up on that.) Something must have really surprised them, as they went from zero to sixty in about two seconds. I jumped up and rushed to the window. In the gray light, I could just make out the blackberry thicket, and there they were, two cardinals, male and female, flipping their tails and flapping their wings and calling *CHIP! CHIP! CHIP!* in a frenzy. *(Audio file 34 has an example of the northern cardinal's alarm call.)* The birds were facing each other, maybe ten feet apart. That surprised me. That was strange. Could it be a domestic spat, not an alarm? If so, I'd never witnessed anything like such tremendous outrage between two birds. Then, as my eyes adjusted to the dim light, I saw the problem: a little screech-owl perched directly between them. This owl must have dropped down for the kill and missed his target, probably thanks to a last-second evasion by one of the cardinals. Or perhaps the cardinals were witnesses to the owl's attack on a mouse. Either way, they were really mad. As I watched, the owl flew up to a higher branch. The cardinals stayed put. The owl went still higher, then higher again. With each short flight of the owl, the cardinals' alarms cooled off, from the sustained screaming *CHIP*s! to sustained *chip*s! to more sporadic *chip*s. Maybe five minutes after the initial attack, the owl finally lifted off and returned to his home, a flicker hole in the locust tree right behind and between the cardinals. When he went inside for the day, the cardinals, still sitting in place, calmed down for good. I learned where this owl lived, and I imagined a huge sigh of relief on the part of the cardinals.

When scaring away an intruder from the nest, the robin has special alarm calls, one of them a high-pitched squeak combined with the rapidly uttered *cheenk cheenk*. The context of this behavior is a giveaway as well. If the intruder is, say, you, the bird will fly perhaps twenty feet up and away, watch you intently from this perch, and complain the whole time with *tut*s and *cheenk*s and *ʒeee-bit*s.

One day, while walking with two young friends in a willow grove beside the Skykomish River, I heard a blast of this special alarm and murmured, "Well, there's the nest."

"Whose nest?"

"The robin's nest, right over there." I pointed. I couldn't see it, but we walked over and there it was, at eye level. We peeked in quickly as we walked by and saw the two little blue eggs. From twenty feet away, the female *tut-tut-tut*-ed with diminishing intensity as we moved off. After discovering a nest, it's always good to get away as quickly as possible, because any ravens, crows, and jays within hearing range will respond to the robin's nest alarm. Some nifty research reported twenty-five years ago by the Wilson Ornithological Society confirmed distinct differences in the test robins' alarms for two different nest-threatening predators—blue jays and snakes. The stuffed snake merited both the *chirp* and *chuck* alarms in equal measure. The stuffed blue jay was significantly more likely to elicit the *chirp*. The robins who then attacked the fake jay included more *chirp*s in their vocalizations, while those who did not attack included more *chuck*s. I'll return to this issue of specialized alarms later in this chapter, only noting for now that juncos, song sparrows, and many other birds also have specialized alarms that designate a threat to the nest.

I've described the junco's companion call as like a tiny tambourine or sleigh bell, or a plaintive, thin, high-pitched *dit*. Its alarm sounds kind of like the noise I can make by putting the tip of my tongue on the roof of my mouth and *almost* clicking, but releasing the air out toward my top teeth: *ttth! ttth! ttth!* As we would expect from this quiet bird, this is a quiet alarm. To my ear, juncos sound as though they are expressing all their vocalizations through absorbent flannel. I saw one junco ascend to twenty feet and broadcast its alarm for a human getting too close to its nest, but a microphone would have to have been pretty close to the junco in order to pick up the call. So it's surprising that juncos are such great bird language allies. Often feeding and nesting on open ground along forest edges — or even in what could be considered open ground, sometimes in tallish grass right next to a walking path — they are terribly vulnerable to just about every possible danger except the highest-flying raptors. They need to have a lot going for them in the way of subtlety and awareness, and all the other nearby birds know this and are tuned in. They hear the little alarms, and if they miss them, they see the flash of white feathers as the junco flits off through the bushes. The dominoes start falling with the robins, the chickadees, everyone — including us. Understanding bird language, we also know what's going on, or at least have the tools with which to undertake an investigation that will yield a pretty clear picture of the situation.

In league with the juncos are the towhees, which can be something of a baseline aberration. Most birds catch everyone's attention with sudden flitting and flashing action that interrupts the stillness, but the opposite is true of the towhees. As we saw in Chapter 3, flitting their wings and flashing their tail feathers is normal baseline companionship behavior for them — it's how they feed. So *stillness* is their important alarm, and this stillness may not be accompanied by any kind of call in the beginning.

Towhees keep the closest eye on one another of any bird species. When feeding, they always arrange their bodies so that they can use their peripheral vision to see as many of their fellow feeders as possible, especially their mates. This adaptation makes perfect sense, since their movements substitute for companion calls. If something alerts one towhee, it will freeze, and a split second later so will all the others. Then they may casually move—almost fade—into denser, safer cover. No noise whatsoever, no big production, but they are gone. It could be a minute or more before the song sparrows look up, notice their absence, look at one another, perhaps *schweep* in cautious alarm, and follow the towhees into hiding. The rest of the birds may still be feeding, but finally all of them become alarmed and scatter off the feeder. What has happened? One morning while I watched just such a scenario, the intruder turned out to be Barney, our beagle. He'd been off wandering for a good couple of hours on the edge of the forest, probably scent-tracking snowshoe hares, as he loved to do. Barney was not much of a predatory concern for the songbirds, but he could disturb them anyway. Well after the early warning stage, a towhee may fly to a strategic post a bit higher up and away from immediate danger, uttering its *tow-hee* call (or sometimes its *wreeeannh* call, especially in the Northwest), but by that time, the danger might already be gone. *(Spotted towhee vocalizations: listen to audio files 36 and 37 for examples of* mews *and* chips *given by towhees.)*

I've noted my hunch that towhees may be able to hear in the subsonic range, because they're the first to leave when a disturbance approaches and the last to return. If you can move through the landscape without disturbing these birds, you've really accomplished something. Consider the towhee as the ultimate motion detector and master mentor of subtlety awareness training for all who listen, watch, wait, and put together the patterns over time. For the bird language student, the useful first warning from the towhee will be the frozen body, the absence of scratching in the dirt, the silence. As with the junco, pay attention if you want to catch the towhee's heads-up—if you want to "count coup," as a fellow instructor learned one day.

The Gift from the Tentative Towhee

At the conclusion of a wilderness skills training session in Washington, where the forest meets the floodplain of the Skykomish, I was walking along the dried sloughs and game trails among the willows and grasses, headed back to the car after a day with other instructors and students. I was taking my usual exploratory time, enjoying a peaceful stroll, picking the occasional blackberry, when I heard the spotted towhee scratching in the duff beneath a hemlock in the shadows of the undergrowth. The baseline version of this rhythmic scratch-feeding is a subtle sound but, once mastered by the observer, never forgotten: *schhhh, schhhh schhh*, followed by three or four seconds of silence, then *schhhh, schhhh schhh*, three or four more seconds of silence, then *schhhh, schhhh schhh*. That's the usual rhythm, with the number of consecutive scratches roughly matching the seconds between the series.

But on this day in western Washington, I heard just a couple of scratches followed by ten, even fifteen, seconds of silence, which felt impossibly long and uncomfortable. This was not baseline feeding. This extended silence was an alarm. But for what? If a predator such as a coyote, bobcat, weasel, or cat were nearby, the bird would have long ago stopped feeding, jumped into a tree at the necessary height, and alarmed *wreeeannh* with a rising inflection. Its consternation would then have been matched by the other birds' dismay. So I knew this wasn't a four-legged ground predator. Was it a hawk? No. There was none of the general commotion, and then the zone of silence, that would confirm this predator. So who was left among the usual suspects? A person. Had to be. Myself? That didn't make sense, because I'd walked past some other towhees that day without disturbing their baseline feeding rhythms. Just in case, though, I conducted a quick mental review of my approach, or a "back-trail analysis." *Was I really tense? Hurried? Unaware as I approached this spot?* No. I'd been moving slowly, stopping a lot, looking around in a lazy if curious manner—nothing to disturb a feeding towhee at thirty feet. Must be someone else. There *were* other people around, colleagues, and they liked to test their scouting skills by trying to sneak up on me. I stopped and looked deeply into the lengthening, darkening shadows of the hemlocks. I didn't see anything or anyone, so I changed my route to bring me farther from the hemlocks in an arc, then went along to the cars.

Some minutes later, I was standing there eating my sandwich when a fellow instructor, Gretje, walked up and said, "Was I that obvious? Did you see me?"

"What are you talking about?" The walk from those hemlocks to the cars had cleared my mind. I wasn't making any connections.

"You know what I'm talking about."

Then I remembered the curious towhee moment, when I had stopped and stared into the shadows. I now realized that it had been Gretje hiding in the hemlocks, because she had known my most likely route back to the cars and wanted to see if I'd pass by her unaware. If I did, she could ambush me and count coup. She had taken her position early enough to let any broad alarm die down, which was the right strategy, but I'd had some help from a certain little bird. Gretje's intent and her position in the towhee's feeding area had given the bird too much to think about, and its unusual scratching alarm had betrayed her.

"Was that you?" I exclaimed.

"Yeah. You looked right at me."

"I didn't see you. I thought someone was in there, though. The towhee gave you away."

"What towhee?"

I wanted to kiss that bird! (I can be competitive, too.)

A Matter of Scale

For a change of pace when it comes to alarms—for a lesson on a radically different scale—find some Canada geese. In Chapter 8, I'll tell an amazing story about one flock of these big birds, but here

I just want to make the point that for alarm purposes, geese are like juncos, towhees, and sparrows, but bigger and slower. Changes in their attitude and alarms are easy to see. Walk toward a feeding Canada goose, and she'll pause for a few seconds, then raise her head a little to look at you and find out if you're going to stop. Move closer, and she'll raise her head a bit higher and give it a little shake. She may stop feeding at this point. Move closer still, and she may give you a muffled, through-the-nose *honk*, and she will probably start walking sideways to your path, then angle away as you draw nearer. Twenty seconds into your approach, when you're about ten yards away, she might walk a bit more briskly, raising her head even more, with a focused stare into your eyes. She may increase the volume of her *honk*, maybe offer a couple in succession. At last, if you keep pushing, she'll open her bill and string together many *honk*s with a raised pitch and volume. (If there's a nest nearby, don't be surprised if she lowers her head and lets out a scary *hisssssss* in your direction.) She's genuinely, justifiably annoyed, and all the other geese in her group have by now joined in her concern. If they have to fly, they'll do so with some drama, as it takes a lot for them to get off the ground. My point: this whole alarm sequence could take a full minute. With the tiny ground feeders, the same sequence wouldn't take five seconds before it reached red-alert status, and the stages can be difficult to differentiate. With geese, it's all slow-motion and crystal-clear. They, too, are good teachers.

Cats and Dogs

I rush to note that annoying the birds is the opposite of my accustomed approach, which is rooted in respect. However, somewhat controlled experiments are great teaching tools, because the reactions and the intentions behind them accurately convey how the generic alarm system works. Walking the same routes each day, getting to know the birds on your path and at your sit spot, all this adds up over time. As these interactions become more personal, the intra- and interspecies alarm system becomes easier to analyze and understand. A tense, stressed coyote moving faster than usual in her efforts to feed those whining pups back in the den will elicit a stronger set of alarms than the more relaxed coyote, maybe responsible only for itself, whose movements seem less anxious and stressed. In the first instance, in reaction to the stressed coyote, the towhee will be intense in its *wreeeannh* alarm call for a cycle or two lasting twenty seconds, and the catbird will join in the rousing with its ducklike *wett* call every five seconds for twenty seconds. In response to the relaxed coyote, the towhee might simply pause while feeding and stop the flash of its tail feathers, hop up a bit into the bush for a better view, and remain quiet. The catbird might emit its alarm only every ten seconds (that is, only once or twice before the coyote is gone). Meanwhile, the birds will note, without alarm, the mother coyote sunning herself and dozing on the mound in front of her den.

The towhee, the catbird, the robin—all of your local birds— know the difference between the housecat seriously on the prowl and the housecat simply walking home (alert, of course, but not actively hunting). The difference between the slinking, start-and-stop, up-to-no-good movements of the hunting feline and the more easygoing actions of the stroller is unmistakable to us humans, and even more so to the birds. Their alarm reactions will be commensurately different. At the very beginning of this book, by way of a teaser, I noted that the alarm for a cat is different from the alarm for a dog. At the time, that claim might have seemed like a bit of a reach on my part. Now I hope it's self-evident: the birds easily pick up the difference in body language between the furtive cat and the rambunctious, definitely bothersome, but relatively clueless and harmless dog who's just trying to cram as much sensory input as caninely possible into his half-hour in the yard. One of those animals habitually hunts and kills birds; the other doesn't. Taking into account the evolutionary pressures exerted down the ages, the resulting instincts, the baseline issues, and energy conservation, how could the robin *not* know the difference? Spend some truly watchful time in a yard with a dog and a cat and confirm this for yourself. In such a yard, the pets essentially become part of the birds' baseline; they're a known quantity. You'll quickly acquire a solid sense of the different treatment they habitually receive from their feathered friends.

"But Jon," I'm sometimes asked, "why do the birds at my feeder five feet off the ground flee when my harmless little terrier rushes out the door? They know him." Well, *some* of the birds know him. Those just passing through the neighborhood don't. The new hatchlings don't. And the birds who do know your dog also have instincts, and a sudden movement toward a feeder is going to elicit an initial response. At first blink, a dog tearing out the door could be a predator charging. (Imagine that you have a raccoon, say, who's always moving around your yard at night. You've seen this animal a hundred times, but that doesn't matter if a dark shape suddenly materializes out of the dark night, right at your feet. You're going to react.) The mere opening of the door is usually enough to get the birds' attention. Over time, they'll get the picture. They'll quickly "correct" their initial response and return to the feeder unless the dog can't resist yapping at them. As long as he does, they'll react with alarm. And if your terrier is out there all day, running around and yapping, the birds might decide that although the feeder is handy, the rest of the baseline in this yard just isn't worth the trouble. Depending on available food sources, they might move elsewhere, even right next door—different feeder, different pets, and different people. All the while, the bird language observer watches and learns.

Chapter 6

THEY'RE ALL IN THIS TOGETHER

T HE ROBIN TWENTY FEET up a tree can see a whole lot farther than the song sparrow a foot off the ground. If that robin discerns a possible problem twenty-five yards away and sounds an alarm with its *chip*s and *tut*s and *ʒeee-bit*s and "whinnies," the song sparrows jump off the ground and are now hanging on to the trees, chest-high, flipping their tails and trying to determine from what direction any fleeing birds might be flying, how far they're flying, and how fast. If their assessment is sufficiently worrisome, they echo the received alarm with their own *shreep! shreep!* Out of the corner of their eyes, the wrens now pick up the sparrows' reaction. At least the wrens stop singing or feeding, rise up through the brush, emit their own little *bzzzz* alert, and make their own assessment. Is the danger on the ground or in flight? Is it now coming this way?

Or: The summer jogger causes a feeding song sparrow to stop, flutter up and away with pumping tail, and *shreep* a first modest alert. The bobcat hears and sees the agitated sparrow and crouches, causing nearby jays to scold. A small herd of whitetail bachelors hear the jays and sneak off, which brings the feeding and singing of the nearby robins to a halt for a few tensely curious moments.

Or: Two arguing male robins overhear the song sparrows' alarm cries and instantly bury the hatchet. Two nearby parents feeding their chicks drop that chore, get very attentive in stillness, and ready themselves for a possible dive into the bushes. If they have picked up the other birds' alarms from a considerable distance, they may fly to a higher branch to get a better view and sense of things — listening, always listening, because the sense of hearing comes online instantly and with a 360-degree scan, while vision requires direction and focus and thus is a little slower. The exodus of all the birds in the vicinity upward (or into thick cover) almost certainly means that something of concern is happening maybe twenty yards away, maybe as far as a hundred yards, and it's very likely *coming this way*. The alarms issuing from that direction tell the birds as much. Careful waiting is warranted. (Yours as well.)

The point: it is never just the robins communicating with the other robins, the song sparrows with the other song sparrows, the juncos with the other juncos. In the yard and in the trees, it's everyone communicating with (because they are eavesdropping on) everyone else — spring, summer, fall, and winter: ripples within ripples, a vast web with many seams and confusions; concentric rings bouncing off concentric rings; subtle sounds, subtle scents, subtle movements. Even the ants on the forest (or the living room) floor are sending out concentric rings of information. The question is, which creatures can perceive them, or need to? In the instance of the ants, only really tiny creatures (I guess) and birds such as the drongos and jays who want to use them for formic acid spa treatments. In the instance of the birds, just about everyone their size or larger, and maybe even some of the bugs.

To rephrase the vital point: alarms must always be universally understood within the habitat, just as the wailing of an approaching ambulance is impossible for any of us humans (or the other creatures, for that matter) to ignore. Obviously, no scientific experiment could prove the "must" and the "always," but enough experiments prove specific interspecies communication to make the inference totally plausible. I don't imagine that any scientist in any related field would now dispute the point. For many years, published studies have demonstrated that Arabian babblers, crows, magpies, quail, and robins use distinctly different alarms for different occasions. Squirrels, gerbils, prairie dogs, and, most famously, vervet and Diana monkeys and baboons in Africa have different alarms for different occasions. *(These audio files have examples of interesting alarms: 72 [black-tailed prairie dog], 65 [black-billed magpie], 66 and 67 [eastern chipmunk's terrestrial threat alarm and aerial threat alarm].)* Among those who study bird language, the sophistication of such *intra*species communication is basic knowledge, but more surprising to those outside the field is the ubiquity of *inter*species communication—one species eavesdropping with benefit on another species' alarms, as in the scenarios sketched at the beginning of this chapter.

In the introduction, as a blatant teaser, I mentioned the perplexed reaction in some quarters to research showing that red-breasted nuthatches understand at least certain alarm calls of black-capped chickadees, including the distinction between "high" and "low" raptors. As it happens, chickadees' alarms are more complex than those of many other songbirds. In fact, they're beyond me. But after reading this study, I'm listening to them a lot more carefully. (Given the chickadees' complex alarms, perhaps it's not surprising that their song also varies from bird to bird, although it is always some version of a set of plaintive whistles.) Their alarm for a hawk or owl on the wing is a quiet *seet* that directs everyone to freeze in place. Their alarm for a hawk or owl perched on a branch, however, is a loud *chick-a-dee-dee-dee*, with as many as a dozen *dee*s extending the alarm and distinguishing between larger, less dangerous birds (such as the great horned owl) and smaller, quicker raptors (such as the pygmy-owl): the more *dee*s, the greater the danger. *(Audio file 51 has an example of black-capped chickadees mobbing a sharp-shinned hawk.)* The extended alarm brings the chickadees into a flock that harasses and maybe confuses the predator, which eventually flies away. As a control in their experiments, the researchers used a perched bobwhite, and the chickadees performed as we would expect: they were unperturbed by this peace-loving bird.

To find out whether a different species—the nuthatches, specifically—pick up on the chickadees' distinctions, the researchers set up a loudspeaker where nuthatches but not chickadees were living. (This was a relatively unusual habitat. The two birds are often found together.) When recordings of the different chickadee alarms were played, the nuthatches reacted as the chickadees do: when the extended *dee-dee-dee* alarm indicated the presence of the more dangerous predator, the nuthatches mobbed together to harass the enemy. (But beware, nuthatches: the chickadees apparently know that you're listening and sometimes produce false alarms, causing the gullible to fly away and leave that much less competition for food. This behavior indicates that the chickadees can make fine distinctions between fake and real alarms and that they—like the jays I suspected in Chapter 1—use audio tools for deception.)

Even more surprising (for those new to this research) than interspecies eavesdropping is inter-order and even interclass eavesdropping, which many other studies confirm. Monkeys and hornbills recognize each other's specific predator alarms, and their reactions vary depending on the nature of the threat. Yellow-bellied marmots and golden-mantled ground squirrels heed each other's alarm calls. Likewise, chipmunks listen to and take appropriate action regarding the alarms of the titmouse.

All in all, perhaps the most easily observed communication symbiosis is between the birds and the chipmunks and squirrels. Anyone who has spent any time in the woods knows that these incorrigible rodents are often making the most noise of any species, and a lot of this chattering and barking while hanging on to the side of a tree, tail twitching frantically, seems to be an all-out alarm of some sort. It may be, but there also may be some territorial behavior mixed in, perhaps even some mild neurosis! For us, the important point is that in more cases than not, the squirrels' alarms are linked to the birds' alarms. Squirrels obsessively monitor their feathered neighbors and then obsessively add their own opinions. There are studies on this point, but experience will be your ultimate teacher: the birds are probably the first ones to hit the alarm button, followed *immediately* by the squirrels. Check it out.

Studies on interclass communication are fairly common now, but it's hard to see how they will ever capture the fullness of this phenomenon. Consider the deer and the junco. If a deer wanders into this bird's nesting territory, the junco will rise up and stand tall, turn toward the deer, and issue its mildest, meekest alarm call. Who could hear this barely audible *ttth! ttth! ttth!*? But the deer does hear. It pivots its ears forward and pauses: *Oh, okay, I get it.* Then it takes a step back and circles around. I wouldn't look for a study on this symbiosis anytime soon (how could anyone set up such a study, including controls, in the forest?), but bird language students have recorded the phenomenon in their journals innumerable times.

In fact, we see this kind of courtesy in the natural world all the time. (I've seen a video of a herd of elephants parading along an African mud flat. As one female is just about to flatten a basking turtle, she pauses midstride and gently rolls it out of the way.) The herbivores, specifically, are not predators and therefore are not dangerous. The birds know this very well. For one thing, the body language of the grazers is so different from that of the predators. For another, how many tens or hundreds of millions of years of experience with deer versus foxes have hard-wired the birds' instincts? So they don't become overly alarmed about a deer or elk or cow. It would be a waste of energy. If, however, a deer should get spooked and move in a way that is obviously not casual feeding, in a way that violates the baseline, the birds and chipmunks will almost certainly respond with mild agitation alarms — not in fear of the deer, just in recognition that something has caught the deer's attention.

Many bird species around the world hitch rides on the backs of cows, rhinos, buffalo, and all the other stolid grazers who provide a fairly dependable platform for plucking ticks. Not many birds ride around on the jumpier grazers, such as the deer, who might be more trouble than they're worth. No birds ride around on cats and foxes. Louis Liebenberg, the South African responsible for the Cy-berTracker software, told me that candidates for one of the credentials offered by the organization CyberTracker Conservation fail one part of the examination if they can't discern the companion or alarm calls of the oxpeckers, who feed off the backs of Cape buffalo resting in the shadows and shade. Those calls often convey trouble brewing in the bush. The guide has to understand this language.

In East Africa, dik-diks, the miniature antelopes (only fourteen inches tall at the shoulder) who live in mated pairs on multi-acre territories on the savanna, heed the *gghhoo-aaawwaaayyy!* alarm calls of the white-bellied go-away birds perched in the treetops, sentinel-style. When anecdotal word of this cross-species, bird-mammal communication reached the Department of Ecology and Evolutionary Biology at UCLA, three researchers—a professor and two undergraduates—pricked up their ears. The scenario seemed eminently testable employing a recording of the go-away birds' alarm calls. The team's subsequent work, which I was prompted to read about in the journal *Behavioral Ecology,* confirmed that the dik-diks, hearing the alarms, usually assumed a vigilant stance or stopped foraging altogether and bolted for cover, while they all but ignored innocuous bird song.

It only makes sense. The dik-diks are as quick as cats, and they need to be, because numerous predators, including some cats, dine on them. The dik-diks are not going to ignore the go-away birds' free warning. The authors of the UCLA study speculate that such eavesdropping by vulnerable animals is much more common than biologists appreciate. I can't speak for biologists, but native trackers and bird language students know that the authors' point about eavesdropping—widespread eavesdropping, virtually universal eavesdropping, *mandatory* eavesdropping—is correct.

The abstract of a piece about related research on monkeys and baboons published in the *Annals of the New York Academy of Sciences* in 2006 states:

Historically, a dichotomy has been drawn between the semantic communication of human language and the apparently emotional calls of animals. Current research paints a more complicated picture. Just as scientists have identified elements of human speech that reflect a speaker's emotions, field experiments have shown that the calls of many animals provide listeners with information about objects and events in the environment. Like human speech, therefore, animal vocalizations simultaneously provide others with information that is both semantic and emotional.

I admire and welcome all the research on "second language" alarm calls, but when I read a passage like this one, I know that "modern" science is not necessarily the leading edge; in bird language and animal behavior, it's just catching up with indigenous knowledge. And most of the academic research focuses on one, maybe a few, species' modes of communication in very specific contexts. The whole story is actually much bigger than that, just as the meaning of human language is not fully addressed by research on the thousands of discrete languages. I've mentioned my hunch that the dawn chorus may serve a meta-purpose of some sort for all the songbirds. I'd love for academic science to tackle that subject—but I have no idea how researchers would go about it. (How would you set up controls for the dawn chorus?) The old-time native scouts were way ahead of the scientific curve, and their present-day protégés around the world still are (most famously, perhaps, the San Bushmen, as well as tribes from the deep rainforests in remote regions of the world). They know in their bones that, for all the creatures, awareness plus instinct rules. Birds, specifically, cannot ignore danger or the other creatures' alarms. It's impossible. Many tightly controlled studies have confirmed the amazing ability of some of the corvids, especially the Clark's nutcracker, to remember and then find hundreds of food caches under deep winter snow. How could this "strategic memory" *not* be utilized for other purposes, specifically recognizing and remembering alarm calls? Such a narrow use of a given mental skill would fly in the face of everything we understand about how brains and evolution work. Learning and using the communications of other species in a particular habitat has provided a selective advantage, by definition, and as a bird survives season after season, accumulating street smarts and survival skills, surely it becomes more aware and less likely to make a fatal mistake.

There Is a Limit

Clearly, the more complex the habitat and the more diverse the species living there, the more complex the alarm dynamics. Habitats with a variety of plentiful nut-producing trees, such as oaks and beeches, are particularly rich zones of biodiversity, with many bird species and many predators. The forest's understory presents us with one dynamic, the midstory with another, and the canopy with yet another. There's a lot of overlap and a lot of opportunity for misinterpretation. Put this diverse forest along an edge with a meadow or a creek, or both, and the complexity increases even more. The presence of people — those who are learning to hear and see and understand, and others completely unaware — adds yet another complicating factor, another source of alarm, and a major one.

Note, however, this vitally important point: the ripples of influence and alarms don't roll on forever; the seamless web does have limits. Otherwise, the birds would be trapped within an almost continuous state of alarm: not 24-7, but about 16-7, a system that would not serve them well at all. As usual, the issues are energy and energy conservation. Therefore, the birds have to make very quick decisions about alarms, downplaying many, ignoring some altogether: *What's more important to my survival right now, this potential threat or continuing to eat and* storing *energy, not* spending *it?* If the bird repeatedly underestimates the gravity of the situation, it will be culled as ruthlessly as if it were a begging chick. Similarly, if it consistently overestimates the threats, the resulting stress will inexorably beat it down and it will probably be culled from the scene (if not so dramatically as the oblivious chick). Over the long haul, these selective pressures have laid down the instincts that guide the birds' decisions today. Alarms provide foreknowledge, which allows the easy fadeaway into the shadows, which is highly preferable to the last-instant mad dash for safety, which may be dangerous in itself and costs energy.

Is There No Privacy?

The prey species listen to the birds. The predator species also listen to the birds. Look at this scenario: A pair of mated coyotes hunting hares along a road detect an intense alarm response from a host of birds, including some common yellowthroats, red-winged blackbirds, and towhees. *(Listen to the following audio files for examples of assorted songbird alarms: 26 [common yellowthroat], 31 [red-winged blackbird], 37 [spotted towhee].)* One possibility is a nest-robbing predator, maybe a weasel, threatening the birds. Understanding this, the coyotes drop everything regarding the hares and sneak toward the scene of the songbirds' alarms, splitting up to come in from different angles. Since the birds are distracted, one or both coyotes have a good chance of arriving undetected and a fairly decent chance of snatching up the weasel, egg dripping from his lower jaw, and maybe a towhee as well. The predators' keen awareness of the birds' alarm calls also explains why commercial "predator calls" work as well as they do. I've used them many times, without at first understanding why the dying-rabbit call, for example, is so effective at luring foxes and owls into close proximity. Then I learned about wake hunting, a means of energy conservation employed at every opportunity by just about every living creature, I now assume—after only forty years of watching and wondering. (What else am I missing? A lot, no matter how adept I am at this bird language business.)

So it's a many-angled dynamic: the birds pick up on the predators and spread the alarm, and the predators pick up on these alarms about themselves. How, then, do the predators ever catch any game? Their best recourse is to manipulate the birds' alarm systems, like the coyotes who took advantage of the weasel alert to avoid an alert about themselves. Clever. The accipiters—especially the Cooper's hawk, in my experience—also take strategic advantage of the birds' alarms. Here's my theory: hearing an alarm for another predator, an accipiter glides in that direction, knowing that the birds are distracted by the first predator, making the second predator's odds just a little better. Joining the coyotes and accipiters as opportunistic students of bird language are foxes, wolves, weasels, housecats, bobcats, and bigger cats. Through careful observation and controlled body language, these animals can sometimes avoid disturbing the birds and, in effect, move invisibly through the forest. Not always, but sometimes. The fact that they sometimes succeed shouldn't diminish our appreciation of the birds' awareness; it should increase our appreciation of the subtlety of this variation on the proverbial cat-and-mouse game. It also explains why leopards and mountain lions choose the night shift for their hunting: it's just too hard to be a big sneaky cat in the daylight. (In the old days, native scouts manipulated and to some limited extent evaded the birds' alarm systems. Today, advanced students of bird language and others mentored in the native traditions can employ certain techniques of body language to greatly further their cause of getting "past" the birds and closer to the fox lolling in the sunshine. Ninja-like, I guess, but rooted in the routine of invisibility discussed in Chapter 4.)

Birds Can Tell Hawks Apart Better Than I Can

For the other birds, hawks are a case unto themselves. The appearance of a sharp-shinned hawk, Cooper's hawk, or goshawk—all of whom will cruise at mid–tree level or even lower, maybe even under the trimmed lower branches of the trees bordering sidewalks —is a universal threat. All of the birds in the right size range will sound the alarm, because all of them, high and low, are in danger from these predators. The alarms for the accipiters can be heard a hundred yards in all directions—first the bird plow alarm, then the zone of silence. (I'll talk a good deal more about this in the next chapter.) By contrast, if the baseline buster is a red-tailed hawk flying along the tops of the trees, the tanagers and blackbirds living up there will surely sound a mild, temporary alarm, but the ground birds—well hidden, well protected, and safe from the redtail's talons—will actually continue their singing and their companionship. If they pause, it's only momentarily. They have quickly analyzed the approaching wave of alarm calls and established their own safety, a marvelous feat of awareness.

Now let's get really specific. In their alarms, the songbirds differentiate among at least five categories of aerial predators: accipiters, buteos, falcons, owls, and corvids. (Corvids are discussed in Chapter 7.)

Accipiters

The accipiters—often known as the bird hawks and including the sharp-shinned hawk, Cooper's hawk, and goshawk—are speedy, adept hunters who are most productive when working in a closed, tight forest, picking off birds, small mammals, lizards, and snakes. If they get close, they provoke the universal alarm: *DIVE! DIVE!* In fact, they're one of five sources of this universal alarm. The others are nest robbers (universal but more isolated); eagles (which propagate a large wave across the countryside, alarming even the largest hawks and ravens); peregrines (whose concentric ring reminds me of the Cooper's hawk's); and some people.

Buteos

The buteos are the soaring hawks, such as the red-tailed, broadwinged, red-shouldered, and Harris's hawks, all of whom focus on small mammals and secondarily on birds that inhabit open or patchy habitats in which the hawks can see their movements. Some also go for carrion, including roadkill. The red-tailed hawk is one of the most abundant large birds of prey in North America, and it is definitely the most commonly seen by us. It may well be the first to a carcass, if only because the vultures, whose beaks are too soft to "open" the harder skin of animals such as wild pigs and deer, have to wait a while for the package to start rotting and soften up. The buteos are slower than the accipiters and therefore need more space for maneuvering as they descend toward a (probably) moving target. Pigeons, doves, robins, and quail feeding on the open ground will clear out quickly, but smaller birds ensconced in thickets, bushes, and stands of trees will often react to the redtail rather casually and won't get agitated much at all. They'll just give the hawk some respectful space. This behavior is especially visible with an entire mixed flock of blackbirds.

Falcons

The falcons specialize in open-sky hunting, taking other birds on the wing. They are really not a threat to birds protected in the bush, but these birds will still pay attention with high-pitched alarms, or maybe silence, as long as the falcon is in sight. For this reason, the alarms for falcons may, in the beginning, be difficult to distinguish from the alarms for accipiters. With experience, the difference will become clear: the response to falcons is less dramatic.

Owls

The nocturnal owls merit a separate mention, relying as they do on stealth, not speed, for their success. (In the story I told in Chapter 5 about the screech-owl and the two cardinals, which happened right at dawn, the cardinals had a smudge of daylight on their side, and this turned out to be enough.) When discovered by chickadees or jays during the day, an owl on its roost will usually provoke a static alarm—an alarm that indicates a "still" predator. The ensuing mobbing may escalate and bring in robins, other jays, cardinals, blackbirds, mockingbirds, and crows. What started out as noisy chickadees can end up with crows so loud and furious they irritate any nearby humans to the point of driving off the owl so that peace can return. Or the owl will often make this choice after a while anyway, because those mobbing birds aren't going away.

The pygmy-owl can cause the same escalation of alarm behavior, but with smaller species of songbird mobbers, and lower in the shrubs, rather than in the canopy of trees. In the northern Santa Cruz Mountains, at my last sit spot, I witnessed a real donnybrook between a pygmy-owl discovered in a chest-high elderberry thicket by chickadees, titmice, nuthatches, sparrows, wrens, juncos, thrushes, and others. It lasted for twenty minutes. Not wanting to disturb the situation but unable to hold out any longer, I had to investigate. I thought the intruder was an owl, but I couldn't be absolutely sure. A nest robber was an alternate explanation, although it wasn't the season for nest robbers. I was with a couple of friends, so we surrounded the thicket. (It's good to have help before pushing into such a fracas. Owls are notorious for sneaking out the back without being seen. Accipiters, bobcats, weasels, and foxes also have a pretty good routine of invisibility.) As we closed in, a small, fluttery-flying, songbird-looking owl—a pygmy-owl—flew out of the thicket and into plain view. It took one look at my friends and me, then shot off to the farther recesses of the thickly vegetated drainage canyon off the meadow. Of course, the alarms instantly kicked in over there and then followed the owl into the distance, until they were drowned out by the running water and the breeze in the leaves.

Land-Based Predators Cause Smaller Alarms

Many beginning birders and students of bird language are surprised to learn that land-based predators pose any problem at all for the birds. *Can't the birds just fly away? That's their whole advantage over the rest of us.* Yes, flight is an advantage, but ground predators utilize a suite of stealthy tactics to grab birds before they get airborne. Some, like the bobcat and housecat, can snatch a bird in the air, but stealth is required to get that close. All of the ground predators use shadows, thickets, and distractions to mask their approach and ambush. Some hunt at night and can pick birds off their nests or roosts.

Alarms for the land-based predators tend to be more localized than those for the hawks and falcons, simply because the land-based predators aren't flying and therefore aren't as fast or as widely dangerous. Their progress can be more easily monitored and reported as necessary. The set of alarms broadcast about a ground predator has a leading edge, and the birds have the luxury of following the progress of this edge and drawing careful conclusions about the predator causing it. With the torpedo-like accipiters, the birds have no such luxury; the leading edge is more like a pressure wave in front of a fast-flying jet. A ground predator can be mobbed in relative safety, although this mobbing may call in other predators, who can sneak up from behind or above the mob, taking advantage of the birds' alarmed focus on the first predator. This is, in effect, an ironic kind of wake hunting, with the secondary predators following in the alarm wake of the primary predator, quite possibly with more success.

One summer in Washington, I had the opportunity to compare and contrast the alarms directed toward two kinds of wild canids. To my surprise, coyotes and wolves were treated entirely differently by the local birds, even though each is a doglike predator trotting around on all fours. The setting for this fortuitous experiment was the sandbar of the Skykomish River in the Cascade Range. Living here were a small family of wolves that I studied closely (large male, medium-size female, and their two offspring, one male, one female) and a family of coyotes that I didn't follow nearly as closely (one pair of mated adults and three or four other adults or subadults that I could hear in the evening at times).

On and around the sandbar, the coyotes always seemed to be up to no good. Their attitude appeared to be, *I'll take advantage of every opportunity I can get,* and their body language exuded anxiety (probably because of the wolves nearby). The song sparrows, Pacific wrens, robins, and spotted towhees responded in kind, never failing (to my observation) to broadcast alarms at the trotting approach of these animals along their brush trails. The wolves, by contrast, always seemed to be totally at ease, masters of their domain: *I have twenty miles of hunting coming tonight.* Or, *My deer carcass awaits nearby. I'm not really after those songbirds, who are a waste of energy for me. Let the coyotes bother with them. If I need to hunt on this sandbar, I'll team up with my partner and stir up a hare.* The wolves' body language exuded confidence and peace of mind, no anxiety about the next meal at all, and the birds responded to them in kind, broadcasting many fewer alarms per wolf encounter than per coyote encounter. The two canines seemed to be almost as different in the birds' estimation as cats and dogs.

Exactly Enough and No More

How far does a bird fly from a predator in its territory? This is just about the most common question about bird-predator behavior, and the law of conservation of energy answers, *Just far enough.* As I've noted, ground birds will not overreact to a cat. They know its "predator reach" and will fly up to a branch five feet, maybe ten feet (but not fifty feet), high. That would accomplish nothing, expose them to danger from wake feeders, and waste energy. The point is perfectly illustrated by the story I told in the introduction to this book, the one about the wrentit, the robin, the sliding glass door, and the cat.

When a weasel or a cat agitates the song sparrows on or near the ground, the robins, juncos, and other ground feeders will take note and probably follow suit. The tanagers and vireos higher up in the trees will hear those alarms and perhaps pause midsong for an instant and look down, but they'll quickly resume their singing. There's no reason to invest much energy in the soap opera down below. (Should the weasel head *up* the tree, the tree-oriented birds will pay some attention, though they've never seen a weasel make it to the top of a tall fir, and this one presumably won't either. The weasel's cousin, the pine marten, may make it all the way up and likely elicit a potent response while doing so.) A pair of black-throated green warblers busily feeding in the canopy may convey code-green baseline status for their patch of the trees, but that might be only because they have set aside the subtle but persistent little *tut* alarm from the Swainson's thrush hovering on the edge of the small ravine below, signaling a skunk meandering along down there. The distant alarm precipitated by the housecat in the neighbor's yard will be heard and monitored, but action will be deferred until the progression of that alarm establishes the movement of the predator.

For the fast-flying accipiter who poses an imminent, life-threatening danger, the various territories of the songbirds are violated in such rapid succession that the alarms triggered over a distance of a hundred yards are almost simultaneous. Territorial considerations don't really come into play. When the predator is on the ground, however, with everything happening more slowly, territory does play a major role in the alarms. With the urgency not so great, the birds are much more vociferous when the danger is *inside* their respective territories. That's how much investment they have in their turf and airspace. I don't think it's an exaggeration to state that when the issue isn't clearly and truly urgent, the territorial instinct subverts the self-defense instinct. Conversely, many birds are noisier with their alarms when they're near the boundaries of their territories. In these cases, the territorial instinct seems to reinforce the self-defense instinct, and maybe that's exactly what's happening.

You'll need a good map to unsnarl the impact on the alarms of *overlapping* territories, especially in richly diverse habitats in the eastern forests of North America. In such bird paradises, the fairly large territory of a single robin, five acres in some cases, could "contain" as many as a dozen or more much smaller and overlapping territories defended by members of almost that many species, including bird language stalwarts such as song sparrows, juncos, wrens, and towhees. That's unusual density. Many places with what seems like a lot of birds will, in fact, feature only a few overlapping territories, if any at all. But even here, knowledge of the territories will clear up any confusion about the alarm responses, because these responses to a cat, say, creeping through the brush will be localized, one territory at a time. Two reasons: the cat can't fly, so time is not absolutely of the essence, and the birds are territorial. Therefore, the robin may sound the alarm about an approaching cat, while several birds with smaller territories within the robin's larger one will not send out an alert unless the cat actually crosses into their respective territories. Or one song sparrow may emit an alarm while its neighbor sparrow just thirty feet away may not, even if that neighbor also sees the cat. The territorial boundary lies between them. The neighbor will probably investigate at least, and quietly. Likewise with the robins. If they happen to be close to one another but with the DMZ between them, the one with the cat actually in its territory will push the button, but the nearby robin may just sit there—agitated, watching, pumping its tail, but quiet for now. A robin may even adopt a watchful attitude if the cat is on the far side of its territory, seventy-five feet away, even though the Pacific wren, whose tiny territory the cat has simultaneously entered, will fire away.

Quirks of the Trade

Also in play with alarms is the factor bird language specialists label "species sensitivity." Some birds are simply more tolerant of threats than others. When you or I walk by, the hermit thrush will disappear into the thicket, while the male red-winged blackbirds perched at the edge of a nearby swamp will continue their duet. *(Listen to audio file 41 for examples of hermit thrush calls. [Note: these are often graded vocalizations, used in a variety of situations—some alarm, some nonalarm.])* Thrushes are much more sensitive than redwings. Juncos are also somewhat sensitive, or, as the field guides say, "shy and retiring." With experience in a given habitat, you will be able to line up the birds on a shy-to-bold scale. A spectacular bird on the shy end of the scale is the great blue heron—not a passerine, of course, nor a dependable ally for bird language purposes, but it does have a wide range in North America, and its presence stalking along the edge of a pond or lake is a good indicator that calm prevails. It's a good indicator, that is, if you actually see the heron, because its lovely, shadowy camouflage coloration and inherent stillness allow it to live among us generally undetected. In the early morning and late evening in late spring and early summer, the great blue migrates between roosting and feeding sites. If you see a heron flying in its ungainly style at any other time, it has probably been surprised by a land-based predator (quite possibly a human being or a dog) or pushed off by an approaching eagle.

The great blue's basic alarm is a deep *CROOOOOAAAAAK,* but other herons and egrets have similar alarms, so it's not definitive for the great blue. (You'll just have to get to know your local herons and egrets!) One year on Vancouver Island, British Columbia, I heard an unfortunate variation of this call. I was visiting my colleague Mark Tollefson's sit spot on a small hill with magnificent old firs, Garry oaks, and maples, overlooking a wide expanse of salt marsh fed by the Chemainus River. A few friends were with us. In midafternoon, we paused in our explorations to watch three trumpeter swans swimming in the twisting river. Our idyll was interrupted by a loud *CRROOOAAK*—the basic heron alarm call, but pitched noticeably higher than usual, I thought, and with much more volume and a sort of cut-off-at-the-end quality. Overall, the sound was, for a heron, frantic and shrill. It was followed by a deafening silence stealing across the marsh, and I got a twisting feeling in my gut. I turned to everyone and said, "I think that heron just bought the farm."

We were looking in the general direction of the alarm, but our view was obscured. We continued our explorations. Some time later, on our way back to our van and following the same soggy, grassy trail we had used going in, we found the recently deposited neck and breast feathers of that great blue, also bits of skin, still pink and dabbed with fresh blood—all of it scattered right on top of the prints we had left walking in. The signs of ripping and tearing were unmistakable. We followed the path of fresh feathers a short distance. When it ended, we looked up to see many other feathers from the heron dangling, dancing, and snagged in the branches of a cottonwood tree. There was no wondering now. We'd seen bald eagles all over the place, and we'd heard several heron alarms, once not thirty yards in front of us. This was the work of an eagle in action. The skittish heron had not been skittish enough.

Generalizing again, the tolerant species are those that seem always to be hanging around, under all conditions, but that is somewhat of an illusion. They do have their moments to disappear, but we may not notice when they do. Or we may notice: dispatch a peregrine falcon across the urban sky, or bring in a Cooper's hawk across the rooftops, and every passerby will see the pigeons scatter with stormlike intensity. I haven't codified my observations in any way, but I feel comfortable picking up messages from pigeon flocks on the wing: a certain way in which they look at each other, the landscape around them, how fast and in what pattern they're flying. The focus of attention, averaged over the group, almost always identifies the "point last seen" of the Cooper's hawk or falcon.

This we know for sure: since all these species are still with us in force, their respective tolerances for danger have worked in evolutionary terms. Over time, observing the scene at your sit spot, you will come up with your own shy-to-bold scale for the local birds. And not just for the different species, but for individual birds, too, some of whom will be *abnormally* shy or bold by the standards of the species. I've decided that these little outliers tend to become our favorite allies.

Chapter 7

A SHAPE FOR EVERY OCCASION

T HE DISCUSSION OF ALARMS in the previous two chapters emphasized the sheer ubiquity of intra- and interspecies, inter-order, and even interclass eavesdropping. There we focused on individual birds, territory issues, and categories of predators (aerial and land based). In effect, we were looking at alarms in three dimensions. In the real world, of course, when viewed in sequence as a collective response to a threat, the birds' individual alarms produce one three-dimensional alarm rolling through *time*, the necessary fourth dimension. This collective alarm, and the accompanying strategic and evasive actions, are dynamic and almost always have a distinctive "shape" within the habitat. Often we can see this shape unfolding. It tells us the nature of the threat, the intent of the threat, and perhaps even the species.

This chapter lays out bird language specialists' codification of twelve alarm shapes, each a time-tested response by the birds to a specific kind of threat: bird plow, sentinel, hook, popcorn, parabolic (or umbrella), weasel, cat, bullet, ditch, hawk drop, safety barrier, and zone of silence.

Bird Plow

Consider the plow mounted on the huge truck barreling down the highway in a heavy storm, shoving aside the snow and anything

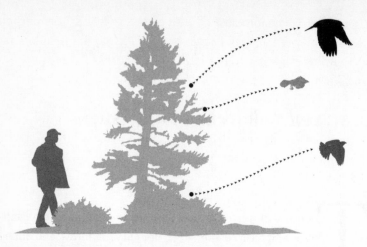

Bird Plow: The bird plow is created when a person (or other perceived and immediate danger) appears suddenly and with a brisk trajectory—somewhat ignoring the impact he is having on his surroundings. The bird plow is marked by a rush of birds flying up and away in a straight-line trajectory from an approaching threat on the ground.

else in its path. It doesn't slow down. It has no respect. *Out of the way!* In the wild, the birds are the first creatures who flee an invaded scene, and they proclaim the alarm for all to see and hear. We call this the bird plow, and it's why Native American scouts could pinpoint the location of invading cavalry troops from two miles away. Those stories are passed down to this day. When I first heard them, I thought a little hyperbole might have seeped in. Now I give the stories much more credence, because I couldn't count the number of times I've seen a relatively new student of bird language predict the arrival of *Homo sapiens* two minutes before the stroller's actual appearance, just as I describe in Chapter 8. For an advanced student, that's a parlor trick. Thus, given the mayhem soldiers on horseback must have caused, it's quite likely that the great scouts could have identified the mortal threat to their tribes from two miles away—or maybe even farther—especially considering their lookouts on escarpments overlooking many miles of country.

The most common cause of the plow is the abrupt, heedless, uncaring entry into a given habitat by people. More unusual instigators include fast-moving vehicles (where they're not common); a spooked herd of deer, elk, or moose stampeding through the woods or across the meadow or tundra; or a pack of wolves, say, in furious pursuit of prey. *(Audio file 73 has an example of white-tailed deer alarm.)* On a pond, river, bay, or lake, the explosive liftoff of ducks, cormorants, geese, and mergansers is a bird plow. And a wildfire, of course, kicks up an incredible bird plow. In all cases, the disruption has consequences. The baseline is disrupted. The birds have to exert a lot of energy and often end up on unfamiliar turf. Riskiest of all, they may become the victims of wake hunters, who know well the opportunities stirred up by a bird plow.

Fortunately, the nature of the danger and conservation-of-energy principles make such all-out flight unnecessary most of the time. Like all the alarm shapes, the bird plow is usually, in one way or another, "contained." The birds always take into account the "reach" of the predator or other danger. In cities and suburbs, where the birds are habituated to our presence, we may elicit no alarm at all. We're practically part of the baseline. The birds may well react to us, as we shall see, but perhaps not with full flight. The bird plow is usually reserved for people entering a natural area where they're more of an unknown quantity and behaving with an "assumption of permission," as I label their imperious attitude. Most traditional cultures would view this intrusion as inconsiderate at best.

As students of bird language become more knowledgeable about contained alarms, they realize the abnormality of the birds' sometimes uncontained reactions to our presence. Spend some time learning the baseline of a given habitat and comparing the birds' reactions to people and to foxes, say. We're not after the birds—foxes are—but the birds may fear us more. The interaction of birds and people is the subject of the next chapter.

Sentinel

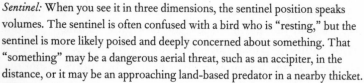

Sentinel: When you see it in three dimensions, the sentinel position speaks volumes. The sentinel is often confused with a bird who is "resting," but the sentinel is more likely poised and deeply concerned about something. That "something" may be a dangerous aerial threat, such as an accipiter, in the distance, or it may be an approaching land-based predator in a nearby thicket.

In 2010, I took my first trip south of the equator. On one of my first mornings in Cape Town, South Africa (a remarkably beautiful city), I was working in the sitting room of my friend's winter rental, a small cottage with a thatched roof overlooking the sea, when I heard what I thought were bird alarms to the north. The birds' singing stopped abruptly, followed by high-pitched calls. I walked out to the veranda in time to see birds of multiple species flying up and perching on just about every available chimney, antenna, and rooftop, calling and looking hard to the north and east. This was alarm behavior, and it went on for many minutes. My friend said, "They're always sitting and looking like that." Always? I didn't think so. Often? Possibly. Regardless, this was not baseline behavior. Posted as high as possible, this collection of birds was at extreme attention. A predator was in the vicinity. This was sentinel behavior — not strictly a shape in terms of its visual appearance, but more of a metaphorical shape. Anyway, it's the most common alarm shape I observe in the field. Why is it so common? Every neighborhood, city, forest, meadow, shoreline, and swamp features some kind of bird-hunting predator, probably more than one, often many. I've never seen an exception to this rule. Maybe such a paradise for birds exists, but I seriously doubt it. Therefore, sentinels post up everywhere.

My friend's comment was typical of the reactions of many beginners in the bird language world: *Certain birds are often up high, looking around, so this must be baseline.* That is a plausible conclusion, but likely mistaken. If the bird looking around from a high post is really in baseline, he will be singing or fluffing his feathers, maybe preening. His attention will not be riveted in one direction. He will not be joined by a number of other birds from other species, all aimed in that same direction, craning somewhat, tails wagging. All this is sentinel, not baseline, behavior. In the discussion of alarms and territory in Chapter 5, I mentioned that birds will often not sound the vocal alarm for a predator they see outside their territory. Instead, they'll post up, watch, and wait for developments: sentinel behavior.

Birders know that certain species often pick a perch in the open or high above everything for either feeding or singing. Naturally, these birds are excellent sentinels. When danger approaches, they're often the first to sound the alarm. The behavior fits into their overall strategy for living. Birds I would count as helpful natural sentinels are robins, flickers, various jays, mynahs, kingbirds, mockingbirds, and, to a lesser degree, various flycatchers, who live in a permanent state of sentinel. (In effect, the sentinel post-up *is* baseline for these birds, but only people who have studied some bird language understand this.) Also good natural sentinels are the eastern and western wood-pewees, who perch on exposed branches and watch for insects to catch on the wing. Flying sentinels (birds that look back toward a threat when on the wing, then usually circle around) include pigeons and doves, flocks of finches, siskins, various shorebirds, and the corvids. (Why do these flying sentinels circle instead of flying directly away from a threat? The reason is simple: a bird's territory is its safety zone, even when currently occupied by a life-threatening accipiter or falcon. If required, evasive action will be taken within this known context. The birds' motto: Keep your friends close and your enemies closer. Pell-mell flight might also put the flying sentinels in jeopardy of predators who have sized up the situation as a good wake-hunting opportunity and are moving in for the kill. Better to stay home and stay organized.) Along waterways, killdeer, plovers, sandpipers, and croaking herons are extra-watchful sentinels, and their various distinctive calls are usually loud and unmistakable. *(Audio files 52–55 have examples of killdeer vocalizations.)*

If the sentinel bird is posted higher than usual, the threat is almost always an accipiter. Logically enough, lower sentinel behavior from one of our favorite ground-dwelling bird allies usually betokens a ground predator nearby. If their alarms are accompanied by alarms from the higher sentinels, an accipiter is the best candidate.

As students of bird language, we comb through the evidence and

Ground Sentinel: A ground sentinel is usually low on a bush or shrub, or sometimes on a low telephone wire. The bird faces in the direction of the threat.

figure out what's happening in context. The birds who we know are telling us something include the shrike who drops its impaled beetle and flies to the top of the hawthorn tree; the robin who broadcasts a series of *zeee-bit* alarms and flies up to a higher perch flipping its tail; the song sparrow who swings precariously on the top of a coyote-brush twig to crane its neck over the hedge; the stalking heron who flies up to a branch in a dead cypress tree; the cedar waxwing or goldfinch flock circling very high, with other birds posted in the treetops; and pigeons in the city circling in quick nervous flight. These are sentinels all. *(Listen to audio file 46 for an example of the American goldfinch's flight call.)*

In a shrubby grassland habitat, quail are excellent sentinels. They're moving around, feeding in a covey. Where I live in California, there can be as many as twenty pairs of eyes in that covey. In the discussion of baseline and companion calls in Chapter 3, I mentioned the quail's "flock call" as the equivalent of a companion call. For us, it may also be an after-the-fact sentinel alarm, because the birds' leader doesn't employ it unless something has scattered his birds. If that scattering was nearby and explosive, as it often is, we already know there has been some disturbance. But sometimes the scattering is less dramatic. Say a group of quail were singing at the edge of the field a few minutes ago, and now we hear the flock call. This means the birds have scattered, but we missed it. The flock call attracts our attention. Numerous times, I've identified the location of people, bobcats, coyotes, and foxes by the quail's after-the-fact sentinel alarm. The same holds true, I'm sure, for all of the quail equivalents around the continent, including the northern bobwhite and the Gambel's, scaled, and mountain quail. *(Audio file 56 has an example of the California quail flock call [aka assembly or rally call]. For quail alarm calls, listen to audio files 57 [California quail] and 60 [northern bobwhite].)*

When the issue is one isolated danger, various birds will often line up in a kind of fence line of sentinels, facing in the direction of the threat. What's really interesting is that the birds on the threat side of the sentinel fence will probably be in some kind of alarm mode, while the birds on the nonthreat side of the sentinel fence will continue singing, feeding, and preening—basic baseline behavior. It's as if the latter birds know that the sentinel birds have their backs. For this reason, I sometimes look at the sentinel fence as the front edge of a concentric ring. As emphasized earlier, birds cannot afford to let an alarm spread forever. The sentinel line says, in effect, *Far enough.*

One more point: in winter especially, the out-of-context song can potentially be a sentinel-like alarm call. I learned this in New Jersey, where the Carolina wrens had the odd habit of bursting out in song—*tea-kettle tea-kettle tea-kettle tea-kettle*—on sunny days when there were patches of snow on the ground. *(Listen to audio files 17, 18, and 19 [19 includes female chatter while male sings] for examples of Carolina wren songs.)* The syllables were the same, but something about this rendition didn't sit quite right with me. A little too much gusto, maybe? Anyway, I was pretty sure the intention wasn't the same as it would be three or four months later. One winter day, I had the opportunity to figure out exactly what was going on. I was walking along a stream below a dam in Monmouth County, following a mink's trail from the day before, looking for the tracks of a muskrat and for fossils dislodged from the sediments along the banks, and checking out prospective fishing holes—all baseline behavior for me. Then I heard a Carolina wren singing its loud, fast song from its post on a south-facing hill. In January, that vantage point can be a little microclimate of warmth, with a cloud of gnats hovering despite the temperature. Hearing the wren's song, I first took it as a spontaneous territorial proclamation, maybe regarding an unexpected bonanza of spiders in the leaf litter below. Then I had a nagging second thought. I left the stream, walked up hill, and discovered in the loose soil and snow patches the very fresh tracks of a gray fox headed away from me. These tracks were not twenty yards from where I thought the wren was perched. The bird would have seen the fox. Could it have used its song to spread the alarm? That was an as yet unobserved behavior for a Carolina wren, but the fox's tracks provided some circumstantial evidence. (Since that time, one other experienced bird language practitioner has described similar wren behavior to me.)

The next day, I was following the same route along the stream when I heard the wren's song, but this time from a different direction. Curious from the day before, I investigated right away. Again I found fresh fox tracks. Now we were beyond the circumstantial or the coincidental, I was sure. The Carolina wren was picking up the gray fox who was sneaking away from me. I saw this as an opportunity to get close to the fox, so the next day I headed along the same trail, hoping to unnerve the animal again. When the wren sang out in alarm, I knew I had a good chance. This time I didn't walk straight toward the bird, but instead doubled back on myself, quickly moving in a wide circle around some concealing brush and sneaking into the area I thought the fox was heading toward, based on the paths I'd taken the previous two days. Sure enough, here he came. He had a furtive posture, using the tree roots at the top of the bank as cover, and he paused to look over his shoulder at where I should have been. As he was looking for me, I was looking at him from behind a tree. I was thrilled and, I'll admit, pretty pleased with my detective work. This is a classic example of how understanding bird language helps us see more wildlife.

The Carolina wren does utilize a regular alarm call—a raspy, harsh *schwep-schwep-schwep-schwep*. *(For Carolina wren alarm calls, listen to audio files 22 [typical male alarm] and 21 [female alarm].)* I think it probably uses its song instead when the issue is twofold: an approaching fox or other ground predator, and its own defense of a territory (in this case, a food larder). Other personal experiences and anecdotes circulating at workshops lend credence to the hypothesis that song can be used as a sentinel alarm. I'm not prepared to state this conclusively as a principle, but it's certainly a good topic for further research. *(Listen to audio file 75 for an example of another songbird using its song as an alarm: the purple finch's "vireo song alarm.")* Another such topic is the "out-of-body song." I cannot begin to explain this oddity of nature, but I've seen a chickadee sitting right in front of me—pumping away, with its bill wide open—and heard its call coming to me from over *there,* many feet away, in midair: nothing less than ventriloquism. In my experience, this phenomenon occurs when the predator is a sharp-shinned or Cooper's hawk, dangerously close and moving in quickly. Just a few years ago, a graduate student at the University of California, Davis's Department of Ecology and Evolution determined that many species of birds, including juncos, finches, and warblers, have ventriloquial abilities. (Her research focused on a yellow-rumped warbler and a stuffed owl.) Other studies followed, all demonstrating that birds can adjust their "acoustic directionality" in order to beam their alarm calls in chosen directions.

Hook

One day years ago in New Jersey, a student I'd been mentoring took off one afternoon for a swim in the creek on the property where our group had been studying bird language for several years. This was the student's sit spot, so he knew a lot of the creatures there, and they knew him. Sitting by the fire waiting for him to return, I saw a wood thrush fly out of the trees, then almost immediately hook back into the forest, about ten feet up. I figured this probably meant that my student was on his way back to camp. The thrush didn't flee his approach in all-out alarm, because he knew this kid well. Besides, the bird was alone in his reaction. This wasn't a bird plow; it was a bird *hook,* the standard evasive response to a known intruder. The hook tells us that the bird has this matter under control. I even took the thrush's hook as a compliment to the student's benign presence in those woods.

In the story I told in the introduction about the wrentit, the robin, and the cat, the wrentit flew from the ground into the bush, altitude

Hook: The hook (compared to the bird plow) is something of a compliment. It suggests that the bird is familiar with the habits of the approaching danger (especially a ground predator) and therefore goes only far enough to escape the intruder's reach. The bird moves in a more casual manner than when using an alarm reserved for a true and immediate danger.

five feet, in order to evade the cat, a known adversary whom the bird could see. Poised five feet off the ground, the wrentit (and the other birds) could always hop a little higher should the cat have a go at it. The cat knows this and will rarely try for the alarmed bird staring down from overhead, because the cat also wants to conserve energy. Many of us have seen a heron in a suburban neighborhood rise up to a branch a mere eight feet off the ground to get away from the largest, meanest-looking dog. The heron knows this dog, as well as its limitations in the "up" direction. There's no reason to fly away. The simple hook works fine.

Most of our best allies for bird language purposes are anchored to a territory, of course, and do not want to venture beyond it. There's an invisible barrier. Once off the ground in the hook alarm, they may choose to follow the disturbance or danger until it has left the territory, then fly back into their own space. (Small ground-dwelling birds with small territories that are easy to see all the way across, such as song sparrows and juncos, can monitor the predator without moving at all. When the threat is gone, they return to the ground, or to whatever they were doing previously.) I've seen thrushes handle foxes and coyotes with a rather casual hook. Why? They know the individual animals. Settle down for weeks of close observation, as many students of bird language regularly do, and you'll discover that those individuals, the thrush and the fox, will have little if any interaction, even though they live in fairly close proximity. I might suggest that *this* thrush has a personal relationship with *this* fox. The thrush certainly knows the fox's habits and limits. A hook is all that's required to handle it.

Compare the hook with the sentinel alarm. If a robin is alarmed in a general way and needs a higher vantage point as a sentinel, it will ascend to 50 feet or higher (the top of a 150-foot tree is not impossible) and look beyond the boundaries of its territory. With the hook, the bird addresses a clear and present danger within its own territory (or immediate surroundings, in a nonterritorial season). The bird hooking up in this way will always take into account the predator's reach. The hook can even look rather casual: high enough but no higher. It's as if the bird is tethered to an invisible shock cord that limits its maneuver to the minimum height required. Generally speaking, a bird's sentinel action takes it higher than any hook it's likely to need.

Think of it this way: In the sentinel alarm, some unidentified disturbance *pulls* the bird higher for a better look. In the hook, some confirmed and identified danger on the ground *pushes* the bird a little higher in a controlled maneuver.

Popcorn

Say an intruder or predator is moving through the neighborhood at a trot. Just ahead of it, the birds hook up and out of the way. What does this series of hooks look like when observed from a distance, one by one, bird after bird? In bird language, it looks like popcorn popping, with each hook a *pop — pop . . . pop . . . pop —* on

Popcorn: One way to look at the popcorn alarm is as a series of hooks with a hint of agitation or surprise, reflected in short vocalizations (as compared to more sustained mobbing when the threat is greater, as with a hunting cat or nest robber). Visually, birds pop up and down in a sequence that mirrors the predator's speed and direction.

down the line as far as the eye can see. If that student in New Jersey who elicited the single hook from the wood thrush before emerging from the trees had instead stayed back and walked (in his brisk pace) a circuit ten yards *inside* the woods, he would almost certainly have sparked a series of individual and intermittent hooks from the thrushes and other birds: the popcorn alarm. This is the birds' basic alarm shape in response to a disturbance on the ground moving at a steady, somewhat fast, controlled pace. The popcorn alarm is sometimes accompanied by the appearance of crows and jays who have overheard the popping and don't want to miss this opportunity to make a comment or even taunt the hapless intruder.

We may not see the intruder, and we are not likely to hear much of its progress (just the odd snapping twig or shaking brush), but we can hear and to some extent watch the birds that are just ahead and above it, and we can know with a good deal of confidence that we're dealing with either a person with a calm, controlled demeanor and body language, maybe also known to the local birds (thus no bird plow is triggered); a member of the canine family following an accustomed trail in moderate cover on quiet ground (ready to take a bird by opportunity but not actively hunting for one); a bobcat in a hurry, trotting instead of walking (usually evoking a more intensive scolding than most popcorn alarms, almost a hybrid with the parabolic alarm described in the next section); or an ungulate "ghosting," or sneaking away, in a somewhat crouched trot or fast walk (which is more common than generally realized). The canine could even be a farm dog on routine patrol, or a tired house dog meandering along a riparian trail. (The fresh, excited dog charging all around the woods is a different story, and we know the more dramatic response she's likely to provoke: a considerable, if localized, bird plow.) If the owners of an off-leash springer spaniel lose sight of their Susie but know a little about bird language, they'll be able to follow the dog as the junco hooks up to a branch four feet high, followed by the same hooking action twenty yards away by another junco, then a little farther on by a towhee, then a sparrow, each bird likely releasing a mild alarm call at the same time. There goes Susie, surprising but not really scaring the birds.

Here's a favorite popcorn story — a puzzle, really, that I needed several weeks to solve, aided by lots of eyes and ears and several birds. The scene was that same Skykomish River sandbar that has featured in a couple of other bird language lessons in this book. In this case, the pertinent section of the sandbar was right at the base of the steep embankment of a railroad right-of-way. One day a group of us had gathered at this recently discovered tracking area, a wonderful setting with the snowcapped Cascades in the distance. Before heading out in the morning, we gathered around a fire pit that was apparently popular with teenagers, judging from the tracks, layered wear patterns, and certain other signs and objects left behind. Most of my group didn't know one another, so we exchanged basic information and described our goals for the day's tracking, nature observation, and bird language work. Before we finished, I caught a popcorn alarm coming from the robins, Swainson's thrushes, Pacific wrens, and song sparrows posted in a salmonberry and willow hedgerow. Maybe a human, but that was unlikely. I figured it was probably a coyote moving along one of its preferred game runs, provoking the individual hooking maneuvers that, when strung together, become the popcorn alarm. The students were brand-new to bird language and had no way of knowing what was happening, so they showed no awareness of the alarm.

As the chatter continued, I had half an ear on them, half on the popping corn. Suddenly, those students facing in the direction of the alarm froze. One of them raised his chin to point. Another surreptitiously raised her finger. Their eyes were big. I leaned over so that I could see what they were seeing, and there it was: a coyote staring out of the hedgerow. Now everyone in the group saw the animal. No one moved. Moments later, the coyote casually turned and was gone without a sound, back to the cottonwood forest beyond the hedges from whence it had come: *pop . . . pop . . . pop . . . pop*.

I explained to the group the alarm I'd been heeding before the animal stopped to study us. Later, I dug into the thickets and found the well-worn coyote run. The tracks in sandy loam were unmistakable. No deer had used this tunnel in the brush recently, just coyotes, and the popcorn alarm confirmed that this was a routinely used pathway. Every time a coyote passed this way, the birds took note, but the alarms weren't frantic.

But why had the coyote stopped to study us? Why had it then so casually turned away? As I discovered with a good deal of tracking (almost daily visits over the following weeks), this area was also used by a second category of humans: steelhead fishermen setting off for and returning from the river 150 yards down the path. Their parade passed right by the fire pit, and this coyote (and others, presumably) had learned the sounds of cars parking on the railroad cinders, doors closing, feet scrambling down the embankment, tackle boxes banging, and people talking loudly and walking fast to and from the river—all of it setting off a considerable bird plow and perhaps some hares as well. Worth checking out every time. And down by the river, the gut piles from the large steelheads were not such a bad offering either. So when my little group showed up, the coyote had every reason to stop by. I like to believe that the bird plow we kicked up during our respectful studies was a big disappointment to him.

Parabolic (or Umbrella)

One evening in early summer, a hungry raccoon, driven out to hunt and scavenge by her also hungry young in the den, ambling along her regular run, picks up some commotion from a pair of mated song sparrows and their newly hatched chicks in the nest. The raccoon veers in that direction, and when she begins climbing the densely trimmed spruce hedge, the parent sparrows perch just a foot from the nest, aim their bodies at the intruder, and at first scold

Parabolic: This alarm, also called the umbrella, is commonly used for nest robbers such as rats, squirrels, crows, ravens, and jays (to name a few common examples). In the nonbreeding season, owls are usually under the parabolic (or umbrella) collection of vocalizing and mobbing birds of multiple species. The birds face the threat as they alarm.

her. *(Audio file 10 has an example of the song sparrow's alarm call.)* As the raccoon keeps coming, the birds' defense escalates to the all-out panic alarm of sharp *TCHI!*/s or *TCHUNK!*/s. Even though it's almost roosting time, the nearby robins hear this frantic alarm and understand that it can mean only one thing—a nest robber—and they add their own alarms. So does a mockingbird, dive-bombing the potential thief. *(Listen to audio file 74 for an example of the northern mockingbird's alarm call.)* The neighboring Carolina wren flies over to investigate and gets caught up in the growing mob. Everyone within fifty yards soon flies over to join the defense. Such a highly energized, focused, multispecies alarm is almost always reserved for egg stealers and nest robbers, who are the lowest of the low, in the birds' estimation. (The birds mobilize just as strenuously, if not more so, in defense of a fledgling that has fallen out of the nest onto the ground.)

In this season, nest robbers come in ground and flying varieties. Among the ground dwellers are the omnivorous opossums, raccoons, skunks, snakes, squirrels and chipmunks (who are not technically or otherwise predators), and rats and mice. All wisely alter their diets to include the highest possible percentage of nutritious and vulnerable eggs, nestlings, and fledglings. Truly, just about any animal that can climb a tree becomes a serious threat. I've already noted that certain birds, including the robin, have a distinctive alarm for nest robbing, because this predation is a mortal threat to all the nests and chicks in the area. In defense of nests and fledglings, the birds set aside all territorial considerations: it's all for one, and one for all. *(Listen to the following audio files for examples of nest alarms: 47 [American goldfinch] and 54 [killdeer].)*

We call the egg-and-nest defense "parabolic" because a tracing of all the countermeasures expressed over time would suggest the shape of a parabola, with all the birds maintaining a consistent distance from the source of the alarm. It could also be called "umbrella," as the birds are often arrayed in an umbrella shape above the threat. If the raccoon does make its getaway, it will not be alone.

Most of the scolders will follow, taking turns dive-bombing the thief at times, but now the various territorial borders will become a factor, with most of the birds dropping out when they reach the borders of their respective territories, and with new scolders taking their place. The parabolic alarm is now on the move. Have you ever been sitting inside the house and heard an incredible ruckus from the birds during nesting season? That was probably the parabolic alarm for a nest robber. Possibly an owl, like that pygmy-owl who was the target in that twenty-minute donnybrook I described in Chapter 6. (The mimicry known as "pishing," a common birder's subterfuge for drawing in new birds, in effect instigates a mock parabolic alarm. Birds just can't ignore this cry; the stakes are too high.)

The parabolic alarm is the best the birds can do, but the marauding raccoon is opportunistic, persistent, and very good at climbing and scrambling into tight spaces, so despite forceful opposition, it may grab the eggs or nestlings anyway and make its getaway in the gloaming. Four hours later, the raccoon and opossum and skunk have an even greater advantage. The birds are roosting, incapable of mounting a concerted defense in the dark against nocturnal predation. This is why I have often seen a nest with half a dozen active fledglings at sundown and no fledglings—none—the following morning. Such is the life of the songbirds, especially where raccoons and opossums abound, and thus the second batch of eggs in the nest in July.

Another scenario, this one in the suburbs: A housecat somehow weathers the parabolic alarm and nabs a fallen nestling blue jay. As it escapes, it intermittently stops to tear at the small quill-like feathers of the bird even as the angry mob of adult jays, cardinals, and robins dive at the cat, with some birds even pecking it, all bursting forth with their most intense vocal alarms: *JAY! JAY! JAY! CHIP! CHIP! CHIP! TUT! TUT! TUT! (Audio file 63 has an example of blue jay calls.)* The cat then finds harbor in a multiflora rose thicket. After fifteen agonizing minutes, the parabolic alarm dies down as the birds return to their perches and nests, and the cat tries to slither out the back of the thorny scrub. One jay spots the cat—*JAY! JAY! JAY!*—but this is a much-reduced version of the earlier parabolic mobbing, because the cat has its meal, and what's done is done. Still, the cat is exhibiting furtive body language, and the jay has a nest to protect, so it will scold the cat. As the cat moves off, its trail will be revealed to the keen observer with either a moving parabolic alarm, if the cat is moving slowly and carefully, or something resembling the popcorn alarm, if the cat is either walking faster or trotting right along.

Parabolic, Part 2: Those Corvids

Even more than the tree-climbing predators, the aerial nest robbers known as the corvids—ravens, crows, jays, magpies, and others—are mortally dangerous during the nesting season, because they, like the defenders of the nests, can fly and hop around quickly. Other aerial predators might elicit a similar response, but in my experience it is almost always the corvids. They are persistent, clever, fast, and dangerous. The shape of the alarm response is parabolic.

Before I get into the alarm details, I'd like to speak in more general terms about these noisy, aggressive birds. Let's begin with a question: why do beginning students of bird language, anxious to run out and find a verbose robin or song sparrow, almost invariably first encounter the distracting *Caw! Caw! Caw!* of a marauding crow or the insistent, repetitive *Jay! Jay! Jay!* of the closely related blue jay? *(Listen to audio files 61 and 63 for examples of noisy corvids.)* When this happens, the students often get confused and think, *I'll never learn bird language. I can't understand anything about the behavior of these corvids!* Truly, corvids are in a league of their own, which has prompted me to compose the Bird Language Corvid Disclaimer Clause: *While these species are technically passerines —perching birds—we can't trust them to follow the rules. We can almost trust them* not *to follow the rules. They do everything backward.*

While robins and thrushes and juncos and sparrows proclaim their territories with their songs—a basic principle—crows and jays are usually silent in their own territories. Vocally speaking, they're hiding. Why is this? Since they're nest robbers, maybe they feel the need to be quiet in their own neighborhoods so their own nests won't be robbed. It reminds me of a saying I heard years ago: "When one's a thief, the whole world's a thief." This might also be called the "takes-one-to-know-one phenomenon." Yet the nesting parents' silence may seem futile, because the begging juvenile corvids put out an amazing number of loud demands. Although the corvids are tenacious attackers, they are also tenacious defenders. They'll try to kill any other corvid that comes close to the nest.

The corvids don't have signature songs, but instead vocalize incessantly with a very complex language and mimicry skills that have been the subject of much research. My friend Brian Knittel—naturalist, tracker, bird language practitioner and researcher—got interested in the mimicry talents of the Steller's jay and looked online to find out everything he could about them. Brian has confirmed (to my satisfaction, at least) the Steller's mimicry of the golden eagle, northern flicker, northern goshawk, white-breasted nuthatch, red-eyed vireo, and Clark's nutcracker; red-tailed and red-shouldered hawks (and maybe also Cooper's and white-tailed hawks), woodpeckers, grackles, and assorted wounded birds; fox squirrels, cats, dogs, and chickens (including roosters); and water sprinklers, telephones, squeaky doors, and RV alarms. So the corvids, as well as their fellow passerines, have a great investment in vocalizations. It's just a different sort of investment, and harder for humans to get a handle on. Bernd Heinrich's *Ravens in Winter* will give you a good idea of what you'll be up against should you decide to study their language.

In the winter, corvids roost together by the hundreds. Try to get a handle on *that*. When they make a racket in any season, it's for purposes of alarm, imitation, trickery, and/or social communication of confusing complexity. Of course, they're notoriously smart and get high marks in the experiments researchers dream up to test them. They are masters of the nick of time, grabbing a road-killed lizard right in front of an oncoming car, or dodging and stealing food from other birds or animals.

Corvids are larger than other passerines, so they're often successful as nest robbers, boldly stalking right onto the nest to grab an egg whole and take off with it. If the mother robin won't give up the egg, the larger corvid can just stun her with a powerful peck on the head and grab *her* instead. The robin knows this, so she has to give up and fly off at the last second. When nest robbing, corvids hop and sit among the shadows of the branches, not actually flying much. And they're deadly silent, of course.

Like a ground-based nest robber, a thieving corvid always elicits the most drastic alarms and defensive measures from all the local birds, right down to the tiniest sparrows and wrens, the orioles, and even the tanagers, who descend from the treetops in a colorful display of aggressive defense. There are no bystanders, because the marauding corvids are a threat to *every* nest in *every* tree. The best defense is to gang up on the invader the moment it arrives, before it can find out where the nests are. Birds dart in from the edge of the parabolic and strike, then return to the edge. The thief hangs in, shifts position, ducks a dive-bombing robin, and bides its time, knowing that victory is likely in the end. The intensity of the defense increases each time the bird moves, then lets up just a little when the bird remains still for a while. The closer the corvid comes to a nest, the harder the other birds fight in defense. In a way, this is a mistake, because this smart predator knows that when the raucous defense gets even more raucous, it's getting closer to a nest. In this manner, the bird zeros in. I've seen many intense, energy-expensive face-offs go on for half an hour.

Watching corvids in action in the spring produces very mixed emotions in me. They're so clever and effective, it's hard not to give them credit, but they grab so many eggs and kill so many chicks, it's disturbing to me as a parent, a birder, and a bird language advo-

cate. At times, the intensity of the birds' parental defense and my ir-
ritation with all the noise provoke me into chasing off a raven, fully
realizing that this may be a lost cause.

In New Jersey, I once rescued a twitching crow I had found on
the ground beneath a group of other excited crows. I assumed this
was a fledgling that had been knocked from the nest by a predator, and the birds raising the ruckus overhead were the angry parents and their aligned cohort. Or maybe a nearby cat or dog had
triggered the ruckus. I learned otherwise when I, the Good Samari-
tan, picked up the bird, balanced it on a nearby branch, and walked
away. To my great surprise, all the other crows went berserk, forming an absolutely furious mob. The crows attacked the bird again,
and again I came to the rescue. When I did, the crows began breaking off sticks and throwing them at me. *We're trying to kill that
thing, and here you bring it back again!* I had to go into the house
to get away. When the birds quieted down, I walked back outside.
They started up again, yelling and throwing more sticks. I took the
injured crow into the house and nursed it back to health. A week or
so later, I drove a few towns north and let it go. At my house, the
crows never forgot the yellow shirt with black stripes that I wore
during the encounter. Anytime they saw me wearing that shirt, they
would shape up into an angry parabolic right above me, as if *I* were
a nest robber. Thinking about all this, I developed a hypothesis. To
test it, one day I wore a jacket over the shirt. The crows did nothing. Then I flashed them, opening the jacket so they could see my
shirt. Hypothesis confirmed: they mobbed. *(Audio file 61 has an example of American crows mobbing humans.)*

Weasel

The long-tailed weasel zigs and zags through its environment,
snakes this way and that, backtracks, loops around, and slips under
some leaf litter. It does have favored runs and freely uses the sub-
way systems of the wood rats, mice, and chipmunks, but the wea-

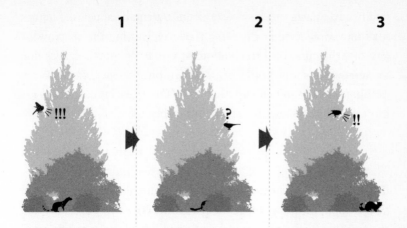

Weasel: Because of their erratic nature, agility, and ability to disappear and quickly reappear in a different spot, weasels create an especially recognizable alarm. When the bird is silent, it's looking very hard for where the weasel will appear next. When the bird is vocalizing, it is scolding the animal.

sel may go anywhere, really. With the help of a finely calibrated GPS unit, a map of its route would show a tangled path. Other animals, including the closely related martens and fishers, as well as the mink, sometimes proceed in such a fashion, but for the weasel such perambulation without any apparent goal seems to be the norm. Thus, the bird language community has named this alarm shape after the weasel.

Actually, this is the shape without much shape. The sparrow spies the approaching weasel, hooks up to a low branch, and emits an alarm. Since the weasel has the approximate reach of a cat, this branch will be about five feet up. Now the weasel disappears underneath the leaf litter. The sparrow's steady tail pumping and intense scolding cease, then become sporadic as it jumps around nervously, peering down in all directions. The weasel pops up from the cover ten feet away, and the sparrow flies directly over to a low branch, broadcasting the alarm. The weasel disappears again, maybe even by clinging to the base of a tree, motionless, much like a lizard or a squirrel. (I've seen one virtually disappear this way; only its yawn finally gave it away.) The weasel can play these disappearing games for quite some time in the same territory, causing the sparrow or any other ground bird tremendous stress. Even after it leaves one territory and starts bothering another bird twenty yards away, nothing says it won't end up back here. The weasel is dangerous for birds precisely because it's so unpredictable.

Cat

The shape of this alarm depends on the intention of the cat. It can be the hook, the popcorn, or the parabolic. Given this diversity and the fact that birds and cats are so closely linked in the public mind (and even more closely linked in birders' minds), I've fudged it a bit and granted them a "shape" all their own. It includes both housecats and their larger, wilder cousins.

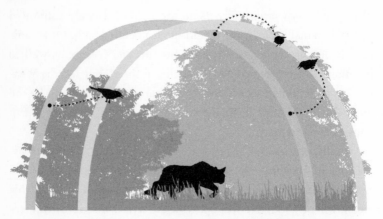

Cat: The shape of this alarm (hook, popcorn, or parabolic) depends on the intention of the cat. Sometimes called a "moving parabolic," the cat alarm is one of the most common ground predator alarms. It can be caused by a hunting or agitated housecat, bobcat, or cougar. I have heard of a tracker in Africa who can find leopards using only bird and animal calls—likely a similar alarm pattern. I met an indigenous hunter from Central America who called this alarm the "ocelot" (in his country, that is the animal who would be slinking below the alarm). At the time, we were in bobcat territory.

As any owner of a cat knows, this animal likes to have things its own way. Except when cats are in a playful mood, they'll avoid anything that makes them uncomfortable or challenges them. Yes, they're intensely curious, but I think they feel as much prey as predator when moving in the landscape outside. (Dogs are a threat in suburbs and towns, and there are more diverse threats in the countryside.) Proceeding from here to there, cats don't want any surprises, so, much more than most people realize, they use well-traveled runs that afford them relative safety and predictability. They use such runs in thickets as well—sometimes their own runs, sometimes those created by other animals. They're not going to snake and pull and drag themselves through a thicket randomly. That may be the weasel's way, but it is not the cat's. From the outside, the thicket may look impenetrable, but get down on elbows and knees, and you'll find a functioning tunnel of some sort.

Watching a cat on its rounds, the birds see the difference in body language between the hunting cat and the fat-and-happy cat and respond accordingly. Any neighborhood cat with a reputation for zealous and effective hunting will be greeted with much more alarm than the known cats that don't cause the birds much trouble. A cat in a hurry—trotting, walking fast, or otherwise moving with non-hunting purposefulness—will generate the series of hooks known as the popcorn alarm. By contrast, a cat that's deliberately hunting will take about ten steps, stop, look around, take ten more steps, stop, look around, take ten more steps, stop, look around . . . It has to do this because it is visually oriented. Since it doesn't have eyes in the back of its head, it has to proceed more slowly than the smell-oriented canine, who can detect precious scents coming from any direction. The cat's start-and-stop behavior generates something very like a parabolic alarm on the move, which is nerve-wracking for the birds, who tend to gather in force and mob a cat moving with hunting intent. If the hunting cat ventures into the open, it will be dive-bombed by the mockingbirds and jays at least, and maybe by others.

Even though the cat isn't disappearing under the leaves and the birds can follow its progress without any problem, the resulting parabolic alarm on the move might strike a bird language beginner as similar to the weasel alarm. A little experience will reveal the difference. With the cat, the mobbing often builds over time, with more birds able to join in. The weasel is probably not around long enough for this to happen (although it may be back, of course, and then back again). Therefore, the alarm for the cat is more intense. That said, the local birds' baseline is ruined for as long as either cat or weasel is in the vicinity with a hunting intent.

Feral cats are more common than we think, and the birds' alarms for these felines can be our clue to their presence. Back in the 1970s, I used to follow up on these situations with my dog, Max, who would dutifully dive into the parabolic moment, scattering the mobsters in a small bird plow, then pick up the sight or scent of the feral cat. The cat, seeing the dog, would quickly climb a tree to safety. I could then walk up and inspect this cornered, hissing, very unhappy predator. I kept a mental list of feral cats and their markings, and they helped me learn about the various alarms they triggered. And Max loved the game.

A bobcat is a cat. The alarm signature for its presence is going to be the same as for a smaller cat, but, logically enough, bigger. In my experience, intense bobcats trigger a really intense popcorn or parabolic alarm. Tracking in northern California with a native hunter and his wife from Central America, I learned that the cat in those jungles (the ocelot) triggers the same alarm signature as a bobcat. I found this out when we came across . . . what? Something was hiding in a ravine, completely invisible to us in the thicket of willow, poison oak, and blackberries, and triggering a powerful parabolic alarm. My new friend and I picked up on this action at the same time, both of us staring in that direction. He spoke one word, quietly. His wife translated, quietly: "Cat." It was a bobcat, not an ocelot, but no matter. My friend knew. Likewise, I understand from my safari-guiding friends in Africa, extraordinary naturalists and trackers all, that the alarm for "their" leopards is functionally the same as what we see for "our" cougars and bobcats. Although there are different species of birds (and cats) in Africa, Central America, and North America, the birds still exhibit the same alarm behavior.

Bullet

The Cooper's hawk, sharp-shinned hawk, and goshawk (all accipiters), as well as the merlin and the peregrine falcons, streak through or above the trees like bullets, hunting birds and anything else small and alive. The falcons specialize in chasing down birds in the open sky or blasting them from above without warning. The accipiters, particularly, will fire right into the trees and chase the songbirds, who dash madly for the highest cover possible. For the smaller birds, these raptors are the very definition of *terror*. They will chase their prey anywhere, even into a thicket so dense we might think it is impenetrable. I've seen the bloody evidence inside such dense brush. The accipiters are amazing birds, probably the most success-

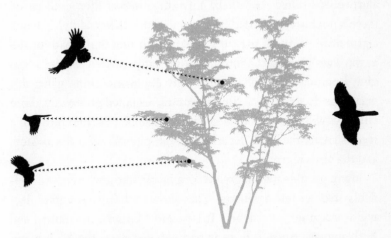

Bullet: A specialized kind of bird plow, the bullet alarm consists of fast-moving birds flying just ahead of an approaching fast-flying threat. It usually indicates surprise or last-minute action and almost always signals an accipiter or sometimes a diving buteo, harrier, or falcon.

ful hunters among all the raptors, and the Cooper's hawk might be the most successful accipiter. When a Cooper's locks on a particular bird, it's a grim prospect for the target.

"Bullet" describes both the raptors' hunting style and the shape of the other birds' reactions. The alarm spreads in tandem with the hawk's flight, virtually instantaneously and universally. Some small bird such as a chickadee often emits, ventriloquist-style, a super-high-pitched *tseee-seee-seee-seee*. *(Audio file 4 has an example of the American robin's high-pitched* SEET *calls.)* Many species emit almost the identical call for the same purpose. There is no time for the sentinel alarm or much of anything else. The hook and parabolic are pathetically insufficient; the threat is too immediate and too deadly. The bullet alarm reminds me of the first stroke in a billiard game, when the cue ball strikes the target balls, which explode in straight lines toward the sides and corners of the table. It's the same with the birds. The impact of a fast-approaching bullet causes them to go up, to the sides, out in front, and straight down from the approaching threat. (If a "bulleting" bird finds cover, it will go into another alarm shape called the "ditch.") To the observer fifty yards away, there's no mistaking what's going on, as the universal flying-hawk alarm slices through the trees. It's easy to follow the path of the hawk, even though the intruder is probably unseen. Steller's jays give a particularly explosive *cac! cac! cac!* vocalization when this occurs, as do scrub-jays. (But be careful. As noted previously, those wily jays will employ that same call as a gambit to scatter birds off a feeder.) After the hawk departs, the high-pitched vocal alarms stop, and the birds regroup.

Many people unwittingly detect a bullet alarm when a bird suddenly smashes into a window. That was very likely a songbird fleeing an accipiter, or maybe a falcon. Most birders, naturalists, and bird language students have a favorite bullet story, though it might not be labeled as such. One of mine dates back to my New Jersey days. One summer afternoon, I was sitting alone outside, on a farm, when a Cooper's hawk flew over the farmhouse, then the barn, along the edge of a field, and across a bunch of transition areas. The path of the hawk must have covered 150 highly visible yards, and the event probably lasted thirty seconds. It was amazing to hear and see the intense tide of alarms that preceded the approaching hawk by about twenty seconds. It was like a storm, but instead of rain and hail and thunder, I heard erratic, frantic, high-pitched vocalizations. That was maybe the longest bullet alarm I've ever witnessed—a rare opportunity. Normally, we don't get to see the full run of a Cooper's hawk, because such a flight in the open is not the bird's most productive tactic. It's too visible, giving the targets too much time to react. Instead, a Cooper's usually takes to the willow breaks, hedges, thickets, or other available cover in the area.

A falcon hunting in the open sky and catching birds on the wing also raises a bullet alarm, but it's different from the alarm for an accipiter. The falcon may come in from the sky above, while the accipiter usually has some cover, and may even come in from below. (Dan Gardoqui, my friend and indispensable collaborator on this book, has seen a sharp-shinned hawk cruising at top speed less than a foot off the ground. Amazing.) As a result, more of the fleeing birds fly horizontally as far and as fast as they can. Some even fly up, to get above the falcon. Others fly across the treetops and down into the trees, where the falcon won't follow. It is common to see mad flights of circling groups of shorebirds, or flocks of starlings so dense that from a distance they look like smoke, banking up and circling around in this dynamic shape—the way baitfish flee from larger predatory fish—swirling, shifting, moving up and away as the predator darts into the mass. (Beautiful to watch, not so beautiful for the prey to experience.) With fewer birds, the pattern is more diffuse and not as noticeable, but still present.

You could think of the bullet alarm as a bird plow in extremis: much more urgent, a lot faster, and often accompanied by that telltale super-high-pitched *tseee-seee-seee-seee* call and wing noise, leaves slapping and shapes darting everywhere. It may be over in a matter of seconds, once the hawk is gone.

Ditch

The Cooper's hawk slices through the air, and the birds broadcast their direst, shrillest alarms. Then what happens? They ditch it. On my lucky day at that farm in New Jersey, positioned with a good view of the Cooper's long run, I watched as all the birds—many dozens of them—scattered every which way, dropping into thickets and anywhere else the hawk might not follow.

With a predator on the ground, the birds hook upward, or fly higher still in a sentinel alarm. With a hawk, either they flee horizontally, evasively zigzagging and using features of the landscape for cover, or they dive straight down as if they've been shot, seeking the nearest, densest cover. Even the tanagers and grosbeaks in the treetops may drop all the way down to the thickets, because the trees are no guarantee of safety from an accipiter. Birds at the very farthest end of the approaching alarm may have time to fly away at a sharp angle from the direction of attack ("quartering," in effect, a tactic used by many prey creatures). Quartering is preferable to ditching, because a bird who ditches into a thicket may be pursued

Ditch: When the danger is from above and appears suddenly (such as a sudden swoop of an accipiter), birds dive for cover in what my colleagues and I call the ditch. When we were young, we used to "ditch" from headlights when we were playing outside at night. This alarm has a similar feeling.

all the way to the end, and it also loses some of its connection with what's happening outside the thicket. (A hide-and-seek analogy is the closely hidden kid who can't see what's going on and may be vulnerable to a quiet ambush.) One time—amazingly—a house sparrow darted out of a thicket straight at me to elude the Cooper's hawk entering on the other side of the thicket. And when I see a certain wren set up near the back door, I know this is a subtle pre-alarm for a hawk's approach that I have not yet detected; the more dramatic alarm is to come. I've seen this wren ditch many times, right into the thickets of multiflora roses and honeysuckles near the door.

Dan Gardoqui has a thrilling postditch story, which also serves as a good companion call story. As Dan relates it:

This was in May 1995, when I was fortunate to spend the afternoon at the home of ecologist Roger "Doc" Locandro, who owned forty acres of land in the Delaware River valley of western New Jersey. This land was exceptionally well cared for, with a variety of fruit trees, timber trees, outbuildings, livestock, gardens, berry thickets, and wild areas.

After gathering some of the delicate green herbs along one trail, I decided to nestle into a little hollow that faced south toward an opening between two rosehip thickets growing under the shadows of a young black walnut grove. I was a little nervous about a presentation I had to make that afternoon on the collapse of the cod fishery in the northwest Atlantic. I couldn't have been too effective with my bird language awareness, but after a short sensory tune-in I did pick up a pair of cardinals calling back and forth, out of sight: *chip . . . chip . . . chip? . . . CHIP. (Listen to audio file 33 for an example of northern cardinal vocalizations. The first part is contact calls, then song, then finally, a male "chrrrr" song.)* A minute or two later, I spied the male cardinal situated a couple of feet from the ground, occasionally on the ground, feeding on some of the older rosehips. His companion soon came into sight, and she was particularly beautiful, I thought, with her creamy brown color and muted scarlet accents in her crest, wings, and tail, and that bright red bill! Wow. I may have been nervous about the presentation, but this bird brought me back to the reality of what we do—both of the cardinals did, exchanging companion calls, feeding peacefully—idyllic baseline on this spring afternoon. I didn't hear any begging chicks, and this couple weren't acting like parents with big responsibilities. Besides, no self-respecting cardinal would feed older rosehips to its offspring.

My mind wandered off, then the tone of the female cardinal's *chip* became *CHIP!* The male didn't answer. I craned my neck to see where he was, and I found him, still as a stone, deep in the rose thicket, dead silent. As I started to analyze the situation, a downy woodpecker I hadn't seen let out a shrieking alarm call that nearly had me on my feet. The downy exploded from its grip low on a decaying maple, and, following its trajectory of escape, I saw the sharp-shinned hawk, cleverly perched in front of a grapevine tangle, glaring directly into the rosehip thicket where the male cardinal remained frozen and silent. The female, farther away, was broadcasting the alarm: *CHIP! CHIP! CHIP! CHIP!* The sharpie just sat there, testing the mettle of the male. Was this cardinal going to stay put at all costs, or would he be tempted back toward the denser, more familiar cover that was protecting his mate?

The female hopped higher in her thicket. This caught both the sharpie's and the male cardinal's attention. The male fidgeted and feigned his move to the other thicket, causing the sharpie to flinch. There was no doubt now: the cardinal was going to make his move, and the outcome would come down to pure speed. When his red flash burst from the thicket, I snapped my neck to spy the sharpie's grapevine perch. It was empty, swaying in the mild spring air. What had happened? Did the cardinal actually get away? My heart racing, my mind dizzy from the intensity, I doubted it. The female had stopped her alarm calls and flown out of sight into an even thicker hedgerow. Because sharpies usually feed on their prey close to the scene of the kill, I scanned the immediate vicinity before moving another muscle. No sharpie. After two long minutes, I rose slowly from my spot. Lying on the trail between the two thickets was a single red feather. Whoa. My breathing stopped. Life and death, here and now. I turned to head back down toward the farmhouse and my presentation about the collapse of the cod fishery.

Just three steps into my walk, my pulse eased and I could hear the sharp *pink! pink!* alarms of white-throated sparrows, and there they were, tails flicking and crests raised, pointing into the thicket. *(Audio file 44 has an example of the white-throated sparrow's alarm call.)* Following their lead, I gazed into the brambles and not five feet from my knees saw a pile of red feathers and caught the gleaming yellow eye of the predator. Frozen in place, his bill stained red, his right wing shielding the cardinal from prying eyes, this bird-killing machine stared back at me. Our eyes locked for a moment. Then the sharpie maneuvered his way out of the shrub and into open air, with half a cardinal secured in his razor-sharp talons.

Though random-looking in the moment, I think a given bird's ditch-and-dive is probably a well-practiced and anything-but-random maneuver. I can't prove this, but I believe it's true, based on a number of observations. When I was a kid playing hide-and-seek in its many variations, I definitely won more often when we played on my home turf. I knew exactly where to run. As the years rolled by and I incorporated my scout training with Tom Brown Jr., I even got bored with the game, because no one could ever find me. Years later, deep into bird language and a veteran observer of many bullets and ditches, it dawned on me: *This is what the birds (and other wildlife) are doing! They know their territories — where to flee, where to swerve, where to hide, where to ditch.*

Have you noticed that a chainlink fence is a favorite venue for songbirds? I believe the reason is that the fence is perfect for losing a sharpie or Cooper's, and the birds have learned this. While feeding or just hanging out, they can work both sides of the fence, confident that should the time come, they can dive through a convenient link to perfect safety. If the attacker isn't ready for the fence, the unexpected encounter could be painful. Shaking its head and preening its mangled feathers, the Cooper's may mutter to itself, *Nobody saw that, right?* (Egregious anthropomorphism, I admit.) I've heard from careful, hardheaded observers that small birds in cities will ditch by flying straight toward glass skyscrapers, accipiter in hot pursuit, and at the last moment turn ninety degrees and glide safely along the surface as the attacking hawk, not quite as knowledgeable about this specific territory, hits the glass with force, maybe leaving a stunned pile of feathers on the concrete — panting, shaking it off, slowly recovering. *Nobody saw that, right?* It happens in the canyons of every city.

So, yes, I have reasons to think that the ditching maneuver is often well practiced. I'm betting that every songbird has had its high-five moments, and I relate them to the bird's overall relationship with its territory. The ditch alarm has to be one of the reasons for territorial fidelity and defense.

The ditch is usually clear and convincing, but it can be misinterpreted. Basic male-to-male territorial aggression can end in a defeat that looks like a ditch. Sometimes a playful chase can look like a ditch. If there's any doubt, consider the following two factors. First, the ditch alarm is widespread — universal for an area twenty yards or more across and moving in tandem with the hawk. One bird will not ditch while its neighbors are singing, chatting, and feeding. Second, the ditch is almost always followed by some serious silence that can last a while as the birds get their wits about them again and figure out where the danger is. The predator may not have left the scene. Having failed to capture a bird, it may double back. (If it has succeeded and stayed right there to eat, which is often the accipiters' behavior, you can expect something more like a parabolic alarm, which will usually induce the hawk to fly off with its meal.) On many occasions in California, I've watched a Cooper's hawk pass through the Douglas firs on one side of my house, then use the house for cover by flying around it and quickly return to the side from whence it came. To judge by the behavior of my local songbirds, they've seen all this before. The mandatory "cool-ing-off period" after the initial ditch pays off.

Hawk Drop

Many folks assume that every songbird is terrified of every hawk. I did when I started out on this journey, but as I observed more and more episodes with the relatively common redtail and other large buteos, I realized that these "soaring hawks" cruise the sky look-ing mainly for small mammals and carrion, and birds only second-arily (and rarely). They don't dive into the trees—they'd get tan-gled in the branches like a hung-up kite—and the other birds know this. Soaring around in the open sky, scanning the ground for meat,

Hawk Drop: A hawk drop is usually caused by a soaring hawk, eagle, or osprey, and occasionally by a vulture or even a gull (perhaps the last two are a result of mistaken identity or caution). The flocks of birds that gather in treetops in great numbers all chatter loudly with a mixture of flock vocalizations. They suddenly and simultaneously get quiet and "drop" a few feet below the crown of the trees they are in. This very short moment of silence (a few seconds at most) is followed by the birds beginning to chatter again, and then a soaring predator flies nearby. A variation is seen when shorebirds clear out at the approach of a similar predator. The hawk drop is not as dramatic as the bullet, ditch, or plow.

they're right there for all to see. Therefore, the alarm raised is much less emphatic than the bullet and ditch alarms for the accipiters. You could think of this as a slower, less dramatic form of the ditch. Songbirds in the trees and bushes probably won't get too anxious when they hear the alarms broadcast by those birds that habitually feed in the open, including pigeons, doves, quail, and shorebirds, who will respond to a diving redtail with a bullet and ditch. Along the beach in California, a sudden flight of gulls from the beach is almost always prompted by a redtail that has just cleared the cliff and loomed into view.

In my old stomping grounds in New Jersey, the deciduous forests along the steep banks of the ravines are pretty much all that's left of the old-growth forests. These remaining narrow strips of older forest are some of the favorite roosting zones of very large mixed-species flocks of blackbirds and grackles—hundreds if not thousands of birds. This particular cacophony of baseline harmony can be incredibly loud, then drop into total silence for just a few seconds. I heard this phenomenon a few times, and each time I then witnessed this mass of blackbirds drop in unison from the tops of the trees to a slightly sheltered vantage point a few feet below. It happened within a few seconds and with no alarm calls, only silence while repositioning. Then the whole mass immediately started yakking again as if nothing had happened, and a red-tailed hawk passed overhead. That's the "drop" for which we name this relatively mild alarm for a soaring buteo. It reflects respect but not panic. It's nothing compared to the total chaos of the birds in the bullet and ditch when a sharpie or Cooper's hawk dives alongside or into those roosting trees.

Safety Barrier

One commonly observed behavior in a sit spot, often construed by bird language beginners as baseline, is actually an alarm. I have a pretty good idea that a student has made this mistake when he or

Safety Barrier: This is a commonly misidentified behavior. A beginner will often consider this a sign that all's clear, since there are birds in view right next to her as she is sitting quietly. In fact, this is usually accompanied by an overall, generally oppressive silence indicating that the predator hidden from view in a nearby tree is likely a Cooper's hawk or other accipiter. Note that the birds are protected from above, they keep cover between themselves and the danger, and they use the person as a shield.

she says, "Jon, there was this nice period of baseline right around me. The birds were so busy feeding that it was quiet."

Quiet? That word is the tip-off, and I ask, "Were the birds feeding with cover over their backs? Were they close to you?"

Often these questions are mistaken for psychic powers. "Well, actually, yes, they *were* really close to me. Some of them were under branches of the coyote brush." (Or the picnic table or the car — you get the point.) Some students also believe that the birds' close feeding proximity confirms that their own presence is becoming so unobtrusive, so baseline itself, that the birds are returning the compliment. If I don't break the news to them, they won't get anywhere in bird language. It's true that their presence must have been reasonably centered and respectful, or there wouldn't have been any feeding birds around at all. In all likelihood, however, these juncos, sparrows, and towhees were using this human being as a safety barrier for feeding during a period of "oppression" caused by a stationary sharpie, Cooper's, or goshawk. These raptors generally don't like to venture too close to us (though exceptions are possible), so the songbirds feel safe feeding in our proximity with cover directly overhead. I have had chickadees, specifically, hang out right next to me, eating away, when the rest of the forest appeared to be utterly abandoned. It was "abandoned" for good reason, but these chickadees had me as a safety barrier.

In such episodes, why wasn't there any bullet and ditch alarms for the arrival of the predator, which then assumed a stationary post? I've come up with four possible explanations: (1) the accipiter avoided detection by the birds, plain and simple, which sometimes (though rarely) happens; (2) there was an alarm, which the person just didn't pick up; (3) these friendly birds at the sit spot were at the far edge of the danger zone and didn't react strongly to the accipiter in the first place; or (4) most likely from my experience, the inexperienced individual had kicked up an initial bird plow while arriving at the sit spot, which called in the accipiters to check things out (a kind of wake hunting). The last possibility — that the person in effect created, or at least called in, the "oppression" — is pretty common for someone in the early stages of a bird language program. It becomes less likely as we become better acquainted with the routine of invisibility.

In that long-ago episode when the chickadees were practically eating out of my hand, I could have missed the preceding alarms, and I could have created the "oppression" myself with a massive bird plow — quite possible back in those days, when I was the proverbial steelhead fisherman with the banging tackle box. I probably had some accipiter working me for all I was worth every day. And it still could happen today. I even saw the San Bushmen kick up a bird plow. We're all always learning.

When we humans are part of the baseline habitat, the birds' use of us as a safety barrier is more widespread than we might imagine. House sparrows hang around our feet at outdoor cafés for more than just the crumbs. In suburban mountain lion territory, deer like to live close to houses, and coyotes press right in for days at a time when they have seen a lion or signs of a lion's current residence. A lot of work with radiotelemetry and motion detector data has confirmed this phenomenon. And then there are the hummingbirds who nest all around Cooper's hawks' nests in order to avoid the nasty nest-robbing habit of jays and other corvids. This phenomenon has been widely observed. (So why aren't the hawks interested in the easy meal offered in the hummingbirds' nests? In the first place, those nests are very small and well camouflaged—almost invisible even when you are staring right at them. Busybody corvids may find them more easily. Second, there's the size of the meal itself: very small. Maybe it's just not worth the effort to the bigger predators.)

Zone of Silence

After the sharpie or Cooper's has left the stage, the terrorized birds act as if they are numb with shock (though considering how frequently this happens, they cannot possibly be in shock). Dead silence prevails. This silence is made more profound by the cheerful singing of the birds in the distance—those beyond the reach of the predator and the alarm. In the incident with the Cooper's above the farm in New Jersey, the bird's long passage over the farmhouse, the barn, the field, and the transition areas created a pressure wave in front of it—the bullet and ditch alarms, fifty yards wide—then a heavy wake of silence behind it, the same fifty yards wide. The small creek on the other side of the hawk's route was clearly audible. Under normal circumstances, the baseline bird song and other vocalizations would drown it out. In the zone of silence, it sounded like Class II rapids (and I exaggerate only slightly). To the left and right, off in the distance, the birds were singing: baseline over there. But right here, full, alert, silent tension: the gravest violation of baseline possible.

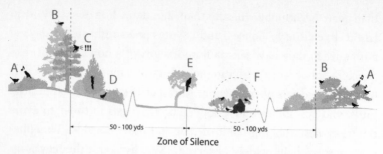

50 - 100 yds   50 - 100 yds

Zone of Silence

Zone of Silence: This diagram tells many stories, and it brings together principles from many of the preceding illustrations. The left and right areas, designated *A,* show that baseline behaviors, such as singing and feeding, are occurring. This relative comfort may be caused by, but is certainly related to, *B,* where the sentinels provide cover, in a way, for the baseline birds. The principle illustrated here is that baseline is often behind the exhibiting sentinel. In the area marked *C,* birds on the edge of the zone of alarm often give alarms, especially when the predator is visible to the bird calling. *D* shows a bird and a squirrel hiding in a thick area and keeping still for protection. A mostly concealed Cooper's hawk is sitting in *E,* perhaps visible only to the bird calling on the left. In *F* a person sits in the midst of a safety barrier and within a zone of silence—also called "oppression."

In its way, the zone of silence is as enrapturing as the dawn chorus. Anyone with developing bird language skills reacts with intense, searching curiosity, gathering more information to answer the unspoken questions about cause, movement, and repercussions. Often insects are the only sounds we hear. Among the birds, a hard-to-miss exception to the silence is the wrentits, who are sometimes so completely encased in their dense thickets of thorny vines and canes of poison oak that they must feel as safe as if they were sitting beside a chainlink fence, impervious to the oppression caused by the hawk. In the coastal scrub of California, it's common for the wrentits' songs to be the only songs for such long periods when accipiters are around that this state of affairs could be mistaken for baseline. The newcomer to the region might believe that only wrentits live here.

In time, the other birds begin to emerge from hiding—and from their silence. One day when a Cooper's hawk finally left its post in an alder top, right in front of more than thirty human witnesses, the singing and feeding among the avian witnesses resumed as if the hawk were pouring that baseline from a net it was towing. Among the song sparrows, Bewick's wrens, and others, the transition from silence to baseline was that efficient and fast. We could still hear the alarms of scrub-jays and Steller's jays in the distance, following the Cooper's progress through the trees. That progress was precisely why the birds left behind felt released from the oppression. In other scenarios, as on the farm in New Jersey, when the birds can't follow the alarms that accompany the departing predator, the return to baseline is slower. When it does happen, bolder birds such as the catbird will tempt fate first, with small snippets of song, followed by a careful silence for evaluation. Then the cascade to baseline picks up, with the goldfinches, red-winged blackbirds, song sparrows, and robins joining in, and the first-out, last-back towhees very likely bringing up the rear. *(The following audio files have examples of assorted baseline songs: 45 [American goldfinch], 28 [red-winged blackbird], 9 [song sparrow], 1 [American robin], and 35 [spotted towhee].)*

The accipiter on the wing propagates the bullet, the ditch, and the zone of silence, in that order. The accipiter who flies into a neighborhood and then assumes a stationary post propagates the initial bullet and ditch, then the subset of the zone of silence that I have labeled "oppression." Most sitting predatory birds induce some kind of oppressive silence, with subtle differences that become clear to bird language students only after they've had lots of experience in one sit spot. (I mentioned earlier that the other birds will occasionally mob a predatory bird. With the slower owls or the soaring hawks, mobbing is relatively safe and therefore fairly common. *[Listen to audio file 62 for an example of crows mobbing a red-tailed hawk.]* It is even relatively safe with an accipiter that is eating prey, but not one that's posted up, hunting. The other birds also will rarely mob a Cooper's or sharpie. I've seen a couple of very brief episodes, then the mobbing birds perhaps thought better of it. The Cooper's and sharpie are too quick and agile; the mobbing could backfire for at least one of the brave antagonists.)

I can usually distinguish between the silences that greet a peregrine falcon and a Cooper's hawk, but I cannot say exactly why. Maybe one day I'll be able to codify this, at least in my mind, but for now it's just an intuitive thing. Distinguishing between the silent alarm for a Cooper's and a sharpie is much easier, at least in coastal California. For a sharpie, the smaller birds—robin size on down—are concerned and silent, while the scrub-jays and Steller's jays are doing their usual thing with mild tension or slight agitation and a series of harsh, nasal *wah*s. The overall zone of oppression is about fifty yards across. For a Cooper's, the zone is much larger, maybe 150 yards across. I know this because various collections of students and I spend a lot of time in one valley just that size, and almost all of the birds across the entire valley—robins, song sparrows, juncos, Bewick's wrens, golden-crowned and white-crowned sparrows, California and spotted towhees, scrub-jays and Steller's jays, flickers, ruby-crowned kinglets, chestnut-backed chickadees, and California quail, to name most of the players—fall into silence when a Cooper's flies in and settles on a high perch. The wrentits, however, keep on singing.

As the birds fall silent, my group does, too. The newer they are to bird language, the more astonished they are at the silence. It's so suddenly quiet that we can actually hear the surf from Point Reyes National Seashore a mile to the southwest. I have seen a Cooper's sit on one perch in that valley for fifteen minutes. Finally flying off toward the ocean, she left behind a wake of relieved singing. In the distance to the west, we could hear the flickers react in alarm to her passage, with the scrub-jays in agreement. Peregrines and merlins also visit this redoubt from time to time, and groups of students have watched and described their various oppression capabilities throughout the year. Given all the hawks around, baseline in this valley always has a slight element of nervousness. It's an amazing place to learn.

I've already described the noisy parabolic alarm that greets nest robbers, including the corvids, who are sharp enough to use that alarm to play the hot-and-cold game (or so I believe): the louder the alarm, the closer they know they are to a nest. But prior to the parabolic, before the raven, say, has any idea where any nest might be located in these trees, or perhaps when he is just flying general patrol during nesting season, the other birds may fall into a judicious silence on his approach, giving away nothing. This temporary silence instantly morphs into an intense parabolic alarm when the raven appears to be moving toward a specific nest. This sequence — silence preceding alarm — is the opposite of the sequence for an accipiter on the wing.

I have another silence story, this one a mystery along the Skykomish River in Washington. I arrived at a favorite tracking area about four thirty A.M. (just before dawn at that latitude in the summer — light enough to see, dawn chorus under way), parked my car, and checked for my friend the towhee, whose territory was a short distance down a hillside. We were on a first-name basis. We know that a towhee's sudden cessation of activity is its first alarm, and that day my friend was sitting halfway up a bush, tense (though not flipping its tail), and completely quiet. Thinking this was pretty strange, I listened for the robin whose nest was in a young cottonwood tree about fifty feet from the towhee. The robin wasn't making any sound either. At that time of the morning, all the robins are usually singing for all they're worth. The Swainson's thrushes were quiet, too. Everybody, in fact, was quiet for a good distance around. It was a beautiful morning, with no wind, and I couldn't find a single reason for the silence. I reviewed my own behavior since I'd arrived, but it all seemed pretty straightforward, giving no cause for alarm. Could this be standard oppression from an accipiter that had flown in prior to my arrival? I knew that a Cooper's hawk did work the nearby sandbar from time to time. But no, the towhee was perched out in the open, unconcerned.

I walked to the edge of the hill and started down, but the towhee didn't move. Usually, I'd honor his intransigence and pass to the side, if only because an alarm cry from him, soft though it would be, would set off the neighboring robin, who'd set off the rest of the birds, and I might just as well shout, "Here I am, outta my way!" I waited a few minutes for something to give, then decided to walk down the hill anyway. That was the last straw. The birds exploded into a red-alert alarm that lasted about ten seconds, then stopped suddenly. More silence.

This alarm pattern—silence, vocal alarm, silence—fit none of the established shapes or sequences of events. It fit no other experience I'd ever had. What was up with the birds that morning? I continued down the hill and found wolf tracks, fresh and easy to read. Aha! According to the tracks, this wolf had been tripping along, doing its thing, then suddenly spun out. Why? I found some of the fur and flesh of a hare, so fresh that it was still warm and hadn't changed color. I followed the tracks. The wolf had caught the hare quickly and carried it onto a little sand mound, where it had met a young wolf coming from the other direction. The first wolf had dropped the hare—I could see the slight impression of the body in the sand—turned to face back up the hill, and then picked up the hare and started to walk away with the young wolf. It had dropped the hare a second time, turned and looked uphill again, picked up the hare, and moved off with its partner at a quick trot, away from my approach. The head turns were evident from the contrast in position between the front and rear tracks and the wolf's line of travel.

That was the raw evidence, so to speak. Correlating that behavior with everything else, I decided that the birds had witnessed the kill, probably just a few minutes before I drove up. The hare, fleeing for its life, and the wolves, pursuing it through willow and salmonberry brush, had gotten everybody's attention. When I arrived, the wolf dropped the hare for the first time. Now the tension among the birds was really thick, thanks to the recent chase and kill, as well as the wolf's nervousness on my arrival. A nervous wolf—a nervous anything—radiates waves of tension that every other creature in the wild senses. The wolf picked up the hare again, but when I started to walk downhill and, unwittingly, toward it, it dropped the hare for the second time. That's when the birds had had enough and exploded from their tense silence. I'm sure the wolf also had had enough, so it grabbed the hare and, according to the tracks, trotted off at a slightly faster-than-normal pace. It knew the territory, where I was, and where it had to go to get some peace and quiet. This wave of movement *could* call the Cooper's.

Does every chase-and-kill episode unnerve the songbirds and induce a micro-silence like this one? Not every one, perhaps, but such silences—short in duration and very localized—probably are regular occurrences. It's a nice little alternative explanation for some of the zones of silence we observe, something else for us to factor into our thinking. Truly, the silent alarm, in its several varieties and infinite specific manifestations, would repay a lifetime's study.

Chapter 8

FROM COLLISION TO CONNECTION

I'M ON RECORD as believing that the most interesting and instructive alarm phenomenon among the birds is prompted by the arrival of the unaware human being. At its most extreme, this intrusion results in the red-alert bird plow. At its most innocuous, it results in a little rebuke, a little hook alarm, and a hop to a branch. Consider that robin in my front yard who is not surprised to see me walk to the mailbox every morning and knows that I pose no threat. He monitors me with his peripheral vision and hearing (predators and worms: those are the targets of the robin's hearing). The bird has "soft eyes." They're not focused on me or anything else. The baseline rules. But one morning I divert from the sidewalk and veer toward the bird's feeding domain. Now he does have to focus on me. Maybe I can even pick up the direct glance in my direction as he recalculates what's going on. He will probably speed up a little bit and maybe vocalize a modest complaint, perhaps one quiet *chip* or *tut* just under his breath. If we think of the bird's state of being as a balloon, it has just been inflated a little beyond the baseline point. Strike one.

He pauses for a second, offering a subtle plea for me to stop on my present course and go back to the sidewalk where I belong. If I do, all is well, and there is an immediate return to baseline conduct. If I continue walking toward him, or if from the beginning I'm bopping along to the beat coming through my earphones (not likely, but for the sake of the argument), or if I'm blindly staring at the ground with my mind chattering away (much more likely), I give that balloon another little blast of pressure. Now the robin will probably raise his head a little higher, stretch his neck, and look me right in the eye. *Hey, aren't you going to stop? Don't you see me?* Most folks don't even notice this body language, and if I'm busy or stressed and thinking a lot, I sometimes miss it, too. Strike two, regardless.

If I don't see, or don't care enough and don't stop, the bird will issue a bolder *TUT* series or maybe even a *CHEENK* alarm as it bursts off and perches on a branch, maybe in a shrub. Strike three, I'm out, and not just with the robin. *(Audio file 3 has an example of the American robin's alarm call.)*

Disturb one, disturb all: *Hey, the robin sounds worried. What's up? What's up?* The other birds have tuned in and probably looked in my direction. With the second and third strikes, everyone definitely sees me: *Oh, there he is, the biped who gives us no respect.* And in case I'm interested, the deer bed fifteen yards from the house is now empty. I *am* interested. I don't care to disturb the bedded deer. In fact, I consider it a compliment to my family that he chooses to sleep near us in the first place. Safe from mountain lions and coyotes? Maybe. But here in the Santa Cruz Mountains, what deer is safe, really? Anyway, I can hear this deer sneaking away from the house through the yard hedge. I now hear another robin in that hedge muttering about the deer, and therefore about me. The Steller's jay also makes a remark about the deer, as does the wren. All with the same message for me: *Should have paid attention, guy.*

Now let's turn to a parking lot at the edge of the suburban woods. A flock of robins are feeding on berries in the trees along the hiking trail as a car pulls into the lot. They are about twenty feet up on average. High enough, one would think, to be untroubled by the humans on the ground. No cars have come into the lot for a good hour anyway. Things have settled back down since the last car brought along the boisterous Labrador retriever that tore all over the place recklessly and almost randomly. The birds see this next car stop, the door open, the trunk open, and Joe the hiker prepare for vigorous exercise. Like the robins in the yard, these birds will interrupt their baseline pattern to pause, look, listen. Nothing drastic, just curious attention. Finally, Joe strikes off on the trail. Typically, he has no consideration of his overall impact, no idea that he's disturbing anyone, no understanding that if he wants to see some animals, he has to get permission from the birds first. That's what it amounts to. People can live near a patch of woods and walk through it every day of their lives but never know that there's a bear around, or an old buck. This is because the bear and the buck have been warned about us by the birds.

Joe creates a mild agitation alarm in the birds. As in the front yard, they try to make direct eye contact. They want to see if this new arrival is paying attention. They are watching carefully to see if he poses a threat. Absorbed in thought, he's not paying attention and does not offer any recognition. Instead, he walks obliviously right under them, and they scatter— *TUT TUT TUT* and *tsreet tsreet*, wings fluttering against the leaves. If Joe was paying attention, he could hear the wind from their takeoffs. Then the juncos scatter— *Shreep! Shreep!*—which in turn causes the Swainson's thrush to stop singing and check things out. When he sees the other birds flying off, he issues his own alarm and follows them in flight.

In this way, Joe has kicked up ripples, waves, concentric rings of disturbance that propagate in every direction. I call this the bird plow, the first of the twelve alarm shapes detailed in the preceding chapter. Now this alarm shape—and the disturbance that causes it —gets a chapter of its own. The broader issue is that important.

Joe is really churning things up. Any deer within earshot hears that junco, stops feeding, raises its head, and focuses its ears intently in the right direction, because it knows that the junco's almost intimate alarm is one of the most reliable for approaching danger on the ground. The squirrels pause in their feeding and climb a bit higher for a better look. Their anxious tails twitch. The song sparrow rises off the ground and hangs chest-high on a tree, flipping its tail and echoing the junco's alarm with its own. *Shreep! Shreep!* The towhee stops feeding. Throughout the area, singing has stopped almost completely, replaced by various alarm calls.

What does it say when the birds shoot off for a hundred feet or more, like clay pigeons randomly fired from spring-loaded traps? It says that they don't know who this biped is, how dangerous he is, or what he's going to do. But they sure don't understand what they see thus far, so the prudent course is to evacuate the area. This would be a fun subject for a controlled study; the only such research I know of was published in the journals *Environmental Conservation* in 2001 and *Biological Conservation* in 2004. These two articles have the same lead author, a researcher at the University of Madrid. The title of the second one is "Spatial and Temporal Responses of Forest Birds to Human Approaches in a Protected Area and Implications for Two Management Strategies." The work was technical, and it didn't analyze bird plows as such, but it goes to my basic point here: birds in relatively "pristine" forest habitats move away from approaching humans, and the larger the bird, the farther away it flies. (This observation may simply reflect the fact that larger birds fly longer distances as a matter of course, though I don't really know.) Regarding policy, the study simply concludes, "We recommend redistributing (but not restricting) human visitation by varying the number of visitors and area of visitation according to the spatial requirements of differently sized species."

The first article is titled "Alert Distances as an Alternative Measure of Bird Tolerance to Human Disturbance: Implications for Park Design." This study confirmed the obvious point that birds want separation from humans, even in the wooded patches of a large park in Madrid. It also confirmed the point about larger birds flying farther away. The policy recommendation: "Alert distance may be used in the determination of minimum approaching areas, allowing people to enjoy their visit to parks, and birds to use patches for foraging and breeding without being displaced."

Does Camo Help?

What about camouflage? Doesn't that help us fit in and keep the disruption to a minimum? I've entertained this question many times, often from bow hunters, but also from unarmed outdoorsmen, and I admit that I ham it up with my answer. "Well, let's think about this," I begin. "Most birds know what people look like. We may perversely use only two of our limbs for walking, and the other two may hang down to no apparent purpose, but those are our problems. Even when we're barging into the birds' world, we're a known quantity. But consider us from their viewpoint when we put on camouflage: *What in the world is this thing? It looks kind of like a bush, but what a funny-looking bush. And whoever saw a bush move? Or is it a pile of leaves? But whoever saw a pile of leaves move? And what about the way the eyes peer out from a hole in the lump at the top? This is* really *strange. What* are *you? Could you be Joe the hiker in expensive camouflage?* The large thing on the ground probably moves furtively, thinking this helps the cause, and it's probably tense, certainly strange. It cannot possibly be up to any good. Alarms ricochet everywhere, especially from the squirrels: *Go away! Whatever you are, go away!* And just think, Joe has paid several hundred dollars for these threads, the best that money can buy."

If I've played my part well, everyone gets the point. To another human being, perhaps even to a deer who wanders into the scene, the camouflaged individual who doesn't move a single sinew *might* be pretty invisible—until he *does* move a sinew. To the other creatures whose homeland has been so invaded—especially the birds and the squirrels—he's not invisible at all, movement or no movement. If one day I walk into my living room and see a pile of shapeless cloth on the floor, I'm going to notice, right? It may be camouflaged to perfectly match the design of the rug, but I'm not that unaware and dumb. In like manner, the woodsman lurking in camouflage is just as jarring a presence for the local denizens as the hunter in a Day-Glo orange vest. All the creatures in the forest speak and read two common languages—bird language and body language—and they react to new behaviors and shapes and vibes. The fact that clothing matches the background in a generic way is irrelevant. They're so far ahead of us in this camo game, it's not even funny.

More important, in the manner of the San Bushmen, we must focus on recognition of, and respect for, all things. Outfits and gear are no substitute for this basic attitude. I always ask people to start not with camo gear, but with their attitude: Proceed with respect, pause frequently, turn the eyes away from direct confrontation, and walk with a relaxed body posture—calmly, with a respectful routine of invisibility. Employ awareness, connection, recognition. Ease around birds who are feeding. Try not to disturb those who are singing. We can do better by invoking the golden rule. The more we adopt a respectful, aware attitude, whether it's in the yard or the woods or the jungle, the more scoutlike we become, and the more respectfully we are treated in return. After, or even while, we learn "invisibility" as an attitude of connection and respectful conduct, putting on the camouflage can be quite valuable in certain circumstances and take us even further in bird language (or tracking or just about anything else outdoors). I just don't want anyone to think that it can be a substitute for the proper respectful attitude.

The Two-Minute Drill

The fact that we are the most common cause of the bird plow is a sad reflection of what we represent to the birds and what our behavior says about us. It is also ironic. Joe the hiker is not dangerous, but the birds don't know that, and their excessive reaction (from our perspective) may now call in the hawks and coyotes in the area, who really *are* a danger. The natural world is a culture of vigilance based on carefully tended relationships and connections, maintained through recognition, mutual respect, and "jungle etiquette" that in the end preserves the baseline and conserves energy. Joe has thrown it into disarray, and anyone watching who has some knowledge of bird language understands exactly what has happened. In fact, the student who sees all the birds flying overhead from the same direction—the advancing forward edge of the bird plow—could set her watch for what we call the two-minute drill.

Justin was a teenager I had agreed to mentor. I had coordinated my schedule so that I would meet Justin just as I finished a meeting with three folks about a rustic building project on some land in Washington State. The four of us were standing at the intersection of two trails seventy-five yards inside the woods. As we stood there, a series of bird alarms came through. "Well," I told my colleagues, somewhat coyly, "I don't know what this is, but something is coming." We quieted down and listened intently, watching the movement of the birds—robins, thrushes, and others I couldn't identify at a distance and through the trees. They were flying straight at us from the direction of a parking lot about a hundred yards away—the leading edge of a bird plow, and an intense one at that. Something had made a mighty big splash, and the ripples were washing right over us. Birds were flying with intense focus and spreading the alarm. *Okay,* I thought. *This isn't a suburban coyote or a hawk. This has to be the animal who no longer seems to follow the local patterns:* Homo sapiens modernus.

I turned and asked if anyone had a watch with a timer. "Start it, would you? Give us two minutes." A woman started her watch, and I pointed with my chin up the trail toward the source. Our little group shaped into a half circle and turned to face the bird plow.

Two minutes is a long time to wait in such circumstances. After an excruciating minute or so, someone asked, "Are they coming?"

"Yeah," I said, "just wait."

Half a minute later, we could hear footfalls and bushes moving. Then, about twenty yards away, popping over a small rise and emerging from the thicket, was young Justin, his body language taut with focus and purpose. Shocked to see this committee of adults who were obviously expecting him, Justin stopped in his tracks, looked down at himself, spread his arms in that "What's going on?" gesture, and then asked with a look of jaw-dropping self-awareness, "Was I that obvious?"

The timekeeper looked at her watch and announced, "Two minutes." We all laughed and explained the scenario to Justin, who was embarrassed but had a sense of humor about it. He had come to the right place.

This is a popular trick in Bird Language 101. I've seen the basic two-minute prediction and confirmation "performed" many times, each in a different context and with a different but telltale result. All such drills are great lessons in the impact of our presence among the birds and other creatures. We really can and do provoke the alarm to end all alarms— *The humans are coming! The humans are coming!* —without even realizing it. The bird plow and the two-minute drill are laws of unnatural nature. The birds flee as if we're one of the greatest dangers ever encountered—and we are if we're hunting some of them. We're also a danger if real predators are drawn to the scene of the disturbance, because they know opportunity when they see and hear it. Picking up the bird plow, the deer pay close attention, but they don't automatically go bounding off. Better, less energy expensive, is to slip into the shadows and see what develops. If the problem is just a human, all is well, because this human will never see the deer who's waiting for him.

Call It "the Vibe"

Years ago, my son Aidan was one of a group of kids out in the field recording their observations at ten-minute intervals. As mentioned earlier, this is a standard mentoring exercise in the art and science of bird language awareness. After forty minutes, they returned with their reports. Everyone had recorded a period of intense alarms vocalized by all the birds within one ten-minute period, and their maps pinpointed the same area. Something had happened *right there.* An intruder had entered the scene, then departed. Before the discussion of possible "culprits" could get going, Aidan spoke up, sheepishly.

"Dad, that was me."

"What do you mean?"

"That intense alarm was for me. I was in a really bad mood, feeling dark and angry, and my body language must have been intense. All the birds around me were alarming like crazy because I was right there in this bad space. They were really responding. I felt bad because I was causing so many alarms, so I got up and left."

Have you ever been in a public place, a plaza of some sort, and seen one individual moving a bit stiffly, seemingly without purpose, making no eye contact, maybe ill or even dangerous, all in all just not fitting in with the general tone and vibe of the place? Something about this person was "off," and you noticed the aberration. You might even have become a little nervous. Well, exactly the same dynamic is in play in the natural world—in spades, because the birds and animals have a lot more to be nervous about in their environment than we have in ours. That's a hard fact of their lives.

Head down, not paying attention to anything outside our thoughts, sudden body movements, all in all just not fitting in—such humans are viewed differently in the natural world (including the backyard) than those who are well into the routine of invisibility. It's going to happen. It still happens occasionally to me (only in minor ways, I hope, with the birds in the front yard), and it's always a powerful lesson. It was a powerful lesson for the group that day. Too bad every kid can't have Aidan's experience at the age of fifteen and learn that the robins, song sparrows, and juncos advise us about the cat, the dog, the hawk, and *ourselves,* if only we understand their language, which is rooted in their *super-natural* awareness (don't forget that hyphen).

If we believe we're in a good mood, or at least an okay mood, but the birds tell us otherwise with their alarms and other actions, who's right? Here's the bird language rule: they're right. If we're in an outright bad mood, if our attitude is arrogant or simply clueless and unfeeling, this attitude will be reflected in our movements as we barge through the trees, and we'll be treated differently by the birds. Just as they read the cat's body language and behavior, they read our body language, behavior, noises, and energy—in short, the overall *vibe*. (Tom Brown calls this the "concentric ring" that we exude.) They read us all the time. (As mentioned in the introduction, one experiment has confirmed that mockingbirds identify and later remember the specific individuals who have approached too close to their nests.)

The good news is that bird language allows us to turn the tables, in effect. If we learn to read the birds—and their behaviors and vocalizations—through them, we can read the world at large. Anyone with a working understanding of this discipline can approach an unknown habitat and quickly draw all sorts of "natural world" conclusions. The types of birds seen or heard, their numbers and behaviors and vocalizations, will reveal the locations of running water or still water, dead trees, ripe fruit, a carcass, predators, fish runs, insect hatches, and so much more. The details of the habitat become very clear. If we don't barge in and kick up a big bird plow—if we replace collision with connection, learn to read these details, feel at home, relax, and are respectful—ultimately the birds will yield to us the first rite of passage: a close encounter with an animal otherwise wary of our presence.

Over the years, I've gotten into quite a few friendly disputes with landowners who've never seen the bobcat or cougar or bear that passes through their property fairly regularly. They've been living there for decades; so how could they be wrong? In the story I told in Chapter 5 about the Pacific wrens, the weasels, and the old VW square-back sedan, the caretaker had never seen one weasel in what was actually a weasel paradise. If the guidebook of mammals didn't say otherwise, the folks who never see a mink might deny that their neighborhood is even within this elusive animal's North American range. They might well blame bad luck, but luck, good or bad, has nothing to do with it. The reason for their lack of success is the birds, who read intruders like us microsecond by microsecond. If we're still a long way off, they read the bird plow our vibe has kicked up among the birds along our line of march. Their alarm calls about the intruding *Homo sapiens* are picked up by the mink and the fox and the deer, who instantly fade from the scene. Or the birds are not alarmed, and the other animals do not flee. Now we find the mink padding along with her babies; the fox in repose, licking her paws; and the deer in bed with her fawn.

This idea that the birds acutely judge our body language and other aspects of our overall energy probably raises more eyebrows among beginning students of bird language than any other proposition. In second place is my promise that close encounters with wildlife are practically guaranteed with good knowledge of bird language, practice with the routine of invisibility, and growing respect, connection, and San-like recognition of the birds and other animals—"jungle etiquette," in the vernacular of bird language. I don't worry about those doubts, whether verbally expressed or implied by furrowed brows, because I've worked and mentored in many different contexts and settings, with people of all ages and backgrounds. Some catch on faster than others, of course, but most, within just a few months, will head into the field one morning and return in the evening with a report of seeing the mother mink traveling with her babies. Personal experience puts the doubts to rest.

In Chapter 4, while discussing the value of the routine of invisibility, I introduced the image of the two spheres, one representing an individual's *awareness* of the natural world, the other representing the *disturbance* this individual causes. I now repeat that crucial point. To understand bird language, we must slowly but surely expand the sphere of awareness and shrink the sphere of disturbance by learning and practicing good jungle etiquette. As the beneficial sphere becomes increasingly larger than the detrimental sphere, we start seeing and hearing many more birds and other wildlife.

Bird Plow Causes "Two-Minute Alarm": This diagram, which also appears in Chapter 4, illustrates the alarm caused by a harried human not paying attention to her impact on the world around her.

Invisibility: Functional invisibility is really about awareness, connection, empathy, and respect. These are common practices among indigenous people who regularly interact with wildlife up close. This illustration, which also appears in Chapter 4, may be more meaningful to you in light of the stories in this chapter illustrating the journey from collision to connection.

Matt, the Deer, and the Robins

I was giving a keynote address to a group in a university town in northern Vermont. Matt, the man who was going to introduce me, had used our mentoring program as a model for years. I asked him to begin his introduction with some little story from that program, because I like to take every chance I get to emphasize the importance of mentoring. So Matt told the audience about his evolving relationship with the small herd of deer who hung out at the edge of the meadow near his house in Massachusetts. In the beginning, when he got home from work in the afternoon, the deer were almost always there, and he sometimes tried to approach them, without success. They bounded into the forest, flags flying. He'd never get closer than a hundred yards. After taking our brief course in mentoring, which included some basics in bird language: awareness, respect, and recognition, Matt drove home intent on using his new tools to get a better look at those deer. The first afternoon, he walked into the meadow slowly, modestly, respectfully, and as aware of everything going on as possible. When the deer were feeding, heads to the ground, he moved forward. When they lifted their heads, he stopped. He made a little progress this way, but then — *boom* — off they went. *(Listen to the white-tailed deer's alarm in audio file 73.)* This happened a few times before he checked in with one of the instructors from the mentoring program, who had invited him to call with any questions. After Matt explained his continuing lack of success with the deer, the instructor asked gently but leadingly, "Got any robins in that meadow?" (Of course, he knew there were robins in that meadow in New England in the summer. It's prime habitat for that time of year.)

After a long pause, Matt said he didn't know for sure about any of the birds, but he'd find out. The next evening, he pulled up near the meadow, and there were the deer on the other side as usual. This time, however, as he stepped into the meadow, Matt looked for robins. They were there, and after a quick glance in his direction, they immediately took off. *CHEEENK!* The deer instantly perked up their ears, lifted their tails, and took off, too. Matt saw the cause-and-effect relationship clearly. Now he understood: The deer were not his immediate problem. First he had to get past the robins, who were the real gatekeepers.

Over the following months, he worked on recognizing these birds. In a meadow in Massachusetts, he learned some jungle etiquette: throwing out that first little string of real recognition, expanding his sphere of awareness, and shrinking his sphere of disturbance. Speaking to the group in Vermont, Matt reported that he had become adept at getting very close to those deer and many other animals. I have many other such stories, but this is one of my favorites — simple, sweet, and heartfelt: collision becoming connection.

Goose Whispering

In Chapter 5, where I contrasted the little towhees' alarms with the big geese's alarms, I mentioned the amazing story about geese that I would tell in this chapter. Here it is — a classic, in my experience, of collision yielding to connection. One rainy, early spring evening at Lake Sammamish State Park in King County, Washington, I was showing a group of about a dozen people how wildlife responds differently to dogs on and off the leash. (For those with a bent for law enforcement, this knowledge can be used to find out where people are breaking the leash laws, because foraging deer avoid dogs' free-run areas, relatively speaking. The forage in those areas will be relatively undisturbed, while elsewhere in the same forest, the deer-pruned forage might be mistaken for bonsai.) At the end of the long day, we were cutting back to the cars across a complex of baseball and soccer fields, and there on the infield of one of the diamonds was a large group of wild Canada geese. Around the country, some Canada geese are practically tame and become the bane of such outdoor facilities. But this gaggle of semi-migratory birds moved between rivers, marshlands, meadows, pastures, and, on this rainy day, the baseball field. They were skittish and obviously nervous about people. There were about forty of them spread over an area about thirty yards wide, right on the path to the cars. Sure, we could easily have diverted around them, but there was also the temptation to move straight ahead, though no one felt good about scattering the geese.

Obviously, these big birds were not as shy as they would be in absolute wilderness. They shared certain territories with people, but they had also had run-ins with humans and were still keenly aware of us. One of the geese had its head up, watching us. As we got closer, it raised its head higher and paid a little more attention. All birds have a species-specific tension sequence (all animals, too, for that matter, including us). In some species (including towhees), it's subtle, and therefore hard for us to differentiate the stages except for the final one, explosive flight. In others, it's obvious, and the geese are one of these species. Feeding or resting on a grassy field, they demonstrate the tension sequence very nicely (as described in Chapter 5).

When this first goose raised its head, we paused. I said, "Well, let's try *this*." We all adopted the "honoring routine," as we call it, which is simply to turn away from the birds (or other animals), maybe forty-five degrees, relax the body posture, and avert the eyes. Ask nothing and expect nothing. Use peripheral vision. The moment we did this, the sentinel lowered its head a little. Not unusual. People are always amazed by how effective this simple gesture is. When we turned back toward the geese and eased forward—relaxed, not "stalking"—the sentinel raised its head again, higher. After a couple of these tit-for-tat exchanges, some of the other geese joined in the ballet. This was becoming an interesting lesson for my group, and we probably could have gone back and forth like that for a long time, with the honoring routine earning a little more respect each time, but without much overall progress for us. At some point, the birds would probably issue a soft *HNK HNK*.

Not a warning exactly, it would mean they were nervous, just paying attention as a group.

I suggested that we pretend to be busy, talking to one another, leaning down in feeding gestures, no threat whatsoever. The geese responded by taking a break from their eating and moving to the dirt area around second base that was puddled with water. They took turns drinking and casually watching us. They were still in our way.

I said to the group, "You know, they're done eating. They're getting a drink after their meal. Let's just tell them that we want to come through."

"How do we do that?"

"We'll turn in unison to face them, take a couple of steps forward, then stop and turn away in the honoring routine. We'll do it all together, like a flock of geese."

So we did, and the most amazing thing happened. The lead goose looked up, another goose looked up, and then they all turned, looked at one another, and separated into two groups, leaving a path for us between them, a few yards wide. My hair stood straight up, no kidding, and so did everyone else's. That was a very high compliment from the geese. We all felt blessed and walked through the flock in single file. I whispered, "Don't turn and look at them as you pass by. The temptation will be to stop, but just keep walking calmly. They've said yes. Don't break the treaty. Just acknowledge them with a nod of thanks as you go by."

All of us were powerfully moved. Setting aside collision in favor of connection always feels deeply *right*. I'm sure the beneficiaries of those geese's courtesy are still talking about that experience.

Two Kinds of Connection

Several years before this goose incident, I mentored a young man who had been diagnosed as having ADHD. No doubt I've had other students so diagnosed, but this was the first one I'd been "forewarned" about. Naturally, I observed him closely, possibly more closely than I watched the others in the group. In the classroom, he was indeed restless. In the field, he was still on high alert, but this restlessness was more akin to the coyote's in her day bed —relaxed tension (looking up at every little sound, ears following unheard sounds in the distance, testing the breeze with a keen nose) and utter curiosity—than to the wired behavior of people who aren't comfortable in the woods. He belonged here. He was attuned to subtle cues and sounds. He had the ears of a native scout. Soon enough, he could monitor and identify bird songs and calls from all directions at the same time. He was always the first to spot the hawk, the first to use the birds' alarms to locate the second instructor, planted for purposes of hide-and-seek. He was sharp about everything, and I asked myself, "Is ADHD a limitation or very possibly a gift?"

Properly channeled, of course, such an omnivorous awareness and connection is a gift. I was convinced that this young man's work with bird language was going to settle him down and help him to focus his quick mind. It would ground him and, in time, bring a profound inner silence that would change his life. I had no doubt about this. Let me repeat the quote from the San Bushman presented in the introduction:

> If one day I see a small bird and recognize it, a thin thread will form between me and that bird. If I just see it but don't really *recognize* it, there is no thin thread. If I go out tomorrow and see and really recognize that same individual small bird again, the thread will thicken and strengthen just a little. Every time I see and recognize that bird, the thread strengthens. Eventually it will grow into a string, then a cord, and finally a rope. This is what it means to be a Bushman. We make ropes with all aspects of the creation in this way.

This is a wonderful image for me, and perhaps it resonates with you more now than it did earlier. I hope so. I also want to point out that the San's concept of seeing without recognizing is practically the definition of the rushed, hectic modern experience. I really don't believe that a daily schedule chopped into quarter-hour segments is who we are instinctively. That is our *acquired* self, not our *evolved* self. Although almost everyone (myself included) uses and enjoys all the specialized electronic connectivity of the modern experience, this is not our natural baseline. That baseline is sitting on a grassy hillock, relaxing in the shade, swimming in the cool river on a hot day, strolling with knowledge and wisdom in the dark forest, eating wild berries, laughing with our children, listening to the stories of our elders around the fire, and feeling the bonds with elders stretching thousands of years behind us. Eons ago, *Homo sapiens* were just as alert and aware as all other creatures, and for the same reason. They needed to be. Now we don't need to be—*or do we, but just don't understand this anymore?* Our sensory equipment and brains are still designed for this awareness. These instincts are still in each of us, just buried, maybe deeply buried. Connecting with bird language begins the process of unearthing them. It changes the whole dynamic of our lives immediately. We now *recognize* the robin. We *recognize* the sparrow. These birds lift us from our troubled minds. They give us a reason to move and see and listen respectfully. They unlock the outdoors. They reflect our knowledge and our attitude, and ultimately they yield the first rite of passage when we're allowed a close encounter with an animal that would otherwise have fled our presence long before.

One of my mentors, Ingwe (of British ancestry, born in 1914 in a rural region of Cape Province, South Africa, grew up in the bush in Kenya among the Akamba hunter-gatherers), said that when he sat alone in the city, he felt "lonely," but when he sat alone in the wilderness, he felt "solitude," which is very different. The natural world folded around Ingwe like a warm blanket and fed his spirit. For many of us, the opposite may be true. The activity and easy excitement of the city is comforting, the forest lonely. Sometimes it seems as if humans might lose the old instinctive baseline altogether, and maybe fairly soon. The high-stress lives that we lead are simply too draining. Immersion in deep bird language is challenging for some people. In a culture in which "connection" usually refers to the strength of the cell phone signal, quieting the mind — even just sitting alone in the backyard, much less in the forest — can be a difficult rite of passage. Instead, we reach for the cell phone, the iPod, the laptop, anything with buttons to push, a mouse to click, or a joystick to manipulate. I understand all this, but I also know that the old instincts can be unearthed, the birds can still speak to us, and lives can suddenly change.

In the introduction, I cited the 2009 study published in *Personality and Social Psychology Bulletin* that confirmed that merely looking at *photographs* of the natural world increased the test subjects' connectedness, empathy, and sharing. Common sense says that actual time spent in, and with real attention paid to, that world out there beyond the pixelated screen should produce even more dramatic benefits. I've seen it many times. Deep bird language is a multidimensional, full-contact nature sport! It influences our psyches much more than any array of pictures or 3-D movies possibly could.

When we train ourselves to listen to the birds with every synapse of our brains (or so it may seem), when we "lose our mind" and "come to our senses" in the fullest possible way, the chattering, texting, e-mailing, twittering mind will eventually quiet down and almost silence itself. This is a sacred and connected silence, and within this zone we can choose to turn on the conscious thoughts or leave them off. It's like a deep, still pond reflecting the stars of the night sky. I believe *this* is the baseline for human consciousness, and I'm convinced that the birds are the best mentors in the natural world for bringing us to it.

APPENDIX A: LEARNING BIRD LANGUAGE

This appendix provides a tool kit for you to use in learning the ancient art of bird language. Refer to the appropriate chapters as needed to provide the context for each exercise. A helpful training resource is a DVD called *Bird Language with Jon Young*.

Introduction: What the Robin Knows

The birds that surround you every day are your teachers. Start paying extra attention to them. Whether you are in the city or the heart of the wilderness, observe the patterns of behavior of the common species around you.

Find a Sit Spot

Adopt a sit spot where you can go every day or as often as possible. It could be in your backyard, on a park bench, or even in front of a window—do whatever you can. A place that is a bit off the beaten path is ideal, but you can learn a lot wherever you are. A spot with a good field of view and a meeting of habitats will yield a higher diversity of birds and animals to observe.

Use your senses fully while you are there. Get to know this place in all seasons, at all times of the day, and in all weather conditions. This is the key to learning the baseline of the place. Going to a place over and over, observing deeply, and asking questions are the main elements of learning the art of bird language.

Keep a Journal

Keep a pocket journal with you to jot down key observations. It is a good practice to transfer your notes—and other observations from memory—into a more permanent journal right when you get home from your sit spot, while the experience is still fresh. There are many styles of journal keeping. Recording bird language events at specific intervals is one method that is especially helpful in learning bird language. We often use this technique, a very focused style of journal writing, during our bird language training workshops.

Plan to stay in your sit spot for at least forty minutes. This allows enough time for any disturbance that you may have caused walking in to settle down and for the animals to resume their activities.

Divide the time period into ten-minute intervals, starting with a zero period that denotes the time in which you walk to your spot. Periods one through four are the actual times during the sit, each lasting ten minutes (for a total of forty minutes), and period five is the time when you walk back from the sit. Write in your journal as events happen during the sit. Label everything in sequence by the period. For instance, "1A" denotes the first event in period one.

1A. Song sparrow actively singing 5 feet up on rosebush, 20 feet to the north. He is countersinging to another male behind me to the south.

1B. Spotted towhee behind me paused his scratch feeding and then hooked up and made a "mew" call.

1C. A junco has hooked off the ground and is chipping, now posted 6 feet up on an apple branch facing the thicket behind me. The song sparrow behind me has ceased his song, while the sparrow to the north only paused his song, then continued to sing.

1D. The junco is chipping still, and now the sparrow behind me is uttering "sweep, sweep" calls.

1E. The calls continue for the rest of the period in the same spot. Farther away, songs are more prevalent, and it is only nearby that several bird species are using focused calls in one area. Could this be an alarm? Who might it be?

Note: Everything is fair game to include in the journal — trucks driving by, planes flying overhead, gusts of wind, animals, people, a sudden downpour, clouds. All of these and more may be tied to the bird language stories that are unfolding before you.

Also note: If you are familiar with banding codes — the shorthand notation developed and used by bird banders — use them to save time. Example: AMRO = American robin.

Create a map using a different color for each time period. Draw in each event and use arrows to depict any movements in position that occurred.

Create a list of questions that were generated from the event and any ideas you have for finding answers. Example: Was the towhee/song sparrow sequence in period one caused by a housecat? I'll check the trail for tracks next time.

Create a list of species seen or heard during the sit. Example: chestnut-backed chickadee, song sparrow, Oregon junco.

The Usual Suspects

Use the range maps in a field guide to list any predators that occur in your range and habitat. Consider aerial predators, ground-based predators, and nest robbers. Avian, mammalian, and even reptilian predators (especially snakes) are all common causes of bird alarms.

1. A Cacophony of Harmony

Watch for these patterns of deep bird language in your sit spot.

What's Happening Today

What food sources are the different birds seeking today? Where are they going to get food? Are any particular weather conditions favoring certain food sources? Could you possibly predict this behavior next year at the same time? Record your observations and questions in your journal.

What's Happening in This Season

What patterns are you noticing on a seasonal scale that might be affecting the behavior of the birds and other animals? How is this autumn the same as or different from the previous autumn? Keeping a regular journal will allow you to make seasonal comparisons and, over time, see larger trends in behavior in relationship to the weather and other factors.

Energy Conservation

When observing bird behavior, consider how the actions you are observing may reflect the need to conserve energy. What is the cost-benefit ratio of a behavior relative to the need to save energy? How abundant is food currently, and how stressful is the environment (cold, wind, rain, competitors, predators)?

Observing Wake Hunting

Predators often use the confusion of disturbances caused by vehicles, wind, people, and even other predators to slip in undetected and catch their prey. Look for this behavior around jogging trails and places that have occasional loud vehicles passing by.

2. In the Beginning Is the Song

Make a concerted effort to learn the baseline of your sit spot.

Learn the Five Voices of One Bird

Pick a common bird, such as the American robin, and get to know all the vocalizations of this species. Put your audio source on repeat and listen to the tracks over and over until you have internalized the sounds. Listen for them in the landscape when you go to your sit spot. After you learn one bird, learn another.

Make a Top-Five List

Make your top-five list of common bird language birds. Pick ones that are commonly seen and heard at your favorite spot. Focus your studies on these five birds. Good qualities to look for include ground feeder, small territory, earth-colored, year-round or nearly so, widespread range, and habitually vocalizes. Some excellent birds to consider are the American robin, song sparrow, Pacific wren, spotted towhee, junco, and cardinal.

Map the Birds' Territories

Map the territories of the birds in your sit spot. Use clues such as song posts, sentinel perches, nests, and skirmish areas to outline the territory of each bird. Observe how territory sizes may shift both before and after nests are established. Persistence is the key. Understanding a bird's territory will bring a whole new layer of meaning to bird language.

3. More Cacophony of Harmony

Listen for the Quietest Sound

Send your hearing across the landscape. Focus on the quietest sounds. Then listen for the silence in between sounds. This will tune your ears so that even quiet sounds become apparent.

Observe Companion Calls

Observe a pair of mated birds (cardinals and song sparrows are great) to listen for the companion calls. Note the rhythm and tone of the calls.

Observe Territorial Aggression

Watch for examples of intraspecies (within the same species) and interspecies (across different species) aggression. Keep your eye on one robin and how he guards his territory. Note how other birds react (or don't react) to two fighting robins.

Observe Adolescent Begging

Locate a nest. Notice patterns of begging calls when the parents arrive at the nest and when they leave. Keep an ear out for nest robber alarms and note any changes in nestling vocalizations. Watch the chicks as they get older and follow their parents. Look for behaviors such as wing flapping and persistent begging prior to feeding.

4. The Sit Spot

Every place has something to teach. Adopting a specific place in the landscape will allow you to develop a relationship with the landscape and the beings there.

The Daily Challenge

Bring back a story about birds or bird language from some place you went today, even if it's just a list of questions you have developed about that place. Share the story with a friend or write about it in your journal.

Get Motivated

Use questions such as these to get you going in your journal.

- Why do I want to learn this?
- What are my learning goals?
- What opportunities do I see at my sit spot?
- How well do I know my spot?
- What questions do I have about my sit spot?

Stating your goals builds motivation to practice. Put a list of burning questions on your refrigerator door or somewhere easy to see every day.

Slow Down

Vary your speed as you walk to and from your sit spot. Try going at half or quarter speed, and pause frequently to listen to the songs and calls (or silences) around you. This will diminish your initial circle of disturbance and cause baseline behavior to return much more quickly once you sit down.

Ask Routine Questions That Connect

When you write in your journal, make it a habit to ask:

- What did I observe?
- What is this telling me?
- What is this teaching me?
- How is this helping me?
- How is it helping me to help others?

Asking these types of questions is at the core of learning deep bird language.

Owl Eyes

When you sit in your spot, remember to open up your peripheral vision wide like an owl. Let your eyes softly gaze across the landscape, taking in their full field of view. Notice movements out of the corners of your eyes—branches moving in the wind, birds flying by, and animals walking. Practice this expanded field of vision until it becomes an intuitive part of your awareness.

Deer Ears

Send your hearing out in one direction at a time—first to the left, then to the right, behind you, ahead of you, and up and down. Listen first for the quietest sounds in each direction. Then let your ears soak in all the sounds at once, and keep track of the direction and distance of the origin of each sound. Try to determine the height off the ground of the maker of the sound.

Sounds and Sights

How many airplanes flew over your spot today? This question can be replaced with many others: What direction did the wind come from today? Did it shift direction at all, and when? How did bird language relate to the wind today?

The Lazy Surveyor

Adopt the following movement pattern as you walk to and from your sit spot. Imagine that you are a surveyor getting paid by the hour, and you are in no hurry to get the job done. Let your senses drift gently across the landscape. This is the opposite of a goal-oriented posture. Release any unnecessary tension in your body. Relax, stop a lot, and look around, but without any hard focus. You are not "trying" to spot birds and animals; you are just taking your time and looking around.

Fox Walking

Keep your gaze up toward the horizon, using owl vision to spot the trail in your peripheral vision. Let your feet "see" the trail and find the way by gently easing into each step, committing your full weight only once the ground has been tested for loud twigs that might snap or other hazards such as rocks or slick spots. Imagine your body adopting the lithe gait of the fox as you ease into an effortless, graceful movement. You are gliding smoothly and quietly, as opposed to bouncing up and down with loud footfalls and obvious body motion.

Waiter Form

Bend your knees very slightly. Let your chin relax and imagine that your head is being held up by a string attached to the top. Relax your shoulders and arms. Imagine that your upper body is held on a coat hanger, allowing your skeletal structure to support your weight. While walking, keep your head level. Imagine a waiter carrying a large tray of wineglasses through a crowded room. His bent knees and relaxed body allow for level and smooth movement; no wine is spilled.

Mountain Lion or Leopard Form

Cats move gracefully and follow very deliberate routes. Their pathways take advantage of patches of shadow and edge areas that lead to good vantage points for observation. They move slowly and deliberately, with precision and planning. Move like a cat. Look ahead on the trail and determine where the feeding birds are and how much space you will give them so as not to alarm them. Stop in the shadows to scan in each direction and allow your ring of disturbance to settle down before continuing on.

The Routine of Invisibility

Combine the previous exercises. Walk slowly with precision and a gentle step, looking up while using owl vision. Pause frequently in the shadows and extend your five senses in all directions. Use the lazy surveyor approach rather than holding an intense focus. Avoid disturbing the birds. Slow down, extend your senses, and soften your body posture. By doing all these things, you will diminish your circle of disturbance while expanding your zone of awareness. At first this may seem awkward. The key is to relax and open your senses. Take it one step at a time.

Inner and Outer Tracking

Analyze your sphere of awareness compared to your current sphere of disturbance. Were you paying attention, or did you get lost in thought? What body language are you using? How does your current emotional state relate to your awareness of the birds? Did you scatter the birds or instead become aware of them first and give them space?

How Bird Language Works in Practice

Learning bird language requires some dedicated time and effort. Over thirty years of experience in helping others learn bird language has told me that this learning can be really fun and full of adventures. Don't think of this as work or practice, just joyful play right outside your doors and windows. There are core routines that really help.

SHY TO BOLD

Use the "shy-to-bold" index as the focus of your sit. This is a great exercise to do at a birdfeeder or in your sit spot after you settle in. After a disturbance, which birds returned to baseline in the first five minutes, ten minutes, fifteen minutes, more than twenty minutes?

PREDAWN SIT

Sit from predawn to dawn. How is this time period unique? What is the first bird to vocalize?

TWILIGHT SIT

Sit from predusk through darkness. What is the last bird to sing or call?

SIT AT OTHER TIMES OF THE DAY

How is early morning in the summer different from early morning at the peak of spring? There are many possibilities, and each has something different to teach about the baseline of that particular season, time of day, and weather condition.

NEVER WALK THE SAME PATH TWICE

Make it a point to vary your path every time you visit your sit spot. Ask yourself, What is this new route teaching me about this place? Is this leading me to any new discoveries? Record your answers in your journal.

SELF-OBSERVATION

What attitude are you carrying when you observe the birds in your sit spot: calm, anxious, nervous, relaxed, grateful? Does this affect your body posture at all?

FLIGHT PATHS

Observe the flight paths of birds. The feeder is a great place for this. Note the entry and exit routes used by different birds, as well as any staging or secondary feeding areas.

JUNCOS AND OTHER QUIET BIRDS

Track down the quietest bird call you can hear. It may take some time to find the source. Don't be in a rush to run right over to the source of the sound. Track the sound each time you are in your sit spot, and try to determine if there is a pattern to the habitat, cover, and height of the sound. By the time you actually spot the bird, you might have learned quite a lot about it. If you don't know the sound of the junco's call, listen to the companion audio or other audio resources. (Visit BirdLanguage.com for a link to some helpful resources.)

TRACKING

Tracking and bird language go hand in hand. A basic understanding of wildlife tracking skills can help you unravel possible causes of mysterious alarms. If you are hearing alarms consistently in one area, take the time to thoroughly search this spot for tracks or other signs of mammals or other animals. "Runs" are worn spots that animals use repeatedly in their travels. Scats (animal droppings) may be deposited along runs. Some animals, such as foxes, often deposit scats at the junction of multiple runs. Sketch any tracks, scats, or other signs left by animals that you find in your sit spot. Digital photography is an easy way to catalog tracks. (Include a ruler in each photo for scale.) Developing an understanding of the animals who may elicit bird alarms is a key to interpreting the story of the alarms.

There are many great tracking field guides available. Mark Elbroch's *Mammal Tracks and Sign* (Stackpole, 2003) outlines an effective program for learning to read the tracks and signs in your area as a complementary approach to learning deep bird language. Another valuable resource is *A Field Guide to Animal Tracks* by Olaus J. Murie and Mark Elbroch (Houghton Mifflin, 2005).

5. An Alarm for Every Occasion

Ask Questions About Alarms

If you hear a possible alarm call sequence, develop some questions that can help you describe the alarm in your journal. This will help narrow down possible causes of the alarm, or possibly even rule out the call as being something other than an alarm. Here are a few questions to get you started.

- Is this a multispecies alarm? (If just one species is calling, could it possibly be an example of intraspecies aggression, such as two robins fighting over territory?)
- What body posture is the bird using? (Tail up or down, tail flicking, wings flicking, beak up or down, beak "pointing" down repeatedly, stillness, preening feathers.)
- How intense are the calls? (Soft, intermittent, light chipping versus harsh, loud, repetitive chipping. This comes with experience, but simply note any impressions you have.)
- Is the alarm static (not moving)? If the alarm center is moving, how fast is it moving?
- Are the alarming birds close to the ground or high up? How high off the ground?
- How widespread is the alarm? Are the alarming birds focused on one small area, or is there a larger pattern of disturbance? How many yards across is the epicenter of the alarm?

- When you hear the sound, does your body register any sensation, such as being relaxed versus tense?
- What predators might be expected to live in this habitat? How would the behavior of each "suspect" correspond to the observed bird alarm? (Coyotes often move quickly at a trot; cats often move slowly and pause for long periods.)

Seek Out Towhees and Other Scratch Feeders

If you have spotted towhees in your area, seek them out for some quality time. Towhees prefer thickets, in which they scratch around on the ground for food. Watch their tails flicking and listen to their baseline rhythm as each mated pair communicates through rhythmic scratching sounds. Start to listen for deviations in the timing of the scratches—longer pauses may indicate a shift in the baseline, and stillness becomes a state of alarm. Constantly compare the state of the towhees with the larger context of bird language in the area.

Observe a Housecat

If you have an outdoor housecat or two, or a friend or neighbor has one, you can put the cat to work for your learning. Watch the cat explore the yard and notice how the birds react. Note the posture of the cat in relation to the birds' reactions (crouching, slinking, sitting, etc.). Note how the birds get out of the cat's path, how close they allow the cat to get, how high they fly to get away, and whether any choose to mob the cat. Listen to and watch the bird language in the area where the cat currently is, where it just was, and where it appears to be headed. Observe as many animals and their alarm shapes as possible in this manner. The animals and birds are the best teachers of bird language.

Cat caveat: Housecats, both domestic and wild, have a considerable effect on bird populations. By suggesting that you look at cats as part of the learning experience, I am not condoning their impact on birds.

6. They're All in This Together

Observe Sentinel Behavior

Make it a focus to observe as many examples of sentinel behavior as possible. A bird that is sitting still on a perch (not preening or singing) is likely on sentinel, just on the edge of a zone of more intense alarm. Try to determine the alarm zone and, behind the position of the sentinel, any zone of baseline song or calls outside the immediate range of danger. Also note any deviation from the usual comfort zone of the species that is on sentinel. For instance, how far was the bird pushed or pulled from its preferred height zone or type of cover?

Observe Variations in Aerial Predator Alarms

Remember that, because of specializations in morphology and hunting behavior, each predator poses a different level of threat.

- Observe a red-tailed hawk flying along the treetops. Note any changes in bird behavior in the canopy as the hawk approaches. Some birds may drop lower into the branches briefly, while those already in cover won't change their positions much.
- Observe the high-pitched universal alarm given when an accipiter is close.
- Observe how birds in the bush may freeze and keep tabs on falcons that are passing by.
- Observe crows and other birds mobbing an owl in the daytime.

Observe Land-Based Predator Alarms

Get to know the mammals that live in your area. Use the range maps in a field guide or online resource to make a list of all the local mammals. Learn to identify the tracks and other signs left by these animals. (Learning tracks and signs can easily represent a multiyear journey all its own.)

7. A Shape for Every Occasion

Study the alarm shapes presented in this chapter: bird plow, sentinel, hook, popcorn, parabolic (umbrella), weasel, cat, bullet, ditch, hawk drop, safety barrier, and zone of silence. Make it a quest to observe and record in your journal several examples of each alarm shape. Understanding these universal shapes will allow you to interpret bird language in many contexts around the world without even knowing the species in a particular area.

When you describe an alarm shape, it helps to use the mapping process explained earlier in the appendix. In addition, draw a side view of the alarm shape that depicts the source of the alarm and the height and distance of the birds from the predator. Use the drawing process to emphasize and support your memory of the event rather than focusing on trying to draw every last whisker on the bobcat and every last tail feather on the alarming song sparrow. Even stick-figure drawings can enhance your journals if they help you to remember what happened.

As your honoring routine skills increase (see the next section), you will cause less disturbance and have a better chance of observing the animals as they move across the landscape.

8. From Collision to Connection

Squirrels on the Brain

How do squirrels react to your presence? At what distance do they take notice of you? Spend some time observing squirrels. What routes do the squirrels in your sit spot take regularly? Do they have certain areas in their home range that they prefer you not to be close to? Play at developing a "squirrel honoring routine."

Body Tension Checkup

Make it a point to continually observe your body and release any stored-up tension. (The shoulders, neck, and arms are common points of tension.) Maintain a relaxed body language while in your sit spot.

The Two-Minute Drill

Sit at your spot. Wait thirty minutes for any disturbance you may have caused to settle down. At a prearranged time, have a friend walk in your direction from farther away. Observe any disturbances in the baseline. Try to catch the "two-minute warning" of his approach. Describe the experience in your journal.

Geese as Teachers

Go to a park and observe some Canada geese. Notice the range of behaviors they express as people, or people with dogs, get close to their feeding area. In particular, watch for sentinel behavior.

The Honoring Routine

The next time you cross paths with a bird or flock of birds, use the honoring routine instead of plowing right through them. Make it a habit to look and listen ahead, as well as on all sides, so that you are aware as much as possible of any birds or animals in your path. Give them space and preserve the baseline state of the area. Describe your experiences with this routine in your journal. Each interaction will teach you more about the particular comfort zone and needs of each species.

Contribute to the Growing Edge of Bird and Animal Language

Share your stories with others who are interested and supportive (even if critically questioning at times). Keep track of your stories in your journal, also logging the date, time, species involved, and habitat. Note who was with you at the time. Share these discoveries with us at BirdLanguage.com. We are always interested.

APPENDIX B: AUDIO

Science editor and colleague Dan Gardoqui has worked to produce a set of professional-quality field recordings of many common birds in a variety of situations that will help you unlock the secrets of the natural world. This audio collection includes many of the baseline voices of backyard birds, such as cardinal songs and chickadee calls, and life-or-death recordings of birds in the presence of imminent danger. It also includes the voices of non-avian species whose calls can be helpful in detecting sneaky predators (such as chipmunks and squirrels), as well as tricky mimics who may throw the budding bird language student a curve ball now and then. To access the audio collection online, visit **www.hmh.com/whattherobinknows** or BirdLanguage.com.

I. Multiple Voices of Common Bird Language Birds

American Robin
1. Typical song: rhythmic, melodic phrases. *(See pages xvi, 159.)*
2. Whinny calls: may be used when agitated, in aggressive encounters, or as a mild alarm. *(See pages xvii, 7, 89.)*
3. *Peek!* and *tut!* alarms: used as alarm calls, often near nest. *(See pages xvi, 7, 39, 165.)*
4. High *SEET* alarm: an alarm call made in proximity to an aerial predator (usually hawk); the high-pitched call is difficult to locate. *(See page 146.)*

Dark-eyed Junco

5. Typical song: a high, metallic trill (sometimes confused with chipping sparrows). *(See page 71.)*

6. Two-part song and *chips:* a variation on a typical song, then contact calls. *(See pages 29, 71.)*

7. *Kew-kew-kew:* calls often used during and after aggressive encounters. *(See page 71.)*

8. *Tsit! Tsit! Tsit!* alarm: subtle, quiet alarm vocalizations of the junco. *(See pages 29, 71.)*

Song Sparrow

9. Typical song: usually begins with 2 to 3 clear notes, then a complex array of notes follows. *(See pages 35, 159.)*

10. *Chip!* calls: calls often used as an alarm call or when agitated. *(See pages 88, 135.)*

11. *Seep* calls: high, clear contact calls used in families and flocks. *(See page 35.)*

12. *Zee* calls: calls given by fledglings. *(See page 44.)*

Bewick's Wren

13. Song: regional variation of song is normal in this species. *(See page 21.)*

14. Variation on song: males have a complex repertoire; here's an example with nasal notes. *(See page 21.)*

15. Alarm: listen to the harsh, raspy notes of this alarm call. *(See page 80.)*

16. Calls: often vary by age and gender. *(See page 30.)*

Carolina Wren

17. Song: this classic loud, clear song says "*tea-kettle, tea-kettle, tea-kettle.*" *(See pages 27, 126.)*

18. Song: another typical variation says "*che-wortel, che-wortel, che-wortel.*" *(See pages 27, 126.)*

19. Song with female chatter: a male sings while a female pipes in with raspy calls. *(See page 126.)*
20. *Ti-dink!* calls: loud notes used as contact calls between birds. *(See page 30.)*
21. *Dit-dit* alarm: urgent alarm calls given by females. *(See pages 88, 127.)*
22. Male alarm: persistent, raspy calls like this mean trouble for the wrens. *(See pages 80, 127.)*

House Wren
23. Song: an example of this unique outburst of song.
24. Alarm: persistent, raspy, scolding alarm calls sound similar to other wren alarms. *(See page 80.)*

Common Yellowthroat
25. Song: a wavering series of melodic notes (variation in song is normal with this species). *(See page 25.)*
26. Alarm: loud *tschat!* calls indicate trouble is nearby. *(See page 107.)*
27. Aggressive chatter: used when combating others of its kind.

Red-winged Blackbird
28. Male songs: a wetland chorus of *conk-a-ree*. *(See page 159.)*
29. Female calls and song: *chack* calls and high-pitched chatter song of females. *(See page 23.)*
30. Contact: loud *chack!* calls used within the flock. *(See page 30.)*
31. Cheer alarm: one of many loud, whistled alarms given by redwings. *(See page 107.)*

Northern Cardinal
32. Song: examples of loud, clear whistles of cardinal songs; variation is common.

33. *Chip* and song: typical contact calls, then a *"cheer-cheer, whoit, whoit . . ."* song with a *"chrrrr"* call tagged into the end (the *chrrrr* is likely meant as a display of fitness, as it's believed to be a very difficult sound to make). *(See pages 31, 149.)*

34. Alarm: *tink!* alarm calls (louder and more urgent than *chip* call notes). *(See pages 88, 90.)*

Spotted Towhee

35. Songs: two examples of their song. *(See page 159.)*

36. *Mew* and *chip: Mew* call used for a variety of purposes (as an alarm when scolding or mobbing, as a contact call when feeding, and in some male-to-male aggressive situations). *Chip* calls usually given in moderately alarming situations (e.g., handling by humans). *(See page 93.)*

37. More *mew* and *chip* calls: slightly different variations of #36. *(See pages 93, 107.)*

Ruby-crowned Kinglet

38. Song: examples of this loud, complex song from one of the tiniest birds in North America. *(See page 86.)*

39. *Chi-dit* calls: used mostly as a contact call (both in flight and when perched); also used occasionally in aggressive male chases. *(See page 86.)*

Hermit Thrush

40. Song: examples of one of the most celebrated songs of all North American songbirds.

41. *Chup-chup* and *vreee:* the functions of these calls are not entirely known, but the *chup-chup* is often an alarm used in hostile situations, while *vreee* may be both an alarm and a contact call. *(See page 116.)*

42. *Weeh:* this raspy vocalization is mostly used by agitated birds as an alarm call.

White-throated Sparrow

43. Song: this easily recognized whistle song says *"Oh-sweet-Canada-Canada-Canada."*

44. *Seep* and *pink!:* the quieter *seep* vocalization is used mostly as a contact call; the louder *pink!* is primarily a general alarm call (but can be heard when going to roost as well). *(See pages 28, 151.)*

American Goldfinch

45. Song: typical long, warbling song of the American goldfinch. *(See page 159.)*

46. *Po-ta-to-chip*: a contact call given both in flight and when stationary. *(See page 125.)*

47. *Bay-bee:* an alarm call, given by distressed birds, often at or near the nest. Also mixed in are nasally *"what-the-hell"* calls, also made by the goldfinches. *(See page 135.)*

48. *Chip-pee:* a begging call given by persistent fledglings as they follow parents around. *(See page 44.)*

Black-capped Chickadee

49. Song: the song of the black-capped chickadee is a loud, clear, whistled *fee-bee. (See page 36.)*

50. *Chick-a-dee:* a variable vocalization with multiple functions, including predator mobbing (in this case, the more *dees* at the end, the more threatening the predator); as an "all clear" call after the predator has left; or as a food source is located. *(See page 50.)*

51. Alarm: a small flock of chickadees vocalizes in the presence of a sharp-shinned hawk. Listen for all the high-pitched *see* and rapid fire *ʒap* notes mixed in with *chick-a-dee-dee-dee-dee-dee* (up to 9 *dees* in this example) alarm calls. *(See page 101.)*

II. Helpful Game Birds

These ground birds are very useful when it comes to predator detection.

Killdeer

52. *Kill-deer:* known primarily as a flight display call often in alarm situations, sometimes simply as an assembly call. *(See pages 18, 124.)*

53. *Te-dit-dit:* an alarm call given by wary birds; often head bobbing is associated with this call. *(See page 124.)*

54. *Deet!:* an alarm call given by birds on the ground, usually near nest. *(See pages 124, 135.)*

55. Aggressive trill: a sputtering alarm call given by a bird chasing predator from nest. *(See page 124.)*

California Quail

56. Assembly or rally call: a common call, *chi-CA-go*, usually given more than 10 times. *(See pages 37, 125.)*

57. *Pit-pit-pit:* an alarm call given when a predator is detected; can be mixed in with a rally call. *(See page 125.)*

Northern Bobwhite

58. *Bob-white!:* made mostly by unmated males in the spring (like a "song"). *(See page 37.)*

59. Scatter call: one of the most common contact calls used to locate and coordinate movement of flock members. *(See page 37.)*

60. Alarm: bobwhites use a variety of alarm calls, starting softly and increasing in frequency and intensity as a predator draws nearer. *(See page 125.)*

III. Corvids

Corvids are known as one of the most intelligent groups of birds, and it's impossible to clearly classify most of their vocalizations. That being said, they're professional nest robbers, and birds know this. Whenever you hear corvids mobbing or when you notice silent corvids during songbird nesting season, pay extra close attention.

American Crow

61. Alarm: in this example, the crows are mobbing a human (who is making field recordings of birds). *(See pages 137, 140.)*

62. Alarm: here the crows are mobbing a red-tailed hawk. *(See page 159.)*

Blue Jay

63. *Jeer:* used as a contact call as well as in mobbing and other alarming situations. Gradation of calls, ability to mimic, complex vocal abilities, and large vocabulary make classification of blue jay calls very difficult. *(See pages 136, 137.)*

Steller's Jay

64. Red-tailed hawk call: here the Steller's jay mimics the call of a red-tailed hawk. Exact function is unknown, but it's often given by a hidden bird, maybe to manipulate other wildlife. *(See pages 14, 55.)*

Black-billed Magpie

65. Alarm: the alarm begins with owl vocalizing and bill snapping (agitation), then magpie scolding calls, more owl hoots, magpie scolds, and so on. *(See page 101.)*

IV. Mammals Useful for Bird Language

While all these calls are not necessarily alarm calls in every context, they're nonetheless worth learning and investigating when studying bird language.

Chipmunk

66. Terrestrial threat: a repeated loud, sharp *chip!-chip!-chip!* warns of ground predators and threats. *(See pages xviii, 73, 101.)*

67. Aerial threat: a repeated low, dull *cluck-cluck-cluck* warns of aerial predators and threats. *(See page 101.)*

68. *Chip!* trill: usually given by a chipmunk diving for cover from threat. *(See page xviii.)*

Red Squirrel
69. Various calls: begins with scold sequence alarm, followed by territorial chatter (also known as chatter-trill), interspersed with whining calls given in social encounters.

Eastern Gray Squirrel
70. Harsh nasal calls: used as both an alarm and in nonthreatening social situations.

Black-tailed Prairie Dog
71. Social calls: typical squeaky, wheezy social calls of prairie dogs.
72. Alarm: typical high-pitched barks of agitated prairie dogs. *(See page 101.)*

White-tailed Deer
73. Alarm: a deer snort sequence, then snorting while bounding away. *(See pages 121, 176.)*

V. More Voices of Alarm

Songbirds in the presence of raptors.

Northern Mockingbird
74. Alarm: a mockingbird mobs a barn owl while making harsh, raspy vocalizations. *(See pages 88, 135.)*

Purple Finch
75. Alarm: with a Cooper's hawk nearby, a purple finch belts out a very strange alarm — a vireo song. *(See page 127.)*

NOTES

Introduction:
What the Robin Knows

xiii *the North American continent:* The ruff, a midsize wading shorebird, breeds in northern Eurasian wetlands and winters across southern Europe, southern Asia, and sub-Saharan Africa. Seeing one in North America, especially for a teenage birder, is a real treat.

xiv *the American robin: Turdus migratorius,* or the American robin, is an example of a "good bird language bird"—notably because it's nearly ubiquitous in North America, it's a ground feeder (save for some winter flocking behavior), and it has a variety of loud vocalizations and physical expressions that are easy to observe.

I know when there's a dog: Species-specific responses are common among wild animals—from rainforest primates (Rainey et al. 2004) to backyard songbirds (Templeton et al. 2005). What's rare today, but was likely very routine in old hunter-gatherer societies, is the ability for humans to interpret these responses accurately.

the robin also advises: Vanderhoff and Eason 2009.

xvi *Any thoughts about:* Bird language interpretation is a very uncommon skill set. At first glance, it may seem "magical," yet there is a very practical, scientific underpinning to it.

xvii *the birds' alarms:* Blumstein et al. 2005.

xix *Such feats:* Gladwell 2005.

xx *I met Tom Brown Jr.:* Naturalist and tracker Tom Brown Jr. founded and teaches at the best-known wilderness survival school in North

America, the Tracker School. Tom's books are mostly narratives and field guides.

xxi *a sophisticated and necessary knowledge:* The rising importance of Traditional Ecological Knowledge (TEK) as an important tool in ecology, restoration, and environmental sciences demonstrates the relevance of an indigenous knowledge of place.

A report of one study: The study is Templeton and Greene 2007. The report appeared in ScienceDaily 2007.

xxii *working with San Bushmen:* Bergen 2009.

crucial for the evolution: Liebenberg 1990.

xxiii *I grew up tracking:* To learn more about holistic tracking, see Young and Morgan 2007.

xxiv *Numerous studies have found:* See, for example, Orians and Heerwagen 1992.

as opposed to the very similar: Sibley 2000.

xxvi *the attitude of the scientist:* Lorenz 1997; Skutch 1997.

They ignore or even deny: On black-capped chickadees, see Ficken and Witkin 1977; on red-breasted nuthatches, Templeton and Greene 2007; and on mockingbirds, Levey et al. 2009.

xxvii *tests measuring connectedness:* Weinstein, Przybylski, and Ryan 2009.

other such studies: These include Berman, Jonides, and Kaplan 2008; DeVries et al. 2003; Faber Taylor and Kuo 2009; and Hartig, Mang, and Evans 1991.

a "denatured" generation: Louv 2005.

1. A Cacophony of Harmony

1 *interpret five vocalizations:* The decision to use the "five vocalizations" terminology in this book is based on more than fifteen years of teaching deep bird language to thousands of birders and nonbirders across the globe. This is a pedagogical construct designed to help students of bird language comprehend and digest bird vocalizations in context. Note that this construct works best with passer-

ines (e.g., perching songbirds of the order *Passeriformes*), with the exception of the family Corvidae (jays, crows, ravens, magpies, and nutcrackers). Different species of passerines have different numbers of vocalizations. Sometimes the number even differs within an individual's own life span. More important, many birds we use as examples have graded vocalizations—that is, they make vocalizations that sound very similar but may vary in duration, intensity, pitch, intonation, or other features. Recent studies (Leavesley and Magrath 2005; Courter and Ritchison 2010) demonstrate that birds "encode" predator information (distance, size, speed, etc.) in their vocalizations and that other birds respond with the appropriate amount of urgency (consistent with the all-important conservation of energy). While graded calls may seem to complicate the five vocalizations construct, they actually fit well within its boundaries. For example, the *tut* of an American robin can fall into one of three categories—companion call, aggression, or alarm—depending on the context of the vocalization, most notably volume, frequency, and duration; body language; and position of the bird.

4 *Ravens preferentially associate:* Stahler, Heinrich, and Smith 2002.

7 *a roosting-time shout-out:* In some species, such as the American robin, many individuals, pairs, and/or families gather for a communal roost just before dark. This gathering is often accompanied by loud vocalizing and active body language.

the blackbird: The European blackbird (*Turdus merula*) is a close cousin of the North American robin (*Turdus migratorius*).

12 *"wake hunting":* This terminology was created by my bird language, tracking, and nature awareness colleagues and me. It is not a term you can Google (yet). The idea is that predators are smart opportunists that learn patterns and take advantage of feeding opportunities that result in prey capture with less effort (that is, distracted prey). Many of these examples may be new to readers. We encourage you to look for these phenomena on your own.

13 *Harris's hawks cooperate:* Coulson and Coulson 1995.

14 *one study of this behavior:* Kennedy and Stahlecker 1993.

18 *the inimitable mockingbird:* Selander and Hunter 1960.

2. In the Beginning Is the Song

20 *The hermit thrush:* See Kroodsma's (2005, 255–67) twelve-page discussion of the song of the hermit thrush.

A study reported: Marcus 2006; Gentner et al. 2006.

23 *fascinating studies have found:* Cristol and Johnsen 1994; Cristol 1995.

the most elaborate songs: A review of this hypothesis, complete with field experiments linking song complexity to reproductive success, can be found in Catchpole 1987.

male canaries actually grow: Nottebohm 1980.

25 *circling the perimeter:* Hofslund 1959.

26 *Like all the wrens:* Sibley 2001.

3. More Cacophony of Harmony

36 *Finding large flocks:* Morse 1970.

37 *One of my favorite birds:* The information regarding vocal and non-vocal communication in bobwhites can be found in Johnsgard 1974 and Stokes 1967.

46 *That's a lot of songbirds:* My personal observation of Cooper's hawk parents feeding adolescent birds to their young is not surprising. One study of Cooper's nests in the Ithaca, New York, region (Meng 1959) documented more than 260 prey items (more than 80 percent of which were birds) brought to the nest of four young hawks over the first six weeks of life. Other studies (e.g., Haskell 1994) have shown a positive relationship between begging and nest predation.

4. The Sit Spot

48 *A lot of careful research:* This research is summarized in Gladwell 2009.

49 *an alternative program:* This teen program was facilitated by the

Wilderness Awareness School of Duvall, Washington, and was known as the Community School.

55 *The body language:* Bent 1946.
   So has the blue jay: Cohen 1977.
57 *outgrown their sockets:* Lynch 2007.
67 *The order of birds:* Fernández-Juricic et al. 2004.
73 *the juncos were making:* Hostetter 1961; Pulliam et al. 1982.
76 *but he never did:* Young, Haas, and McGown 2010.
79 *the junco's modest* t-th!: Hostetter 1961.

5. An Alarm for Every Occasion

80 *alarm calls from the Pacific wrens:* Bent 1948.
86 *feeding their own young:* Meng 1959.
87 *the alarm call is phonetically:* Many birds use similar-sounding vocalizations; this is what ornithologists refer to as "graded" (Miller 1979).
89 *Its big alarm:* Mack and Yong 2000.
90 *Just short of this:* Marler and Slabbekoorn 2004.
91 *the robin has special alarm calls:* Howell 1942.
   Some nifty research: Gottfried, Andrews, and Haug 1985.
96 *geese are like juncos:* Whitford, 1987.
97 *the towhee might simply pause:* Long stoppages may be an indicator of a state of alarm (Orians and Christman 1968), and resumption of said maintenance behavior may indicate that "all's well" (Sullivan 1984).
98 *a dog tearing out the door:* Miller et al. 2001.

6. They're All in This Together

100 *enough experiments prove:* Interspecies, intergenus, interfamily, inter-order, and even interclass eavesdropping has been demonstrated with a wide variety of organisms. Examples include anurans (frogs), Phelps et al. 2007; chipmunks, Schmidt et al. 2008; and primates, Schel et al. 2010.

Arabian babblers: On the context-specific alarms of Arabian bab-
blers, see Naguib et al. 1999; on crows, Brown 1985; on magpies,
Stone and Trost 1991; on quail, Johnsgard 1974; and on robins,
Gottfried, Andrews, and Haug 1985.

101 *Squirrels, gerbils:* On the context-specific alarms of squirrels, see
Greene and Meagher 1998; on gerbils, Randall and McCowan
2005; on prairie dogs, Slobodchikoff et al. 1991; on vervet and Diana monkeys, Zuberbuhler et al. 1997 and Seyfarth 1980; and on
baboons, Fischer et al. 2001.

red-breasted nuthatches understand: Templeton and Greene 2007.

the more dees*:* Templeton et al. 2005.

102 *chickadees apparently know:* Zachau 2011.

Monkeys and hornbills: Rainey et al. 2004.

Yellow-bellied marmots: Shriner 1998.

chipmunks listen: Schmidt et al. 2008.

There are studies on this point: On interspecies communication between squirrels, chipmunks, and birds, see Randler 2006b; Schmidt
et al. 2008; Randler 2006a; Goodale and Kotagama 2005; and
Goodale and Kotagama 2006.

103 *Studies on interclass communication:* Aschemeier and Maher 2011;
Rainey et al. 2004.

hitch rides: Dean and MacDonald 1981.

104 *When anecdotal word:* On the UCLA study, see Lea et al. 2008.

research on monkeys and baboons: Seyfarth and Cheney 2006.

105 *Many tightly controlled studies:* Balda and Kamil 1992; Bednekoff et
al. 1997; Raby and Clayton 2010.

106 *culled as ruthlessly:* Leech and Leonard 1997; Tozier et al. 2009.

107 *The prey species listen:* A classic example that illustrates this is
the practice of "pishing" by birders. Many birders mimic passerine alarm calls vocally in order to get otherwise reclusive birds to
show themselves (Langham et al. 2006).

The predator species also listen: Mosher, Fuller, and Kopeny 1990.

wake hunting: The concept that wildlife will take advantage of
specific situations that are advantageous for acquiring food is not
new. Examples in the literature include marsh hawks on a military

bombing range, Jackson and Sehardien 1977; seabirds hunting over tuna and dolphins, Au and Pitman 1986; coyotes hanging around badgers hunting ground squirrels, Minta et al. 1992; and arctic foxes scent tracking to polar bear prey sites, Anderborn et al. 2003.

109 *songbirds differentiate:* Templeton et al. 2005; Gyger et al. 1987.

112 *Alarms for the land-based predators:* "Localized" refers to the geographic spread of the alarm (a smaller "concentric ring"). Most likely this can be attributed to the urgency with which birds must react to adept aerial predators (such as hawks) versus less speedy land mammals and reptiles. Predators that require an urgent response elicit louder alarms in many species (Manser 2001).

115 *Some birds are simply:* Blumstein et al. 2005.

117 *almost always identifies:* Jones et al. 2007.

7. A Shape for Every Occasion

121 *abrupt, heedless, uncaring entry:* Studies show that previously believed "low-impact" behaviors such as ecotourism and bird watching can have a detrimental effect on the success rates of breeding birds. Many species of birds simply do not habituate to humans in their habitats (Burger and Gochfeld 1991; Fernández-Juricic, Jimenez, and Lucas 2001; Mullner, Lunsenmair, and Wikelski 2004).

122 *"They're always sitting":* Fernández-Juricic, Jimenez, and Lucas 2001; Cresswell et al. 2003.

123 *sentinels post up everywhere:* Wright et al. 2001.

Birds I would count: On mockingbirds, see Burhans 2000. On the Florida scrub-jay, see McGowan and Woolfenden 1989.

125 *quail are excellent sentinels:* Lott and Mastrup 1999.

127 *an as yet unobserved behavior:* This anecdote, of a Carolina wren (*Thryothorus ludovicianus*), cannot be confirmed in the current scientific literature. However, very similar behaviors by other species of songbirds (some wrens) have been documented, including the splendid fairy-wren (Greig and Pruett-Jones 2009), skylark (Cresswell 1994), and eastern towhee (Richards 1981).

128 *a graduate student:* Yorzinski and Patricelli 2010.

Other studies followed: On acoustic directionality, see Collier et al. 2010 and Brumm, Robertson, and Nemeth 2011.

129 *Most of our best allies:* Blumstein 2003.

135 *Such a highly energized:* Altmann 1956; Gottfried, Andrews, and Haug 1985; Gottfried 1979; Stake et al. 2005.

137 *Even more than:* Bent 1946; Kilham 1989; Andren 1992; Chalfoun, Thompson, and Ratnaswamy 2002; Angelstam 1986.

138 *The corvids don't have:* Brown 1964; Kennedy and Stahlecker 1993; Hope 1980.

140 *the crows never forgot:* On individual recognition by songbirds, see Heinrich 1991 and Levey et al. 2009.

147 *a sharp-shinned hawk cruising:* For an example of a goshawk using this behavior, see Rutz 2006.

148 *dropping into thickets:* Using gravity to evade aerial predators attacking from above is not limited to songbirds but extends to primates as well (Lenz and Dos Reis 2011).

152 *use the house for cover:* Many raptors, especially accipiters, practice "fast contour-hugging flights": they travel at high speeds, usually below canopy/rooftop level, flying close to structures (trees, cars, fences, etc.) to conceal themselves from their prey until the very last moment (Fox 1981).

154 *This particular cacophony:* Similar predator-elicited "breaks" in critical vocalizations (such as song) have also been documented in singing insects (Faure and Hoy 2000).

156 *the birds' use of us:* Prey species using humans to avoid their predators has been documented in many groups of animals (Berger 2007). Examples include the gelada baboon and spotted hyena (Kummer 1995), axis deer and tiger (Sunquist and Sunquist 1989), and vervet monkey and leopard (Isbell 1990).

157 *In suburban mountain lion territory:* For relevant research on the "ecology of fear," see Brown, Laundré, and Gurung 1999 and Altendorf et al. 2001. For studies on "mesopredator release," see Courchamp, Langlais, and Sugihara 1999.

This phenomenon has been: On smaller, more timid birds, such as hummingbirds, nesting close to raptors—specifically, black-chinned hummingbirds and Cooper's hawks—see Greeney and Weithington 2009. On curlews and kestrels, see Norrdahl et al. 1995. On wood pigeons and hobby falcons, see Bogliani, Sergio, and Tavecchia 1999.

8. From Collision to Connection

165 *I can hear this deer:* On listening to the alarm calls of birds, see Riney 1951.

167 *The title of the second:* Fernández-Juricic et al. 2004.

The first article: Fernández-Juricic, Jimenez, and Lucas 2001.

170 *"jungle etiquette":* Kipling 1968.

173 *one experiment has confirmed:* Levey et al. 2009.

The types of birds seen: A strong connection to many bird species includes a deep understanding of their natural history and behavior. This allows one to make fairly accurate predictions of nearby habitats, food sources, predators, and so on. This skill is sometimes known as "predictive tracking."

178 *One of the geese:* The social dynamics (flock behavior) of Canada geese in alarm situations can be found in Whitford 1998 and Bartelt 1987.

182 *the 2009 study:* Weinstein, Przybylski, and Ryan 2009.

REFERENCES

Altendorf, Kelly B., John W. Laundré, Carlos A. López González, and Joel S. Brown. 2001. "Assessing Effects of Predation Risk on Foraging Behavior of Mule Deer." *Journal of Mammalogy* 82 (2): 430–39.

Altmann, Stuart. 1956. "Avian Mobbing Behavior and Predator Recognition." *Condor* 58 (4): 241–53.

American Ornithologists' Union. 1998. *AOU Check-list of North American Birds*. 7th ed. Washington, DC: AOU.

Anderborn, A., et al. 2003. "Arctic Fox." In *Canid Action Plan*, edited by D. W. MacDonald and C. Sillero-Zubiri. Gland, Switzerland: International Union for Conservation of Nature.

Andren, Henrik. 1992. "Corvid Density and Nest Predation in Relation to Forest Fragmentation: A Landscape Perspective." *Ecology* 73:794–804.

Angelstam, P. 1986. "Predation on Ground-Nesting Birds' Nests in Relation to Predator Densities and Habitat Edge." *Oikos* 47:365–73.

Aschemeier, L. M., and Christine R. Maher. 2011. "Eavesdropping of Woodchucks (*Marmota monax*) and Eastern Chipmunks (*Tamias striatus*) on Heterospecific Alarm Calls." *Journal of Mammalogy* 92 (3): 493–99.

Au, D.W.K., and R. L. Pitman. 1986. "Seabird Interactions with Dolphins and Tuna in the Eastern Tropical Pacific." *Condor* 88:304–17.

Balda, R. P., and A. C. Kamil. 1992. "Long-Term Spatial Memory in Clark's Nutcracker, *Nucifraga columbiana*." *Animal Behaviour* 44 (4): 761–69.

Bartelt, G. A. 1987. "Effects of Disturbance and Hunting on the Behavior of Canada Goose Family Groups in East Central Wisconsin." *Journal of Wildlife Management* 51:517–22.

Bednekoff P. A., R. P. Balda, A. C. Kamil, and A. G. Hile. 1997. "Long-Term Spatial Memory in Four Seed-Caching Corvid Species." *Animal Behaviour* 53 (2): 335–41.

Bent, A. C. 1946. *Life Histories of North American Jays, Crows and Titmice, Order Passeriformes.* United States National Museum Bulletin 191. Washington, DC: U.S. Government Printing Office.

———. 1948. *Life Histories of North American Nuthatches, Wrens, Thrashers, and Their Allies.* United States National Museum Bulletin 195. Washington, DC: U.S. Government Printing Office.

Bergen, Molly. 2009. "In Botswana, Merging Tradition and Technology." *Conservation International,* October 6 (online edition).

Berger, J. 2007. "Fear, Human Shields and the Redistribution of Prey and Predators in Protected Areas." *Biology Letters* 3:620–23.

Berman, M., J. Jonides, and S. Kaplan. 2008. "The Cognitive Benefits of Interacting with Nature." *Psychological Science* 19 (12): 1207–12.

Blumstein, D. T. 2003. "Flight Initiation Distance in Birds Is Dependent on Intruder Starting Distance." *Journal of Wildlife Management* 67:852–57.

Blumstein, Daniel T., et al. 2005. "Inter-specific Variation in Avian Responses to Human Disturbance." *Journal of Applied Ecology* 42:943–53.

Bogliani, G., F. Sergio, and G. Tavecchia. 1999. "Wood Pigeons Nesting in Association with Hobby Falcons: Advantages and Choice Rules." *Animal Behavior* 57:125–31.

Brown, E. D. 1985. "Social Relationships as a Variable Affecting Responses to Mobbing and Alarm Calls of Common Crows (*Corvus brachyrhynchos*)." *Zeitschrift für Tierpsychologie* 70:45–52.

Brown, J. L. 1964. *The Integration of Agonistic Behavior in the Steller's Jay,* Cyanocitta stelleri *(Gmelin).* University of California Publications in Zoology 60. Berkeley: University of California Press.

Brown, Joel S., John W. Laundré, and Mahesh Gurung. 1999. "The Ecology of Fear: Optimal Foraging, Game Theory, and Trophic Interactions." *Journal of Mammalogy* 80 (2): 385–99.

Brumm, H., K. A. Robertson, and E. Nemeth. 2011. "Singing Direction as a Tool to Investigate the Function of Birdsong: An Experiment on Sedge Warblers." *Animal Behaviour* 81:653–59.

Burger, J., and M. Gochfeld. 1991. "Human Distance and Birds: Tolerance and Response Distances of Resident and Migrant Species in India." *Environmental Conservation* 18:158–65.

Burhans, Dirk E. 2000. "Scanning Behavior by Wintering Northern Mockingbirds." *Florida Field Naturalist* 28 (2): 41–49.

Catchpole, Clive C. 1987. "Bird Song, Sexual Selection and Female Choice." *Trends in Ecology and Evolution* 2 (4): 94–97.

Chalfoun A. D., F. R. Thompson, and M. J. Ratnaswamy. 2002. "Nest Predators and Fragmentation: A Review and Meta-analysis." *Conservation Biology* 16:306–18.

Cohen, S. M. 1977. "Blue Jay Vocal Behavior." Ph.D. diss., University of Michigan, Ann Arbor.

Collier, T. C., D. T. Blumstein, L. Girod, and C. E. Taylor. 2010. "Is Alarm Calling Risky? Marmots Avoid Calling from Risky Places." *Ethology* 166:1171–78.

Coulson, Jennifer O., and Thomas D. Coulson. 1995. "Group Hunting by Harris' Hawks in Texas." *Journal of Raptor Research* 29 (4): 265–67.

Courchamp, Franck, Michel Langlais, and George Sugihara. 1999. "Cats Protecting Birds: Modelling the Mesopredator Release Effect." *Journal of Animal Ecology* 68 (2): 282–92.

Courter, Jason R., and Gary Ritchison. 2010. "Alarm Calls of Tufted Titmice Convey Information About Predator Size and Threat." *Behavioral Ecology* 21 (5): 936–42.

Cresswell, W. 1994. "Song as a Pursuit-Deterrent Signal, and Its Occurrence Relative to Other Anti-predation Behaviors of Skylark (*Alauda arvensis*) on Attack by Merlins (*Falco columbarius*)." *Behavioral Ecology and Sociobiology* 34:217–23.

Cresswell, W., J. L. Quinn, M. J. Whittingham, and S. Butler. 2003. "Good Foragers Can Also Be Good at Detecting Predators." *Proceedings of the Royal Society of Biological Sciences* 270:1069–76.

Cristol, D. A. 1995. "Early Arrival, Initiation of Nesting, and Social Status: An Experimental Study of Breeding Female Red-winged Blackbirds." *Behavioral Ecology* 6:87–93.

Cristol, Daniel A., and Torgeir S. Johnsen. 1994. "Spring Arrival, Aggression and Testosterone in Female Red-winged Blackbirds (*Agelaius phoeniceus*)." *Auk* 111 (1): 210–14.

Dean, W.R.J., and I.A.W. MacDonald. 1981. "A Review of African Birds Feeding in Association with Mammals." *Ostrich: Journal of African Ornithology* 52 (3): 135–55.

DeVries, S., R. Verheij, P. P. Groenewegen, and P. Spreeuwenberg. 2003. "Natural Environments—Healthy Environments? An Exploratory Analysis of the Relationship Between Greenspace and Health." *Environment and Planning* 35 (10): 1717–32.

Faber Taylor, A. F., and F. Kuo. 2009. "Children with Attention Deficits Concentrate Better After Walk in the Park." *Journal of Attention Disorders* 12 (5): 402.

Faure P. A., and R. R. Hoy. 2000. "The Sounds of Silence: Cessation of Singing and Song Pausing Are Ultrasound-Induced Acoustic Startle Behaviors in the Katydid *Neoconocephalus ensiger* (Orthoptera; Tettigoniidae)." *Journal of Comparative Physiology A: Neuroethology* 186:129–42.

Fernández-Juricic, Esteban, et al. 2004. "Spatial and Temporal Responses of Forest Birds to Human Approaches in a Protected Area and Implications for Two Management Strategies." *Biological Conservation* 117 (4): 407–16.

Fernández-Juricic, E., M. D. Jimenez, and E. Lucas. 2001. "Alert Distances as an Alternative Measure of Bird Tolerance to Human Disturbance: Implications for Park Design." *Environmental Conservation* 28:263–69.

Ficken, M., and S. Witkin. 1977. "Responses of Black-capped Chickadee Flocks to Predators." *Auk* 94:156–57.

Fischer, Julia, et al. 2001. "Baboon Responses to Graded Bark Variants." *Animal Behaviour* 61 (5): 925–31.

Fox, N. 1981. "The Hunting Behaviour of Trained Northern Goshawks." In *Understanding the Goshawk*, edited by R. E. Kenward and I. M. Lindsay, 121–33. Oxford, UK: International Association of Falconry and Conservation of Birds of Prey.

Gentner, Timothy Q., Kimberly M. Fenn, Daniel Margoliash, and Howard C. Nusbaum. 2006. "Recursive Syntactic Pattern Learning by Songbirds." *Nature* 440 (27): 1204–7.

Gladwell, Malcolm. 2005. *Blink: The Power of Thinking Without Thinking*. Boston: Little, Brown.

———. 2008. *Outliers: The Story of Success*. Boston: Little, Brown.

———. 2009. "How David Beats Goliath: When Underdogs Break the Rules." *The New Yorker*, May 11.

Goodale E., and S. W. Kotagama. 2005. "Testing the Role of Species in Mixed-Species Bird Flocks of a Sri Lankan Rain Forest." *Journal of Tropical Ecology* 21:669–76.

———. 2006. "Vocal Mimicry by a Passerine Bird Attracts Other Species Involved in Mixed-Species Flocks." *Animal Behaviour* 72 (2): 471–77.

Gottfried, Bradley M. 1979. "Anti-predator Aggression in Birds Nesting in Old Field Habitats: An Experimental Analysis." *Condor* 81 (3): 251–57.

Gottfried, B. M., K. Andrews, and M. Haug. 1985. "Breeding Robins and Nest Predators: Effect of Predator Type and Defense Strategy on Initial Vocalization Patterns." *Wilson Bulletin* 97:183–90.

Greene, Erick, and Tom Meagher. 1998. "Red Squirrels, *Tamiasciurus hudsonicus*, Produce Predator-Class Specific Alarm Calls." *Animal Behaviour* 55 (3): 511–18.

Greeney, Harold F., and Susan M. Weithington. 2009. "Proximity to Active Accipiter Nest Reduces Nest Predation of Black-chinned Hummingbirds." *Wilson Journal of Ornithology* 121 (4): 809–12.

Greig, E., and S. Pruett-Jones. 2009. "A Predator-Elicited Song in the Splendid Fairy-wren: Warning Signal or Intraspecific Display?" *Animal Behaviour* 78:45–52.

Gross, A. O. 1923. "The Black-crowned Night Heron (*Nycticorax nycticorax naevius*) of Sandy Neck." *Auk* 40:1–30.

Gyger, M., et al. 1987. "Semantics of an Avian Alarm Call System: The Male Domestic Fowl, *G. domesticus*." *Behaviour* 102:15–40.

Hartig, T., M. Mang, and G. W. Evans. 1991. "Restorative Effects of Natural Environment Experiences." *Environment and Behavior* 23 (1): 3.

Haskell, D. G. 1994. "Experimental Evidence That Nestling Begging Behaviour Incurs a Cost Due to Nest Predation." *Proceedings of the Royal Society of Biological Sciences* 257 (1349): 161–64.

Heinrich, Bernd. 1991. *Ravens in Winter*. New York: Vintage Books.

Hofslund, P. B. 1959. "A Life History Study of the Yellowthroat, *Geo-*

thlypis trichas." *Proceedings of the Minnesota Academy of Sciences* 271:144–74.

Hope, Sylvia. 1980. "Call Form in Relation to Function in the Steller's Jay." *American Naturalist* 116 (6): 788–820.

Hostetter, D. R. 1961. "Life History of the Carolina Junco, *Junco hyemalis carolinensis* Brewster." *Raven* 32:97–170.

Howell, J. C. 1942. "Notes on the Nesting Habits of the American Robin (*Turdus migratorius* L.)." *American Midland Naturalist* 28:529–603.

Isbell, L. A. 1990. "Sudden Short-Term Increase in Mortality of Vervet Monkeys (*Cercopithecus aethiops*) due to Leopard Predation in Amboseli National Park, Kenya." *American Journal of Primatology* 21:41–52.

Jackson, J. A., and B. J. Sehardien. 1977. "Opportunistic Hunting of a Marsh Hawk on a Bombing Range." *Raptor Research* 11 (4): 86.

Johnsgard, Paul A. 1974. "Quail Music: The Complex Calls of a Bird Contain Clues to Its Evolution." *Natural History* 83 (3): 34–40.

Jones, K. A., et al. 2007. "Vigilance in the Third Dimension: Head Movement, Not Scan Duration Varies in Response to Different Predator Models." *Animal Behaviour* 74:1181–87.

Kennedy, P. L., and D. W. Stahlecker. 1993. "Responsiveness of Nesting Northern Goshawks to Taped Broadcasts of 3 Conspecific Calls." *Journal of Wildlife Management* 57:249–57.

Kilham, L. 1989. *The American Crow and the Common Raven.* College Station: Texas A&M University Press.

Kipling, Rudyard. 1968. *The Jungle Book.* Santa Rosa, CA: Classics Press.

Kroodsma, Donald. 2005. *The Singing Life of Birds: The Art and Science of Listening to Birdsong.* New York: Houghton Mifflin.

Kummer, H. 1995. *Quest of the Sacred Baboon.* Princeton, NJ: Princeton University Press.

Langham, Gary M., et al. 2006. "Why Pishing Works: Titmouse (Paridae) Scolds Elicit a Generalized Response in Bird Communities." *Ecoscience* 13 (4): 485–96.

Lea, Amanda J., June Barrera, Lauren M. Tom, and Daniel T. Blumstein. 2008. "Heterospecific Eavesdropping in a Nonsocial Species." *Behavioral Ecology* 19 (5): 1041–46.

Leavesley, A. J., and R. D. Magrath. 2005. "Communicating About Danger: Urgency Alarm Calling in a Bird." *Animal Behaviour* 70:365–73.

Leech, S. L., and M. L. Leonard. 1997. "Begging and the Risk of Predation in Nestling Birds." *Behavioral Ecology* 8 (6): 644–46.

Lenz, B. B., and A. M. Dos Reis. 2011. "Harpy Eagle–Primate Interactions in the Central Amazon." *Wilson Journal of Ornithology* 123 (2): 404–8.

Levey, D. L., et al. 2009. "Urban Mockingbirds Quickly Learn to Identify Individual Humans." *Proceedings of the National Academy of Sciences* 106 (22): 8959–62.

Liebenberg, Louis. 1990. *The Art of Tracking: The Origin of Science.* Cape Town: David Phillip.

Lorenz, Konrad. 1997. *King Solomon's Ring: New Light on Animal Ways.* New York: Penguin Books.

Lott, Dale F., and Sonke N. A. Mastrup. 1999. "Facultative Communal Brood Rearing in California Quail." *Condor* 101 (3): 678–81.

Louv, Richard. 2005. *Last Child in the Woods: Saving Our Children from Nature-Deficit Disorder.* Chapel Hill, NC: Algonquin Books.

Lynch, Wayne. 2007. *Owls of the United States and Canada: A Complete Guide to Their Biology and Behavior.* Baltimore: Johns Hopkins University Press.

Mack, D. E., and W. Yong. 2000. "Swainson's Thrush: *Catharus ustulatus.*" In *The Birds of North America,* edited by A. Poole and F. Gill, 540. Philadelphia: Birds of North America.

Manser, M. B. 2001. "The Acoustic Structure of Suricates' Alarm Calls Varies with Predator Type and the Level of Response Urgency." *Proceedings of the Royal Society of Biological Sciences* 268:2315–24.

Marcus, G. 2006. "Startling Starlings." *Nature* 440:1117–18.

Marler, Peter, and Hans Slabbekoorn. 2004. *Nature's Music: The Science of Birdsong.* San Diego: Elsevier Academic Press.

McGowan, K. J., and G. E. Woolfenden. 1989. "A Sentinel System in the Florida Scrub Jay." *Animal Behaviour* 37:1000–1006.

Meng, Heinz K. 1959. "Food Habits of Nesting Cooper's Hawks and Goshawks in New York and Pennsylvania." *Wilson Bulletin* 71 (2): 169–74.

Miller, E. H. 1979. "An Approach to the Analysis of Graded Vocalizations of Birds." *Behavioral Neural Biology* 27:25–38.

Miller, Scott G., et al. 2001. "Wildlife Responses to Pedestrians and Dogs." *Wildlife Society Bulletin* 29 (1): 124–32.

Minta, S. C., et al. 1992. "Hunting Associations Between Badgers (*Taxidea taxus*) and Coyotes (*Canis latrans*)." *Journal of Mammalogy* 73 (4): 814–20.

Morse, Douglass H. 1970. "Ecological Aspects of Some Mixed-Species Foraging Flocks of Birds." *Ecological Monographs* 40 (1): 119–68.

Mosher, J. A., M. R. Fuller, and A. M. Kopeny. 1990. "Surveying Woodland Raptors by Broadcast of Conspecific Vocalizations." *Journal of Field Ornithology* 61:453–61.

Mullner, A., K. E. Lunsenmair, and M. Wikelski. 2004. "Exposure to Ecotourism Reduces Survival and Affects Stress Response in Hoatzin Chicks (*Opisthocomus hoazin*)." *Biological Conservation* 118 (4): 549–58.

Naguib, M., R. Mundry, R. Ostreiher, H. Hultsch, L. Schrader, and D. Todt. 1999. "Cooperatively Breeding Arabian Babblers Call Differently When Mobbing in Different Predator-Induced Situations." *Behavioral Ecology* 10:636–40.

Norrdahl, K., J. Suhonen, O. Hemminki, and E. Korpima. 1995. "Predator Presence May Benefit: Kestrels Protect Curlew Nests Against Nest Predators." *Oecologia* 101:105–9.

Nottebohm, Fernando. 1980. "Testosterone Triggers Growth of Brain Vocal Control Nuclei in Adult Female Canaries." *Brain Research* 189 (2): 429–36.

Orians, G. H., and G. M. Christman. 1968. "A Comparative Study of the Behavior of Red-winged, Tri-colored, and Yellow-headed Blackbirds." *University of California Publications in Zoology* 84:1–81.

Orians, G. H., and J. H. Heerwagen. 1992. "Evolved Responses to Landscapes." In *The Adapted Mind*, edited by J. H. Barkow, L. Cosmides, and J. Tooby, 555–79. Oxford: Oxford University Press.

Phelps, Steven M., et al. 2007. "The Mixed-Species Chorus as Public Information: Túngara Frogs Eavesdrop on a Heterospecific." *Behavioral Ecology* 18 (1): 108–14.

Pulliam, H. R., et al. 1982. "The Scanning Behavior of Juncos: A Game-Theoretical Approach." *Journal of Theoretical Biology* 95:89–103.

Raby, C. R., and N. S. Clayton. 2010. "The Cognition of Caching and

Recovery in Food-Storing Birds." *Advances in the Study of Behavior* 41:1–34.

Rainey, Hugo J., et al. 2004. "Hornbills Can Distinguish Between Primate Alarm Calls." *Proceedings of the Royal Society of Biological Sciences* 271 (1540): 755–59.

Randall, Jan A., and Brenda McCowan. 2005. "Alarm Signals of the Great Gerbil: Acoustic Variation by Predator Context, Sex, Age, Individual, and Family Group." *Journal of Acoustical Society of America* 118 (4): 2706–14.

Randler, C. 2006a. "Anti-predator Response of Eurasian Red Squirrels (*Sciurus vulgaris*) to Predator Calls of Tawny Owls (*Strix aluco*)." *Zeitschrift für Saugetierkunde* 71:315–18.

———. 2006b. "Red Squirrels (*Sciurus vulgaris*) Respond to Alarm Calls of Eurasian Jays (*Garrulus glandarius*)." *Ethology* 112 (4): 411–16.

Richards, D. G. 1981. "Alerting and Message Components in Songs of Rufous-sided Towhees." *Behaviour* 76:223–49.

Riney, Thane. 1951. "Relationships Between Birds and Deer." *Condor* 53 (4): 178–85.

Rutz, C. 2006. "Home-Range Size, Habitat Use, Activity Patterns and Hunting Behaviour of Urban-Breeding Northern Goshawks, *Accipiter gentilis*." *Ardea* 94:185–202.

Schel, Anne Marijke, et al. 2010. "Predator-Deterring Alarm Call Sequences in Guereza Colobus Monkeys Are Meaningful to Conspecifics." 2010. *Animal Behaviour* 80 (5): 799–808.

Schmidt, Kenneth, et al. 2008. "Eastern Chipmunks Increase Their Perception of Predation Risk in Response to Titmouse Alarm Calls." *Behavioral Ecology* 19 (4): 759–63.

ScienceDaily. 2007. "Eavesdropping Nuthatches Appear to Understand Chickadees in Distress." ScienceDaily, March 19.

Selander, R. K., and D. K. Hunter. 1960. "On the Functions of Wing-Flashing in Mockingbirds." *Wilson Bulletin* 72:341–45.

Seyfarth, R. M. 1980. "Monkey Responses to Three Different Alarm Calls: Evidence of Predator Classification and Semantic Communication." *Science* 210 (4471): 801–3.

Seyfarth, R. M., and D. L. Cheney. 2006. "Meaning and Emotion in Animal Vocalizations." In "Emotions Inside Out: 130 Years After Darwin's 'The Expression of the Emotions in Man and Animals,'" edited by P. Ekman, J. J. Campos, R. J. Davidson, and F. de Waal. Special Issue. *Annals of the New York Academy of Sciences* 1000:32–55.

Shriner, W.M.K.E.E. 1998. "Yellow-bellied Marmot and Golden-mantled Ground Squirrel Responses to Heterospecific Alarm Calls." *Animal Behaviour* 55:529–36.

Sibley, David Allen. 2000. *The Sibley Guide to Birds.* New York: Alfred A. Knopf.

———. 2001. *The Sibley Guide to Bird Life and Behavior.* New York: Alfred A. Knopf.

Skutch, Alexander. 1997. *The Minds of Birds.* College Station: Texas A&M University Press.

Slobodchikoff, C. N., et al. 1991. "Semantic Information Distinguishing Individual Predators in the Alarm Calls of Gunnison's Prairie Dogs." *Animal Behaviour* 42 (2): 713–19.

Stahler, Daniel, Bernd Heinrich, and Douglas Smith. 2002. "Common Ravens, *Corvus corax,* Preferentially Associate with Grey Wolves, *Canis lupus,* as a Foraging Strategy in Winter." *Animal Behaviour* 64 (2): 283–90.

Stake, Mike M., et al. 2005. "Patterns of Snake Predation at Songbird Nests in Missouri and Texas." *Journal of Herpetology* 39 (2): 215–22.

Stokes, A. W. 1967. "Behavior of the Bobwhite, *Colinus virginianus.*" *Auk* 84:1–33.

Stone, Eric, and E. H. Trost. 1991. "Predators, Risks and Context for Mobbing and Alarm Calls in Black-billed Magpies." *Animal Behaviour* 41 (4): 633–38.

Sullivan, K. A. 1984. "Information Exploitation by Downy Woodpeckers in Mixed-Species Flocks." *Behaviour* 91:294–311.

Sunquist, F., and M. E. Sunquist. 1989. *Tiger Moon: Tracking the Great Cats in Nepal.* Chicago: University of Chicago Press.

Templeton, C. N., and Erick Greene. 2007. "Nuthatches Eavesdrop on Variations in Heterospecific Chickadee Mobbing Alarm Calls." *Proceedings of the National Academy of Sciences* 104 (13): 5479–82.

Templeton, C. N., et al. 2005. "Allometry of Alarm Calls: Black-capped Chickadees Encode Information About Predator Size." *Science* 308 (5730): 1934–37.

Tozier, D. C., E. Nol, D. M. Burke, K. A. Eliot, and K. A. Falk. 2009. "Predation by Bears on Woodpecker Nests: Are Nestling Begging and Habitat Choice Risky Business?" *Auk* 126 (2): 300–309.

Vanderhoff, E. Natasha, and Perri K. Eason. 2009. "American Robin *Seet* Calls: Aerial Alarm or a Contact Call?" *Wilson Journal of Ornithology* 121 (2): 406–11.

Weinstein, Netta, Andrew K. Przybylski, and Richard M. Ryan. 2009. "Can Nature Make Us More Caring? Effects of Immersion in Nature on Intrinsic Aspirations and Generosity." *Personality and Social Psychology Bulletin* 35 (10): 1315–29.

Whitford, P. C. 1987. "Vocal and Visual Communication and Other Social Behavior in Canada Geese." Ph.D. diss., University of Wisconsin, Milwaukee.

———. 1998. "Vocal and Visual Communication of Giant Canada Geese." In *Biology and Management of Canada Geese*, edited by D. H. Rusch, M. D. Samuel, D. D. Humburg, and B. D. Sullivan, 375–86. Proceedings of the International Canada Goose Symposium, Milwaukee, WI.

Wright, Jonathan, Elena Berg, Selvino R. DeKort, Vladimir Khazin, and Alexi A. Makalakov. 2001. "Cooperative Sentinel Behavior in the Arabian Babbler." *Animal Behaviour* 62:973–79.

Yorzinski, J. L., and G. L. Patricelli. 2010. "Birds Adjust Acoustic Directionality to Beam Their Antipredator Calls to Predators and Conspecifics." *Proceedings of the Royal Society of Biological Sciences* 277 (1683): 923–32.

Young, Jon, E. Haas, and E. McGown. 2010. *Coyote's Guide to Connecting with Nature*. Shelton, WA: Owlink Media.

Young, Jon, and Tiffany Morgan. 2007. *Animal Tracking Basics*. Mechanicsburg, PA: Stackpole Books.

Zachau, C. E. 2011. "Alarm Calling in the Context of Flying Predator Stimuli: A Field Study of Carolina Chickadees (*Poecile carolinensis*)." Master's thesis, University of Tennessee, Knoxville.

Zuberbuhler, K., et al. 1997. "Diana Monkey Long-Distance Calls: Messages for Conspecifics and Predators. *Animal Behaviour* 53 (3): 589–604.

INDEX

Page numbers in *italic* type refer to illustrations.

baseline behavior
  alarms and, 87
  body language and, 17–18
  as daily routine, 8–9
  energy conservation and, 9–17
  in generic mixed-forest habitat, 3–8
  human intrusion and, 64, 65, 66
  introduction to, 1–3
  song and, 22
  as species specific, 15
  territory and, 22
  See also adolescent begging;
    companion/contact calls;
    songs; territorial aggression; wake hunting
bears, 40–41, 213n
Behavioral Ecology, 104
Bewick's wrens
  alarms and, 80, 159
  companion/contact calls of, 30
  recordings of voices of, 200
  song of, 21
  territorial aggression and, 42
biking, 62
binoculars, 55–56
Biological Conservation, 167
bird counts, xiii–xiv
bird language
  baseline behavior and, 2
  bird watching and, xviii–xix
  codification of, 78
  empathy and, xxvi–xxviii
  human intrusion and, 169
  interpretation, as skill set, 207n
  jungle etiquette and, 51
  learning, 7, 183–98
  meaning in, xvii

San Bushmen and, xxv–xxvi
  science and, xxi–xxv
  stories of, xx
  training, 60
  types of vocalizations in, 1
  understanding vs. translating, 38
  See also adolescent begging;
    alarms; companion/
    contact calls; deep bird
    language; sit spots; songs;
    territorial aggression;
    territory
bird plow
  alarm shapes and, 132, 133–34,
    144, 145, 147, 156
  bird language and, 173, 174
  human intrusion as cause of, 169
  red-alert, 164
  sit spots and, 51, 64, 65, 67, 68, 75
  two-minute alarm drill and,
    170–71, 175, 175
  See also bird plow alarm shape
bird plow alarm shape, 109, 119–21,
    120, 166
bird whisperers, xix
black-billed magpies, 101, 205
blackbirds
  alarms and, 107, 109, 110, 111,
    116, 154, 159
  baseline behavior of, 7
  companion/contact calls of, 30
  recordings of voices of, 201
  as songbirds, 19
  songs of, 23, 159
  territory and, 25
black-capped chickadees, xxvi, 36,
    50, 101, 203, 208n
black-chinned hummingbirds, 215n

black-headed grosbeaks, 27

black-tailed prairie dogs, 101, 206

black-throated green warblers, 27, 114

Blink: The Power of Thinking Without Thinking (Gladwell), xix–xx

blue jays, 55, 136, 137, 205

bobcats, 99, 108, 111, 112, 125, 132, 142, 144–45

bobwhites, 210n

body language

alarms and, 88, 89, 97, 103, 108, 113, 172

as baseline behavior, 18

camouflage and, 169

communal roosts and, 209n

human intrusion and, 172, 173, 174

in learning bird language, 191

in sit spots, 197

vocalizations and, 209n

Botswana, xxii–xxiii

Brigantine National Wildlife Refuge, xiii–xiv

broad-winged hawks, 109–10

Brown, Tom, Jr.

background of, 207–8n

on baseline behavior, 2

on birds and our attitude, xxvii

on "concentric rings," 173

introduction to, xx

learning about birds with, 29, 56, 66, 151

on "sacred question" teaching tool, 50

sit spots and, 72, 75, 77, 78

walking style taught by, 61

bullet alarm shape, 145–47, *145*, 159

Bushmen. *See* San Bushmen

Butch Cassidy and the Sundance Kid (film), xxiii

buteos, 109–10, 145, 153, 154

California

hawks in, 152, 154, 160

jays imitating hawk calls in, 14

mentoring center in, xv

quail in, 125

robins in, 41

sit spots in, 54

thrushes in, 3

tracking in, 144

training in, 49

wrentits in, 158

See also Santa Cruz Mountains

California quail, 37, 125, 160, 204

California towhees, 7

camouflage, 168–69

Canada geese, 95–96, 177–79, 198

canaries, 23–24

Cape May, 20

cardinals

alarms and, 87–88, 90–91, 110, 111, 136, 149–51

companion/contact calls of, 31–34

as one of "top-five" birds to study, 187

as songbirds, 19

territory and, 25

vocalizations of, 149, 199, 201–2

Carolina wrens

alarms and, 80, 88, 125–27, 135, 213n

companion/contact calls of, 30

Lorenz, Konrad, xxvi
Louv, Richard, xxviii

magpies, 100–1, 137, 205, 209n, 212n
maintenance behavior. *See* baseline behavior
mammals
    observing/learning about, 196
    recordings of voices of, 205–6
Mammal Tracks and Sign (Elbroch), 193
marsh hawks, 212n
meadowlarks, 6
medicine areas. *See* sit spots
mentoring, xv, 176, 179–81
merlins, 145, 160
mesopredator release, 214n
migration, 1, 40
minks, 64, 71, 82, 141, 173–74
mobbing, 159–60, 195, 196, 203, 204, 205
mockingbirds
    alarms and, 88, 111, 123, 135, 206
    bird language and, xxvi, 208n
    body language of, 18, 37, 88
    at night, 7–8
    territory and, 25
monkeys, 101, 102, 104–5, 212n
morning bustle, 3–6
mountain quail, 125
Murie, Olaus J., 194
music, xxvii
mynahs, 123

native people
    alarms and, 108, 120

on animals as teachers, 71
on cardinals, 34
functional invisibility and, 175
understanding bird language, xxi–xxiii, 105
walking style of, 62
Nature, 20
nest robbing, 134, 135, 136, 137–40, 157, 161, 204
neuroscience, xxi
New Jersey
    alarms and, 126, 128, 140, 146, 148, 154, 157
    bird language awareness in, 52
    companion calls of cardinals in, 32–33
    juncos in, 29
    land of Locandro in, 149
    mockingbirds in, 7–8
    ruffs in, xiii
    sit spots in, 53, 71, 77, 80
    wake hunting in farms of, 12–13
    weasels in, 82, 83
    white-throated sparrows in, 28–29
    yellowthroats in, 25
New Yorker, The, 48
nighthawks, 18
North American robins, 209n
northern bobwhite, 37, 125, 204
northern cardinals
    alarms and, 88, 90, 149–51
    companion/contact calls of, 31
    vocalizations of, 149–50, 201–2
northern mockingbirds, recordings of alarms of, 206

as one of "top-five" birds to
study, 187
recordings of voices of, 200
as songbirds, 19
songs of, 35, 159
territory and, 27, 42
sparrows
adolescent begging calls of, 44
alarms and, 81, 91, 99, 113, 115,
125, 129–30, 134–35, 141,
148, 151, 155, 156, 159, 160,
167
baseline songs of, 159
companion/contact calls of, 31,
34–35, 38
nest robbing and, 132, 133–34, 138
recordings of voices of, 200, 203
sit spots and, 67
as songbirds, 19
territory and, 25, 27, 42
"Spatial and Temporal Responses
of Forest Birds to Hu-
man Approached in a
Protected Area and Im-
plications for Two Man-
agement Strategies," 167
species sensitivity, 115–18
spheres of awareness/disturbance,
64, 65, 65, 174–75, 177, 191
spotted towhees
alarms and, 81, 107, 113
body language of, 18
companion/contact calls of, 36
observing, 195
as one of "top-five" birds to
study, 187
vocalizations of, 93, 159, 202

squirrels
alarms and, 101, 102–3, 134, 135,
167, 168, 212n
interspecies communication
regarding, 212n
observing, 197
vocalizations of, 199, 206
wake hunting and, 213n
starlings. *See* European starlings
Steller's jays
alarms and, 146, 159, 160, 165
mimicry of, 138
recordings of voices of, 205
red-tailed hawks and, 55
at sit spot, 55
territorial aggression and, 42
wake hunting and, 14
Swainson's thrushes, 89, 114, 132,
161, 166
swallows, 6

tanagers
alarms and, 109, 113–14, 148
nest robbing and, 139
as songbirds, 19
song of, 21
territory and, 27
territorial aggression
baseline behavior and, 2,
39–43
ditch alarm shape and, 152
observing, 187–88
as type of bird vocalization, 1
territory
alarms and, 114–15, 124, 127,
129–30
baseline and, 22–27

territory (*cont.*)
    corvids and, 138
    mapping, 187
    See also territorial aggression
thrashers, 7, 25
thrushes
    alarms and, 89, 114, 116, 128,
        130, 132–33, 161, 166
    baseline behavior and, 3
    companion calls of, 89
    in late afternoon, 6
    recordings of voices of, 202
    sit spots and, 67, 68
    as songbirds, 19, 20
    song of, 22, 210n
    territory and, 25, 42, 138
Tollefson, Mark, 116
touch, 59–60, 62
towhees
    alarms and, 81, 92–95, 97, 107,
        113, 155–56, 159, 160,
        161–62, 167, 177
    baseline songs of, 159
    companion/contact calls of,
        36–37, 38
    morning bustle and, 5
    observing, 194
    recordings of voices of, 202
    sit spots and, 67, 69
    as songbirds, 20
    territory and, 25
Tracker School, xx, 208n
tracking
    alarms and, 132–33
    baseline behavior and, 4, 7
    holistic, 208n
    learning bird language and,
        193–94

native people and, xxii–xxiii
predictive, 215n
skills and sit spots, 69–70
Traditional Ecological Knowledge
    (TEK), 208n
two-minute alarm drill, 170–71, 175,
    175, 198

umbrella alarm shape. *See* para-
    bolic/umbrella alarm
    shape
University of California, Davis, 127
University of California, Los
    Angeles (UCLA), 104
University of Madrid, 167–68

ventriloquial abilities of birds, 128,
    146
vireos, 27, 113–14
vision, 57–58, 62, 99, 100, 189,
    190
vocalizations. *See* adolescent beg-
    ging; alarms; companion/
    contact calls; songs; terri-
    torial aggression

wake hunting
    alarms and, 112, 156
    described, 12–15, 107, 212–13n
    learning bird language by
        observing, 186
    origins of term, 209n
walking style, 61–63, *65*, 190–91
warblers
    alarms and, 114
    in late afternoon, 6
    sit spots and, 67
    as songbirds, 19